Experiences in Serving African American Churches in Context: Urban, Suburban, Rural

George F. DeFord

xulon
PRESS

Experiences in Serving African American Churches in Context: Urban, Suburban, Rural
by George F. DeFord

Printed in the United States of America

Edited by Xulon Press

ISBN 9781498459693

www.xulonpress.com

Sheila,

My secretary for life is a truth. Thank you for your support over the years and the many projects that you helped me with while serving as Pastor of Metropolitan.

You are a very important cog in the wheel of the life of Metropolitan. Keep up the great work that you do and I know God is going to continue to bless you beyond measure.

Blessings,

[illegible signature]

Dedicated to Four Special Ladies

The late Reverend Sallie Peterson Hayes, (maternal grandmother)

The late Inez Joan Hayes De Ford (mother)

Margret L. McRae (mother-in-law)

Lila A. De Ford (My girlfriend and wife who is one and the same)

Preface

The purpose of this book is to share my experiences with churches in various settings: urban, rural, suburban, and rural. My goal is to provide information to prepare newly appointed pastors and/or seminarians with an awareness of the cultural values and nuances that exist in the churches in the said settings. This book is a summary of my twenty-nine years as an active ordained pastor in the Baltimore-Washington Conference of the United Methodist Church until my retirement in May 2011. While serving as pastor of primarily pastoral-size congregations in Washington, DC and Laurel, Baltimore, and Indian Head, all in Maryland, I had the privilege to serve also on District Committees of Ordained Ministry and the Board of Ordained Ministry for a period of twelve years. In addition, serving as a mentor and regional guide to pastors in the Annapolis-Southern Region of the Annual Conference afforded I the opportunities to work alongside many pastors in various settings. From this experience, it was evident to me that many of the pastors could have benefitted from awareness and prior training to prepare for possible challenges in ministry before assuming their appointments to small churches in suburban and rural settings. In light of this, I share my experiences and reflections in chapter format with a representative sampling of vernacularisms made by some of the laity. My hope is this book will be of value to newly appointed pastors and/or seminarians that eventually will serve in African American churches in suburban and rural settings.

Chapter 1 is a brief recapitulation of our Methodist heritage with an emphasis upon the Washington Conference prior to its merger in 1965. The churches of the Washington South District, currently the Washington East District, are alluded to in this recapitulation. A comment is made with regard to beginning ministers and their assignments to small rural churches.

Chapter 2, entitled "We are Family," is a reflection upon my first appointment while an ordained deacon serving St. Mark's United Methodist Church, Laurel, Maryland. Attention is given to the key players in the life of the church in Laurel. I reflect upon my ministry under the headings of Nurture, Outreach, and Witness. During my eleven-year pastorate, the average worship attendance grew from 70 to 140-plus. I bonded with the families of the church, baptized, confirmed, married, and buried many at St. Mark's. I became thoroughly involved in community and social justice ministries while becoming a familiar face at City Hall. There is some discussion about conflict that I experienced during my pastorate in Laurel. My announcement of going to a new appointment was a traumatic event for the church as well as for me. I leave this chapter with tips for newly appointed clergy and some of the lessons that I learned.

Chapter 3 is what I called, "Interregnum," a seven-year gap between serving suburban and rural congregations. I spent the in-between time from July 1993 to July 2000 in urban churches in Baltimore, Maryland and Washington, DC. Mount Zion and Ebenezer United Methodist Churches both enjoyed the reputations of being middle- to upper-middle-class African American congregations that operated as program-sized churches, with paid administrative and clergy staff. Both churches were in decline and were in actuality pastoral congregations. Mount Zion is located in Ashburton, northwest Baltimore. Ashburton community was a symbol for educated and successful African Americans; however, the community was feeling the encroachment of lower-income persons. I reflect upon my ministry at Mount Zion through the lens of Nurture, Outreach, and Witness ministries. The matter of conflict is discussed, and I offer some valuable lessons learned.

Ebenezer United Methodist Church, Washington, DC, like Mount Zion United Methodist Church, can be classified as a middle- to upper-middle-class congregation on Capitol Hill. It enjoyed the reputation of being the first public school building for African American children in the District of Columbia. It operated as a program church but in recent years declined. The physical plant was in dire need of repair that triggered a capital building campaign. It was at that point I was appointed to Ebenezer with the mission to get the renovation done. I make mention of the key players in the life of the church and discuss renovation, looking through the lens of Nurture, Outreach, and Witness ministries to narrate on those areas of ministries. Significantly, with the demographic change on Capitol Hill and new families that moved into the community, conflict emerged. I share my candid feelings about that situation and the lessons learned.

I labeled Chapter 4, "Exurbia: the New Rural Community." After seven years in urban settings, I moved to the formerly rural bedroom community to what is referred to as "exurbia." Although I went to Metropolitan United Methodist Church, Indian Head, Maryland, to use the expression, "kicking and screaming," it proved to be a great and blessed experience of ministry. Metropolitan is a pastoral-size congregation; the original building was razed in 1975 and a new edifice constructed on the same site. The church enjoys the reputation of having a number of educators in membership. At my appointment, the church was entering a building program. Within three years, we were able to build a multipurpose center costing nearly one million dollars. Through the lens of Nurture, Outreach, and Witness ministries, I discuss the said ministry areas. I was able to initiate a Lenten series of services that continue to the present; organize an alumni chapter of Morgan State University; and participate in Safe Nights, a social justice ministry by Lifestyles of Maryland. Moreover, I helped facilitate the establishment of the Metropolitan-Indian Head United Methodist Churches Cooperative

Parish. Interestingly, Indian Head United Methodist Church was a predominantly white congregation that chose to join with us, an African American congregation, despite the fact there were several other white congregations that they could have joined with. In July 2008, I began to serve as an adventure guide, an extension ministry with the Baltimore-Washington Annual Conference.

Chapter 5 is sort of a recapitulation of my ministry as an adventure guide with the Annapolis-Southern Region with team leader Rev. Dr. Ianther M. Mills, District Superintendent, Washington East District and Rev. Chris Holmes, District Superintendent, Annapolis District. I share my experiences of visiting three pastors in their historical African American rural congregations in St. Mary's County, Maryland. I give a profile of the rural pastors and an example of their administrative support, offering tips for newly assigned pastors.

Chapter 6 is an excursus relative to African American clergy women in the Baltimore-Washington Conference of the United Methodist Church, based on my visits and observation of African American clergy women in the Southern region. This is not an exhaustive work on clergy women of color but just some interviews and observations. I begin with a reflection on my maternal grandmother as a clergy woman who did not experience full parity with her male counterparts in the Baptist church. I point to the late Rev. Dr. Emma P. Burrell as a trail blazer for clergy women and the ripple effect that she created. I give sobriquets to the clergy women based upon the decade in which they became probationary members, or commission: 1970s "First Ripples"; 1980s "The Rush" (Rev. Mamie Williams's description); 1990s "The Surge"; and 2000 "The Millennials." Several clergy woman shared their experiences of successes and push-back from congregations and the emotional impacts as a result of the negativity. I give some closing thoughts on African American clergy woman.

Chapter 7 is entitled "Leaving the Regional Guide Ministry," an account that serves as a lead-in to my ministry as a retiree and a district superintendent's hire as the lead pastor for the Pisgah Charge (Alexandria Chapel and Smith Chapel). Kermit C. C. Moore, Certified Lay Minister, joined with me to serve as the associate pastor. We eventually developed an agreement to become the Smith Chapel-Alexandria Chapel Cooperative Parish. My retirement became effective July 1, 2011.

Chapter 8 is entitled "Smith Chapel-Alexandria Chapel Cooperative Parish" and discusses the histories of the two congregations. A profile of each pastor from 1971 to 2003 is presented as well as descriptions of key families and players in the life of each church. Attention is given especially to the matriarchs and patriarchs of each congregation and their influences in the life of the churches. I address these, again, through the lens of Nurture, Outreach, and Witness ministries. Pastor Moore offers his reflection on his ministry at Alexandria Chapel, and I give my closing thoughts on the church. Meanwhile a similar approach is followed with Smith Chapel by looking at Nurture, Outreach, and Witness ministries. In addition, I report on Smith Chapel's participation with the Ministers Alliance of Charles County and Vicinity, and finally I address the matter of expansion of Smith Chapel.

Chapter 9 is entitled "In Retrospect." I look back at the events leading up to beginning this journey and the lessons learned. At every step of the way, the Lord was, is, and continues to be my "Walk-Buddy." My hope is that what I have shared can be of help to clergy now and in the days to come.

Chapter 10 is entitled "The Pastor's Wife: In Her Own Words." My wife gives her own brief candid reflection of what it is like to be the pastor's wife in the congregations that we served over the years.

Acknowledgments

I wrote this book after reflecting over my twenty-nine years of ordained ministry in the Baltimore-Washington Conference of the United Methodist Church and my colleagues and friends in the Gospel ministry of Jesus Christ.

I am particularly grateful to Dr. Cain Hope Felder, Professor, Howard University School of Divinity, Washington, DC. It was Dr. Felder who encouraged me to embark on this journey of writing a work that focuses upon the African American small membership rural church. I am further grateful to my mentor and friend Rev. Dr. Alfonso J. Harrod, who helped me hone the message that I wanted to convey to colleagues and seminarians. Moreover, I am especially grateful to Bishop Forrest Stith who gave me pointers early in the development of this project and subsequent review. Rev. Obie Wright, Jr., my teacher and friend, took the time to review my drafts and offer substantive critiques. I am particularly grateful to Bishop Marcus Matthews for the opportunity and privilege to serve as a retired pastor of Smith Chapel United Methodist Church,

Washington East District, Baltimore-Washington Conference, The United Methodist Church.

I take this opportunity to thank all of my clergy colleagues and friends that took the time to share with me their experiences in ministry. And I thank the many lay persons that responded to interviews, either one-on-one or by telephone. Without their sharing, this book may not have become a reality.

I thank Margaret L. McRae, my mother-in-law, who is always encouraging and supportive.

Finally, I want to thank my wife Lila, "my girlfriend and wife who is one and the same," a praying woman who offered encouragement and support when I was ready to stop writing. Most of all, I thank God for her being with me on this journey of ministry, all these many years, through the ups and downs. Praise God!

Thank You, Lord!

Contents

Chapter 1

Our History in Brief

The Methodist Episcopal Church was formally established by a gathering of Methodist clergy in Baltimore, Maryland, during the last week of December, 1784. The conference of Methodist ministers began on Christmas Day, hence it was called the Christmas Conference that lasted until January 2, 1785 at Lovely Lane Church. During the Christmas Conference, significant actions were taken, such as adopting the name, The Methodist Episcopal Church, adopting a prayer book known as the Sunday Service (a shorter version of the Book of Common Prayer), and electing two men as bishops (Francis Asbury and Thomas Coke) and twelve other men as elders. The impact of the Christmas Conference continues to be felt in the twenty-first century. [1]

African Americans have a unique history with the Methodist Episcopal Church and subsequently the United Methodist Church. The late Reverend Dr. Horace L. Wallace documents *"A Chronological Account of The Washington Conference of The*

Methodist Episcopal Church." The said account spans from 1772 to 1968 when Methodists united to become the United Methodist Church. [2] On October 31, 1864, the Second Mission Conference approved the establishment of the Washington Conference at Sharp Street Methodist Church in Baltimore, Maryland, and Bishop Levi Scott made the first appointments. [3] The Washington Conference Journal noted:

> On that day, Colored Preachers of the State shall go forth—raised to the dignity of an Annual conference, preaching to their people, freedom from the "Law of Sin and Death" . . . During its existence, its people, who were "born in slavery, weaned in segregation, and reared in discrimination," sought freedom and equality for all people through the church.[4]

The Washington Conference at its merger with the Baltimore Conference in June, 1965, had 42,756 members, 152 ordained pastors, 72 supply pastors, 174 pastoral charges, and 311 church buildings. Further, the racially segregated conference founded Morgan College and N.M. Carroll Home for the Aged. Six bishops came from this conference. [5]

The former Washington Annual Conference with the Washington South District was comprised of sixteen charges in Washington DC and southern Maryland. The Saint Mary's Parish was organized into six churches (Bethesda, Valley Lee; Galilee,

Mechanicsville; Mt. Calvary, Charlotte Hall; Mt. Zion, St. Inigoes; St. Luke, Ridge; and Zion, Lexington Park) I served several of the said churches as their regional guide from the period of 2008 through 2011.

The present Baltimore-Washington Conference (BWC) consists of 642 churches spanning from the western boundaries of the panhandle of Maryland and part of eastern West Virginia to the western shores of the Chesapeake Bay and from the southern shores of the Potomac River to Northern Maryland that borders southern Pennsylvania. The BWC is organized into eight regions: Annapolis-Southern, Baltimore, Washington, and Western Regions. Each region is divided into two districts under the supervision of a district superintendent. The Annapolis-Southern Region, where my ministry was primarily situated, consists of 142 churches. Moreover, the Washington East District (WED) under the superintendence of Rev. Dr. Rebecca Iannicelli consists of sixty-eight churches. Of the sixty-eight churches in the WED, thirty-eight of them report an average worship attendance of 100 or less. Thus, 52 percent of the churches in the WED are small membership congregations. Further, 34 percent of the small-membership churches in WED are African American churches primarily located in rural settings. Thus with this in mind, particularly for African Americans who are bishop-appointed ministers or District Superintendent hires to the WED can expect assignment to a rural church. Kemp comments, "Small-membership churches serve as the training ground for entry level pastors, and they also contribute disproportionate number of their own people into Christian service." [6] It is not unusual for a seminary-trained young pastor to aspire placement after a few years to a pastoral-size or program-size church. (A pastoral sized church typically has an average worship attendance from 70 to 150 while a program-sized church benefits from 150 to 500 worshipers and an administrative and ministerial staff.)

The appointment of pastors to congregations in the BWC typically takes place during the spring with the effective date beginning in July, which is the beginning of the conference year. There are some unusual circumstances wherein pastors are appointed or hired during other times of the year, however. The Board of Ordained Ministry recommends to the annual conference those candidates who possess the gifts and graces for pastoral ministry. The cabinet, upon review of the candidates for provisional membership, deploy the approved ministers. The newly appointed pastors for the most part are current seminarians, recent graduates of divinity schools, lay persons that have received license to preach, or lay persons currently enrolled in the course of study. Also retired pastors are among district superintendent hires who serve rural churches. "Despite the practice among several black denominations of placing beginning ministers or seminarians in rural churches to test their commitment and develop their skills in less demanding environment, the clergy who continue in the rural ministry tend to be older."[7] Yet many of the newly appointed pastors that serve rural churches are fresh out of divinity schools and whose ministerial experiences have been as associates and/or staff members in primarily in mid-size to program churches. This is potentially a problem for the new ministers appointed to the small rural congregation.

Chapter 2

We Are Family

A key feature of the African American small-membership churches is they are made up of several dominant families who are descendants of the founders. The families are continuous sources of support of their small church as reflected through ministries of nurture, outreach, and witness. St. Mark's United Methodist Church is such a church. I had the opportunity to serve there for eleven years when significant growth occurred. The church progressed to become a full-time appointment. Over the years I was there, the average worship attendance increased from 70 to 147. While statistically it was raising the roof to become a program church, attitudinally, we still functioned as an overgrown family congregation. There is a warning for such congregations: "Chapel-mode congregations are inwardly focused. They generally have a presiding matriarch or patriarch who dominates the decision-making process . . . the . . . focus (is) on avoiding change, maintaining the status quo, and keeping the dominant family's leader happy." [1] After my appointment change, St. Mark's experienced conflict with its first woman pastor as an elder, loss of full-time status, and subsequently another new pastor appointed with less than full-time status. Martin, in his book, asserts, "These transitional churches are really overgrown pastoral churches that will probably adjust to a small size when there is a change of pastors" [2] Yet, the "leading" families continued to remain and support "their church."

The Context

St. Mark's United Methodist Church is located in the western section of Laurel, Maryland in an area known as "The Grove." As a newly ordained deacon and probationary member in 1982, I was on my way to my first appointment. St. Mark's is a representative example of the "family church." According to the church's anniversary booklet of 1987, the following comments are made:

> Records do not indicate when blacks began to settle in the section of Laurel known as "The Grove," where St. Mark's Episcopal Church as it was first called, was organized in 1890. A large oak grove once stood across the street from the church. Gigantic oak trees, some more than 200 years old, grew there. Hence, the local community became known as "The Grove."
>
> Few Blacks lived in the Laurel area prior to the Civil War, according to the 1860 census. By 1880 the number had

increased slightly . . . According to a city directory reprinted in the 1970 Laurel centennial booklet, 57 people resided in The Grove in 1894 . . .

The families that lived in The Grove at that time were the Adams, Bacons, Blues, Carters, Hebrons, Johnsons, Matthews, Millers, Levis, Scotts, Snowdens, Suscos, Thomases, and Woods . . . Today, the majority of the members of St. Mark's Church are descendants of these families. [3]

The Centennial Anniversary Journal 1990 contained the following:

In 1890, the spirit of the Lord led Frank and Sarah to organize the home mission known as St. Mark's Methodist Episcopal Church. Their home was located at 618 8th Street, then known as Church Street . . . The mission was part of the Bladensburg Circuit of the Potomac District within the Washington Annual Conference, an all-black mission conference of the Methodist Episcopal Church. The Washington Conference was organized in 1864 at Sharp Street Church in Baltimore. In 1890, Reverend McHenry J. Naylor, a circuit rider preacher, was appointed on trial to the Washington Conference and assigned to the Bladensburg Circuit. According to the Laurel Charge Historical Record, the mission consisted of 28, was organized under Reverend Naylor's supervision. [4]

Many picnics, baseball games, and other community and church-related activities were held in the old oak grove. The facility belonged to the Stanley family . . . Charles Stanley . . . and other members of his family allowed the sponsors of the various activities to use the property free of charge. In the late 1950s, the Maryland State Road Commission constructed Route 198 through the grove. Since that time, homes have been constructed on much of the rest of the site. [5]

The once rural community transformed into a suburban bedroom community, with a significant number of apartment dwellers, not only indigenous members but newcomers ("strangers," as referred to by the old timers) to Laurel who work either in metropolitan Baltimore, Maryland, or Washington, DC areas. There is a sense of pride for those whose generational roots are in Laurel and in particular from "The Grove." Yet, there is still a prevailing attitude of the family church in St. Mark's.

Key Players

I learned the meaning of "family church" and the key players that help make up the family church as I observed them in one such congregation in the formerly rural community transformed into suburban bedroom community—Laurel. My first appointment was to St. Mark's UMC in Laurel, Maryland. It is a historic church that was established in 1890, and the descendants of the founders continue to reside in the community and play an active role in the church. My appointment to St. Mark's began on July 1, 1982, as an ordained deacon who was trained under a senior pastor in a program-administered congregation. On my first Sunday, I experienced a wave of mixed emotions ranging from feelings of confidence to anxiety about the flow of the service to being alone without the guidance of the senior pastor, not to mention fear of having a memory lapse. Immediately after the worship service, my wife and I were introduced to and overwhelmed by a number of welcoming members whose names we struggled to keep in mind. Key players such as Mrs. Ernestine Gibson, Chairperson of the Administrative Council and point of contact; Mrs. Eleanor Moore, Chairperson of Pastor-Parish Relations; Mrs. Shirley Carey, Worship Chairperson; Mrs. Bernice Brooks, Treasurer; Mrs. Ellen Gibson, matriarch of the Gibson Family and her husband William Gibson, chair of Trustees; and Mrs. Viola Wooten, Lay Leader, were those who readily stuck in our minds.

Mrs. Moore took her role very seriously as the chair of the Pastor-Parish Relations Committee, and to a point early on became *in loco parentis* to us during my early stages of ministry at St. Mark's. Later during the month, I learned that the church was made up of basically four dominant families: the Gibsons, Johnsons, Matthews, and Moores. There were other families that were interconnected to at least one or each of the dominant families. As I continued to try to remember the various names, I soon discovered there were nicknames for just about each and every member, such as Bitsy, Bunny, Bush, Collie, Elly, Dutta, Babs, Lynnie, Pennie, Tubby, Glenny, Ginny, Little Helen, and Piccolo (Pic). Also, there were titles of endearment and respect to the senior members such as Miss Ethel and Miss Katie (the Pillsbury Sisters), Miss Pearl, Aunt Easey, Miss Bertha Brooks, Miss Margaret, Miss Catherine, Miss Alice, and Mr. Lewis (Rev.), Miss Laura, Miss Dorothy, Miss Ida, Miss Mildred, and Miss Thelma; each were held in high esteem because of their longevity within the church, their spirituality, or the wife of the local pastor and son of the church.

A key characteristic of the small-membership African American church is family ties, which play a very important dynamic in the life of the church. The selection of those to serve in positions of leadership, serving in the hospitality ministry area, or in various areas of the worship ministry can depend upon the individual's family connection. "Kinfolk ties are important in the small church" is the comment by Lyle Schaller. [6]

Sundays at St. Mark's were family days. The sanctuary generally was filled especially on special and annual celebration Sundays. The Gibson family choir typically filled the choir loft in excess of fifteen persons. After worship services, members generally flocked to their parents' homes where they enjoyed family meals. On Sundays, when there was an afternoon service, Sis. Helen Johnson, known to members as "Ginny," cooked meals in the church kitchen and made certain that the pastor "had a plate." Periodically, members of her family would drift into the church kitchen to get a meal although inactive in their membership. On the occasions when Ginny was not present, Dutter would send one of her daughters with a plate of food for the pastor. Similarly on the days I would be at the office, she made certain that I had something to eat before a meeting.

The administrative machinery of the church was ably maintained by Mrs. Ernestine Gibson (Bitsy), and I soon began to refer to as "Ms. E" because of her high energy. She was an upper-level manager in the federal government and brought administrative and managerial skills to the local church. As an extroverted "A" type personality, she cared for the weekly publication of the church bulletin, announcements, and responsibilities as chairperson of the Administrative Council. Early on, I observed that she strongly advocated for church policies and procedures and getting things done on time. This was clearly demonstrated during my initial charge conference in the fall of 1982. Having been guided by the Rev. Dr. Alfonso J. Harrod, senior pastor of Ebenezer United Methodist Church, Washington Central District, on the preparation of charge conference reports, I gave my guidance and recommendations as to how the charge conference reports were to be prepared. Ms. "E" assembled the reports in booklet format and provided each authorized member of the charge conference with the booklets. At the conclusion of the charge conference, the late Rev. Dr. Joshua Hutchins, District Superintendent of the Washington Central District, complimented the church for having excellent, well-organized reports that were on time. Mrs. Gibson would become my right arm, administratively speaking, during my tenure at St. Mark's. "Ms. E" would eventually become one of the lay leaders of the church; furthermore, she would serve on the district board of ordained ministry and the conference board of ordained ministry and enabler for the local pastor's school. She continues to serve in various leadership capacities within St. Mark's.

"Ms. E's" husband, Mr. George Gibson was very active in the church. He assumed the office of treasurer and remained in the said position for over twenty years, long after I left the church. He was a member of the male chorus and the Gibson Fammily choir. George was noted for his quiet humor and protective care of the church's funds. He served until such time his health militated against his continuance as treasurer.

The late Eleanor Moore, Ms. Elly, served as the chairperson of Pastor-Parish Relations Committee and was noted for being a very stylish lady. During our initial meeting at the church, Ms. Moore was very affirming to Lila and me. On the first Sunday in July 1982, she enthusiastically introduced us to the St. Mark's church family; we both would soon discover that Ms. Elly would be quite maternal to us during our ministry at St. Mark's. In my pursuit to be ever-present and responsive to the needs of the parishioners, Ms. Elly said, "Reverend De Ford, you do not need to run up here to Laurel every time one of these members stumps their toes!"

Before the matter of boundary issues became very prevalent, Ms. Elly protected me from an incident. I was working late in the evening at the office when a young woman came into the fellowship hall and wanted to speak with me about a matter. Naively, I invited her into the office and closed the door. Moments later, Ms. Elly came up to the church, knocked on the door, and came into the office. She told the young woman, "You don't need to be bothering the pastor at this time and let him go home to Mrs. De Ford . . ." The young woman, with attitude, abruptly left. Ms. Elly explained to me some things about her and cautioned me not to close the door of the office when this particular young woman was present. Take it for what it was worth; I was glad Ms. Elly came when she did. She was watching out for the pastor.

Mrs. Moore was very supportive throughout my tenure, even when she was not the chair of the PPRC; especially when my mother died, she was one of those who rallied the church to be in support of my family during that difficult time in January, 1990. She regularly served dinner to us at her home on some of those Sundays when Ginny did not cook at the church; in fact, Ginny would be at Ms. Elly's home dining with us. Years later, at her home-going service, I remarked on Ms. Elly's hospitality and kindness extended to my family during our pastorate: there was a great row of laughter and head-shaking after that comment. Mrs. Moore leaves me with some very fond memories.

The late Mrs. Shirley Carey served as the worship committee chairperson. She was also my barometer in terms of how well the worship service was going on any given Sunday morning. Among her responsibilities was to update the marquis with the sermon title for Sunday; she was very diligent to carry out this responsibility. On one such occasion, when at the last moment I changed the title of my sermon, Shirley became very upset with me. She described the event. While angry and hastily walking back to the church from her home, located three and one-half blocks away and muttering about the pastor, she stumped her foot on the dirt path beside the church. Shirley took the incident as a warning from the Lord not to criticize the pastor! She often times laughed about that situation. However, after that, each time I called to give her my sermon title, I assured her there would be no changes.

Ms. Shirley, as a member of several of the choirs, was very emotive and conspicuous with her natural curly short reddish natural. She was enthusiastic with a unique bouncing rhythmic processional step (slightly like a college marching band leaving the field) as she led the choir at the beginning and conclusion of worship service. She contributed to setting the tone of worship. "She marched down the aisle with majestic rhythm. You could really feel the spirit with every step. She prepared the atmosphere for a spirit-filled worship service" is the comment by her daughter Mrs. Sandra Johnson made. Shirley was the bellwether; I could gauge if my sermon was connecting. When the "Spirit hit her," she would shout in her own unique way, "Yes Sir! Yes Sir! Oooh, Yes Sir!" In a manner of speaking, I reached the *"hum thoughts"* as described by Dr. Evans E. Crawford [7]. However on the occasions, I preached a "dud" Shirley would comment, "Gee whiz, Reverend, you'll do better next time." She continued to serve as worship chairperson long after my appointments to other churches. Mrs. Carey passed February 18, 2004.

Mrs. Bernice Brooks, aka Aunt Easey, grew up in "The Grove" and St. Mark's. Her late mother, Mrs. Pearl Matthews, was the Mother of the Church. Mrs. Brooks served in many capacities of leadership such as the chairperson of the Adult Fellowship and was a very strong supporter of the church. At the time of my appointment to St. Mark's, she was the treasurer and had been so for many years. In addition, in years past she served as lay representative to the Annual Conference. When the Charge Conference voted on the change of officers, she reluctantly gave up her position of church treasurer, after which our relationship was strained for a period of time.

Mrs. Brooks subsequently resumed her duties as lay member to the Annual Conference which she thoroughly enjoyed again. Later on during my ministry I could call her Aunt Easey, and she responded with a chuckle. Aunt Easey was very influential in the local community. There was one incident in which some of the local guys were gambling on the church grounds. She is reported to have gone up to the fellows, chastised them, took the dice, and shewed them off the property. She was able to do this because of her prominence in both the church and the community. In later years long after my ministry at St. Mark's, Mrs. Brooks who is in her '90s and still active is the Mother of the Church.

The late Mrs. Ellen Gibson, aka Dutta, was the matriarch of the Gibson Family. She was the mother of thirteen children. She and her husband William were faithful members of St. Mark's. She served as president of the United Methodist Women and a member of the choir. Dutta wore the old-fashioned hearing aids and occasionally joked about them. On the evenings when I was working in the church office, she made certain that a "plate" was sent to the pastor. There were occasions when I visited Dutta and her family in her kitchen. It was quite evident that Mrs. Gibson was the matriarch of the Gibson Family by the quiet manner in which she directed the children, grandchildren, and great grandchildren. The matriarch supervised the adult daughters who lived in the home as if they were still teenage girls. She was the center of the family's life, and her death was a severe trauma to the family and entire church community.

Mr. William Gibson, husband of Ellen, was a very quiet man who served as the chairman of the Board of Trustees. Any time that he came into the church, he took his hat off out of respect for "the Lord's House." He was diligent in keeping the church clean along with trustee Philip Gibson, nephew, aka Bush. As both Mr. Gibson and Bush grew older, Gordon a younger son of William followed in his father's footsteps. After the death of Mr. William Gibson, nephew Bush became the chair of the trustees, and eventually he turned the reigns of leadership over to Gordon who began to train his identical twin middle-school sons, Kyle and Corey, in the work of trustees. The twins could be seen together on the riding mower and sharing turns cutting the grass on the church campus. Sadly, Corey died in a tragic car accident on September 30, 2003, at 9:44 pm; because of the huge response to his death, the funeral was conducted in the sanctuary of a neighboring Baptist church. Being a member of the board of trustees was seemingly a family tradition for the members of the Gibson family.

The late Mrs. Viola Wooten, Lay Leader, was a quiet and serene senior lady, rather portly with an infectious, welcoming smile. Her fashionable hats were very conspicuous. She made a person feel quite comfortable in her presence. Her particular gift was public prayer. During the earlier years of my ministry, the morning prayer would be given by the lay leader. Mrs. Wooten usually sat on the third row, first seat center aisle side. Without any difficulty, she would get up come to the chancel rail and kneel. "Father, I stretch my hands to thee, no other help I know; if thou withdraw thyself from me, ah! Whither shall I go . . . Lord we come this morning . . ." [8], would be our lay leader's opening to the morning prayer. She prayed with a gentle yet moving fervor that elicited talk-back from the congregation. At the conclusion of her prayer, there was a sense that she had ushered in the Spirit of the Lord. Mrs. Wooten passed during the late 1990s.

Reverend Louis D. Conway, son of the church, served in numerous ministry areas such as Sunday School superintendent, choir director, and assistant pastor. He was licensed as a local preacher in 1947, ordained deacon in 1949, and local elder in 1952. Rev. Conway, affectionately known as Mr. Louis, was appointed in 1953 as pastor of Ridgley-Huntsville Charge. He was appointed to Mt. Zion United Methodist Church in "Bacon Town" (located in the eastern section of Laurel) where he served until his retirement in June 1986. He returned to St. Mark's where he was honored as pastor emeritus. Rev. Conway was very supportive of my ministry and participated in my ordination as elder in June, 1988, at Western Maryland College, presently now McDaniel's University. Mrs. Alice Conway, his wife and Roman Catholic by faith, was a very articulate and dignified lady noted for her hospitality. Reverend Conway's words of wisdom to me were: "Reverend, don't preach so hard. Take care of yourself." Occasionally, he would comment, "I would rather be a good pastor than a great preacher."[9]

Two young women who bonded with Lila during our tenure and continue to be very good friends are Denise and Carolyn, whom I affectionately called the "Corrupters." The two sisters would take my wife to local shopping malls between worship services. On one such occasion when they brought Mrs. De Ford back to the afternoon service late, I asked, "Are you two corrupting my wife by bringing her back late?" The both of them laughed hysterically like two mischievous teenagers; from that point on I called them, "Corrupters." I still use that sobriquet. I had the honor to perform both of their weddings and baptize their children. Denise, a seamstress, visited with us at each of our appointments. She occasionally takes on projects for my wife especially when it comes to fabricating dressings for the pulpit. When her husband Rick died suddenly of a heart attack, it was a severe shock and painful experience. It was as if we had lost a son-in-law. Denise continues to be like a daughter to us.

There were newcomers to St. Mark's who were assimilated into the church. Grace Catching, elementary school educator and her family, served as superintendent of the church school. Charles and Barbara Gregg, who served with hospitality, were taken under the wing of Helen Johnson, aka Ginny. Mrs. Eunice Dumas who became president of the Usher Board continues in the same role today. Albert Whiel, who worked with the young people, was criticized for getting several of the youngsters to matriculate at Delaware State University. We always had some contrived competition between us for encouraging our high school students to consider going to Delaware State or Morgan State Universities. Our intent was to encourage our young people to seek higher education, especially historical black colleges and universities (HBCUs) or any other schools of their choices. He eventually relocated to Richmond, Virginia.

George and Gloria Maxine Still were not newcomers; George grew up in St. Mark's while Maxine, Ernestine Gibson's sister, transferred her membership from the African Methodist Episcopal Church. Maxine, a retired supervisor with the federal government, became chair of the Pastor-Parish Relations Committee during the latter part of my tenure. Mr. Orris Fletcher and his wife transferred from a Baptist church. He became a lay speaker and Sunday school teacher; both eventually returned to Buffalo, New York, due to job relocation. The Fletchers periodically visited St. Mark's when they were traveling to his native home in Florida.

The foregoing persons played key roles in the choreography of leadership in St. Mark's United Methodist Church during my tenure as a probationary member of the annual conference. The administrative machinery of the church functioned smoothly due to the commitment and efficiency of Mrs. Ernestine Gibson. Ms. Eleanor Moore, Pastor-Parish Relations chair, took her responsibilities very seriously while advocating for the pastoral family. Worship services within St. Mark's were very important and publicized in the community via the marquis. Worship services were emotive and certain key players were expected to be participants and serve as indicators of the spiritual atmosphere. The roles each member played contributed to the overall manner in which the church operated. Many of the members were interconnected: aunts, uncles, cousins, nieces, nephews. The newcomers were adopted into one, several, or more of the families of the church. I began to get a glimpse of the family church.

I looked at this family church through the lens of the Nurture, Outreach, and Witness ministries exemplified through St. Mark's during my tenure. "Nurture identifies the need for Christians to be nurtured in the Christian faith if they are to cultivate the spiritual resources necessary to provide effective outreach and witness ministries."[10] Outreach is a responsibility of United Methodist churches regardless of their size. We are to endeavor at the local, state, national, and international levels. It is also a mean by which to get people involved.[11]

> The ministry of witness gives people the opportunity to share their faith understanding of personal and corporate salvation, reconciliation, worship celebration, spiritual development, and discipline. It . . . provides people with opportunities to share their faith with other persons and to work for justice, righteousness, and the redemption of the world. [12]

Nurturing Ministries

Members of St. Mark's could expect to receive some expression of care from the church during unusual occurrences. Before worship services, Ms. Gibson would bring me up to date on recent hospitalizations, sick members, deaths, and community issues, not already brought to my attention. When the choir assembled in the fellowship hall for prayer, prayer concerns were shared. I remembered an occasion when one of the choir members that had been missing for two Sundays was back in the prayer circle said, "Reverend you know I was in the hospital, and you did not come to see me." I replied, "No one told me." From that point on, I routinely stated from the pulpit, "My gift of mental telepathy is gone. Please let me know if you are scheduled for hospitalizations or if there are certain prayer concerns. Please let me know."

There was a certain expectation of care to take place on the part of the pastor and the church. "When someone is sick, ill or injured or when a baby is born or when a loved one dies—is another way to demonstrate care and love."[13] I also learned to listen with a second ear and observe with a keen eye; listen to the small talk about members whose nicknames were used and keep in mind the persons absent from their normal seating location. Or when a member would ask me about how so-and-so is doing, I took that as a hint to inquire or let them know they were seen and doing fine. The testimonials that were given and/or response to the sermon were opportunities to get some insight as to some of the issues going in the lives of the people. A caring response was expected from the pastor and the church.

Learning the nicknames, sobriquet, was an asset to me in the area of pastoral care. Nicknames in some cases capture the spirit of an individual, a distinguishing characteristic, reputation, or something that an individual is to be remembered for.[14] I found that rapport with the members was strengthened, and they would chuckle and inquire, "Who told you my name, Reverend?" It helped me as I heard conversations within the church also when visitations needed to occur within the community or at the local hospital.

Membership care through visitations to the sick and shut-ins was an important part of the nurturing ministry and pastoral care. Hospital visits to my members eventually served as a means for my becoming a part of the volunteer chaplaincy program at Laurel Regional Hospital, where my training in clinical pastoral education (CPE) was invaluable. Moreover, I met members from neighboring congregations and other United Methodist churches. In some cases, those visited turned out to be extended family members connected to other churches, and they made known to me their family ties at St. Mark's.

Sunday school was very important to the membership. Grace Catchings, an extroverted, gregarious, and personable lady, with two sons used her gift of teaching within the church. Assisted by Denise Patterson, the late Johnnielee Greenleaf and Orris Fletcher, kept an active church school, averaging about thirty-two students, including ten adults. There were two multipurpose rooms and the pastor's office adjacent to the fellowship hall. The adult class met in the sanctuary. One year, I am uncertain of the exact year, we had twenty-two youths for confirmation. I have not had that many since! There is a picture of the members of the confirmation class sitting on the front steps of the church prior to our going to a conference-wide gathering at Morgan State University. Many of them now are adults with their own children.

A funeral service at St. Mark's was a communal event with an every-member response to nurture the grieving family. Funeral services at St. Mark's were conducted in their cultural context.[15] The Snowden Family of Montgomery County typically was entrusted with the final services; the late Mr. George Snowden, known as "Junior" and his sister Irene usually worked with us. The members that were employed took leave time from their jobs to serve in one or more capacities to celebrate the life of the deceased member, participating in various parts of the program: singing on the choir, ushering, helping as pall bearers, cooking the repast meal, and serving as hosts to those assembled in the fellowship hall. It was not unusual to have a full sanctuary and overflow seating in the fellowship hall. The attendees were diverse: co-workers, friends, local politicians, and other ethnic groups. Funeral services for sudden and tragic deaths, young adults, and youths were most difficult. On the occasion of a young adult murder victim, there was media coverage and a publication of my sermon in the local paper, *The Laurel Leader*, November 9, 1989 edition. An unusual service was for the late Gilbert Nicholson, a postal carrier; his truck with a black sash was parked outside of the church.

The funeral service was an occasion to get a glimpse of the family ties and those that were inactive with their membership.

In fact, some of the local fellows that were reputed alcoholics and drug users would be in attendance.

For some of the grieving families, the emotionality would be extremely high and required great effort on the part of the pastor to lead the service. Such was the case with the late Frances Davis, a young woman who suffered a heart attack, leaving behind a husband and two young daughters. In addition, keeping reins on visiting clergy tempted to give a sermonette was a chore. On one such occasion, a grandson with aspirations for ministry "high-jacked" the service and gave the eulogy. When my time came to deliver the eulogy, I said, "The eulogy has been given . . ." and proceeded toward the closing segments of the service. An old layman from our sister church Queens Chapel in a very fatherly way said, "Reverend, the members always want to hear from the pastor."

At the conclusion of a funeral service, the vehicle procession to the local cemetery typically caused traffic inconveniences through Laurel to the county line. For some families, the committal service was a very emotional moment. Upon return to the church, the repast was a tribal feast that could last until late afternoon or early evening. At the conclusion of the repast, the late Helen Johnson, aka Ginny, supervised the clean-up in "her kitchen" and made certain that the pastor "had his plate to take home." Such days were very grueling, and I definitely needed the rest. On the following day, I usually called to see how the family was doing. On the following Sunday, a card would be sent to the congregation and expressions of appreciation would be made by the family. I cited above the response from the church family when there was a death in the community.

There were occasions when persons not connected with the church or local community wanted a private and/or graveside ceremony. There was an occasion, in 1989 I believe, when a single mother and the father of her child wanted a private service for their deceased infant. The parents of the deceased infant child were not residents of the immediate community. The child lived only a few days and succumbed to certain complications after birth. Although it was evident that the parents of the infant were unchurched, the young woman was convinced her child should receive a Christian funeral service and burial. I agreed to help them by conducting a service of Death and Resurrection for a Child.

I would be unprepared for what I was about to experience on the day of the funeral. The service would be the most difficult one that I officiated at that point in my ministry. Two limousines and two cars parked beside the church. Anticipating a hearse carrying the remains, the funeral director pulled from the back seat of the first limousine a large ornate shoe-box-like casket. He lined up the parents and few family members in preparation for processing into the sanctuary. The director nodded to me to lead them into the empty sanctuary. As I led the small troop into the sanctuary while reciting the processional sentences, I could hear uncontrollable weeping from the young mother. The little casket was placed on a table that served as a bier for the service but was normally used for bulletins, attendance sheets, and visitors' cards.

When the funeral director opened the casket, there was a beautiful doll-baby-like girl child with a little white baptismal-like dress with laces and ruffles and tiny little booties. My heart fluttered, and my eyes teared up as an indescribable flood of emotions overwhelmed me. Momentarily, I was speechless. Only after the funeral director inquired if I was okay, I regained my composure. From that moment on, I mechanically went through the service while not remembering a word that I said. There was no music, no pulpit assistant with me—just a brief order of worship. At the conclusion of the service, we left the sanctuary and drove to the cemetery.

The director disclosed that he tried to persuade the young mother to have the service at the funeral home, but she was resolute to have the service in a church. After the interment, the young parents promised to come to church the following Sunday. They never visited. This type of funeral is very difficult because as pastors we can become too empathetic and become swept up in the vortex of emotions that can render us helpless at the very time we need to be a means of support, hope, and encouragement to the grieving families. At such times we really need to rely on our training in clinical pastoral education (CPE) but most of all on the Word of God.

Such was part of the mosaic of the nurturing ministry within St. Mark's during my tenure.

Outreach Ministries

Ministry beyond the walls of St. Mark's was limited to several social justice agencies. The Laurel Advocacy Referral Service (LARS), a Lutheran-sponsored social justice ministry with a focus of helping the displaced, homeless, and marginalized families and individuals was an agency to which the church regularly contributed. During the Lenten season, a series of offerings were received during Wednesday night services and donated to the agency. Currently, Mrs. Ernestine Gibson works as a case manager for the agency.

The late Collie, a recovering alcoholic, was instrumental in the church providing a meeting space for Alcoholics Anonymous (AA) on Friday evenings. Collie was very committed to the self-help recovery group and made certain, as a trustee, that the fellowship hall would be open and clean in preparation for receiving the participants. In addition, provisions were made for Narcotics Anonymous (NA) to meet, but the meetings fizzled after several months because some of the local pushers and users were too close by the church, and there was too much of a temptation for the participants to be able to abstain. (I will speak about this later.) Collie complained that the church was duped into allowing the NA group to meet in the fellowship hall on Monday nights because the ulterior motive of some of the members of the group was to get drugs after the meeting. Later on, I concurred.

Reality House, a drug rehabilitation long-term treatment program, was another social justice ministry we attempted to be connected with. The connection was made when I pursued training as a certified addictions counselor. After a few months of training, I took the risk of persuading the administration to allow some of the residents to attend worship services at St. Mark's. Initially, this was a great idea. One Sunday morning, eighteen persons attended. The following Sunday a comparable number attended; however, that would be the last time. Several of the individuals relapsed because of the temptations availed to them by some of the "local fellows."

I attempted to establish a prison ministry at the church. While this also was a great idea, the support was very minimal. There were only three persons who volunteered to be a part of this ministry with me. We cleared the security requirements mandated by the detention facility in Upper Marlboro, Maryland, and made scheduled visits. This, too, like the NA ministry, petered out due to other obligations claiming more of time of the several volunteers.

Mr. Charles Gregg, a newcomer and retired professional regional sales manager for a well-known company, was instrumental in developing the church's bread ministry. He was able to get donated breads and pastries from various supermarkets and bakeries weekly. The products were made available in the fellowship hall for members and residents in the community. A number of persons in the community came to the church to obtain the free bread and pastries. It is to be noted that Ginny immediately took Charles under her wing and put to work in "her kitchen."

At the conclusion of my tenure at St. Mark's, the most vital outreach ministries were with LARS and the bread ministry that continue to this present time.

Witness Ministries

Our witness ministries were somewhat anemic. Younger women did not join the United Methodist Women (The Women's Society) because it was viewed as an organization for older women. The United Methodist Men sporadically met at the push of the pastor. When Bro. Nicholson died, the men agreed to serve as surrogate fathers for the boys with single mothers. Their own young sons, along with nephews, were invited to join the choir. The youngsters joined with the adult men to form the male chorus of St. Mark's, and many of the boys grew up in the choir until it was merged into a mass choir.

The reactivation of Lenten services in 1984 among our sister churches, Mount Zion, and Queen's Chapel was a significant ministry that facilitated a revitalization of connection among the United Methodist Churches in the Laurel area. I developed lasting friendships with Reverends James Harrison and Leon C. Kess, respective pastors of the sister churches. We agreed upon scheduling a series of Lenten worship service on Wednesday nights. We called the event,

"Journey Around the Circuit." The visiting pastor was responsible for the order of worship while the offering received during the said service would be donated to a charity of the host church's choice. A benefactor of the generous offerings was the Laurel Advocacy and Referral Service (LARS). Several other churches joined us the following year: First Church of Laurel UMC, Community UMC of Maryland City, and Faith African Methodist Episcopal Church. Each year, one of the pastors agreed to serve as coordinator of the event.

The Journey Around the Circuit culminated with the Good Friday Service of the "Seven Last Words of Jesus from the Cross." This signature event of the season, typically hosted by Queen's Chapel, was a standing-room-only experience. After the service, a fish dinner was provided in the lower fellowship hall. Needless to say, this was a great time of fellowship along with relatives that were connected to the respective churches. There was strong support of the Lenten services until the mid-to-late 1990s when subsequent pastors did not feel or see the need to conduct the services beyond their local churches. As one of the organizing pastors, I was disappointed to hear of the decline of this particular worship ministry.

The first Saturday after Labor Day was a high time in the Grove. It was the Emancipation Day picnic and parade. This was a celebration commemorating President Abraham Lincoln's issuance of the Emancipation Proclamation in 1862 that went into effect on January 1, 1863; it freed all slaves in slave-holding states. The event drew family members and friends from metropolitan Baltimore, Maryland, Washington DC., and the surrounding counties.

Members of the church provided vendor stands while Sis. Helen Johnson and others cooked chicken and fish for dinners and sandwiches to be sold. Several marching bands' cheerleaders, and lodge members participated. The matriarchs of the church were chauffeured in expensive convertibles during the parade. Mrs. Pat Mundell, a quick-witted and humorous woman, chauffeured the pastor in a Corvette. The local volunteer fire department and civic leaders usually attended and participated in the annual event. Revenue from the event helped the church meet its financial obligations to the conference and other expenses. Significantly though, the community was aware of the event sponsored by the church. My initial reaction was I did not like being on exhibition in the community but later learned to appreciate the significance of the event as it related to the families of the Grove.

I began attending city council meetings at the urging of Ronnie Matthews, a community activist for social justice. We advocated for better services from the department of public works. On one occasion, Mrs. Ellen Gibson, along with one of her granddaughters, was walking toward home but in the street because there was no pavement parallel to the church's property; it was very dangerous. I made it a point to get on the agenda at Laurel City Hall where I complained about the pavement. Shortly thereafter, Mayor Donnie Donohue inspected the area, and she directed the officials at the

Department of Public Works to install pavement running parallel to the church's property and to complete an unfinished part of a pavement near the front of the church. Periodically, local politicians would visit the church.

The other significant ministry in the witness area was the "pumpkin heads" ministry (orange hats). We needed to initiate a community effort to combat against the invasion of drug trafficking and usage in the community. After having made a statement before the city council of Laurel where I requested additional police presence in the community, I volunteered to organize and lead a group of community members in an effort to stop drug trafficking in the community. We called ourselves Citizens Patrol Against Drugs (CPAD) that would come out at unannounced times to demonstrate against drug selling and usage in the Grove. The members of the group primarily church members were George Gibson, David Burley, Bernice Brooks, Mildred Awkward, Gail Gibson, Patty Wallace, the late Collie Moore, and the late Ronnie Matthews and me. I am certain there were other persons who joined in with us, but their names escape me.

On one occasion, I saw a drug pusher selling drugs. I chased him down the streets and through a wooded area where I lost sight of him. He was a member of one of the families of the church. (Years later after serving a period of incarceration, the drug pusher was transformed by Christ and now is an ordained Baptist minister in Laurel where he is building a church. Rev. Devan Hebron spoke at one of my former congregations and remarked, "Reverend De Ford chased me through the woods and lost me, but Jesus caught me." Well, at least I can say, "I chased someone to Christ." It may not have been conventional evangelism, but it worked.

We received newspaper coverage in the beginning. Like most newsworthy situations, there was some attention given until the pushers moved to another location. But a few months later, we were back at square one! We resumed the patrols in the community, but weather and discouragement of some of the members contributed to the petering out of the effort.

NOW THEN

The NOW ministry model was not defined during the early 1980s as in later years, but the principles were operant within the local church. St. Mark's was nurturing, although its focus was insular. This is congruent with what C. Eric Lincoln wrote, "One of the great strengths of black rural churches . . . is their loyalty of their members . . . they have continued to hold the loyalty of the faithful remnant."[16] Concern for the sick and shut-ins or being supportive to bereaved families was a core value reflected in St. Mark's members. Outreach, on the other hand, was not extensive but appropriate for this family-pastoral size congregation. Pertinent to witness in the community, St. Mark's was known for its ministry of social justice in the Grove.

The Matter of Conflict

Conflict is part of the human condition. There are a plethora of biblical accounts regarding conflict such as in the relationship between Jacob and Esau (Genesis 25:19–34), Abimelech and the citizens of Shechem (Judges 9:23–24), Jesus and the people in the synagogue (Luke 4:16–30), and the disagreement between Paul and Barnabas (Acts 15:36–41), to name a few. The Corinthian correspondences emanate from conflict experienced in the First-Century Church.

There is conflict in the church, regardless of its size. I found this to be evident while serving at St. Mark's. Although not labeling the types of conflict that existed, I saw manifestations of such. David Canada describes types of conflict: inner, intrafamily, interfamily, cultural and racial, and fear.[17] Moreover, G. Lloyd Rediger classified conflict into three types: normal, abnormal, and spiritual.[18] There were intrafamily conflicts due to some of the members acting out as a result of alcohol and substance abuse. Interfamily conflicts because of issues from interpersonal relationships in the community and/or in the church. Cultural and racial conflicts based upon previous encounters with the local police or white racists groups in the community.

The administrative council meetings occasionally posed the potential for conflict. Policy changes, new initiatives or issues related to finances were sources for normal conflict. Generally, when attendees at the council meetings were reticent, I could anticipate that after the meetings the Parking Lot Committee (PLC) would convene shortly thereafter. Our meetings were for the most part very civil. Some of the members would speak with me on the following Sunday mornings for the purpose of further clarification of the matters discussed at the administrative council meeting. Typically, I heard, "Oh! I see. Well that seems right. Thank you, Reverend."

An abnormal conflictive situation occurred early in my ministry at St. Mark's. The church provided sleeping space for a local homeless man that had steady long-term employment with a local government agency. He suffered from some mental disorder yet was able to maintain his job as a custodian. The house he lived in since childhood was condemned by the city and torn down. The church agreed to allow him to sleep inside until such time permanent arrangements could be secured for him. However, he refused to accept rental offers and preferred to remain in the church. Finally, after much discussion and prayer, we evicted him. However, each night after the eviction he devised a way to jimmy the locking mechanisms of the doors by placing small pebbles and stones, thus jamming the locks. It was apparent he slept in the church because the smell of his body odor lingered. He was not arrested in view of his family ties and steady employment. I along with the leadership of the church felt very conflicted over this matter.

The matter was finally resolved. The human resources department from the homeless man's job contacted me. The personnel staff member disclosed that our homeless man was caught by security in the nude washing himself in a hallway utility closet. He was remanded to a psychiatric facility for evaluation. Upon his release from that facility, his estranged wife and her paramour allowed him to live in a trailer on their property.

I experienced a clash with the church historian who was collecting historical data for the church's anniversary journal in a very boisterous and heated exchange on a Sunday morning after worship service. Members were shocked at my behavior. On the following Monday evening, I called to apologize for my outburst. That next Sunday morning during "The Peace," I had a keen and powerful overwhelming sense of what it means to say, "Let us offer one another signs of reconciliation and love."[19] Miss Margaret forgave me for my actions.

I did not feel the impact of itineracy along with the associated inner conflict until the Sunday morning in March 1993 when District Superintendent Mary Brown Oliver came to inform the Staff Parish Relations Committee that I would be appointed to another church. I was unprepared for the emotional response from the congregation. It brought into focus the reason Miss Ethel and Miss Katie, in their late 80s, would get so anxious each time I went to conference. After service that morning, Lila and I went to see the Pillsbury sisters and informed them of my soon change of appointment; both were deeply hurt. I felt guilty that I was abandoning them after an eleven-year pastorate. I was severing the bond of "marriage" between pastor and members. This was my inner conflict.

The foregoing would be teaching moments that would leave an indelible impression upon me for years.

Tips for the Newly Appointed Pastor: Lessons Learned

I am certain many have heard a variety of the three preachers' jokes. While not attempting to bore the reader with the verbatim of one such joke, there were three preachers who went fishing. Two of the older preachers got out of the boat and walked on the water to the shore and returned to the boat. Finally, the younger preacher stepped out the boat and fell into the water. The two older preachers conferred and asked, "Do you think we ought to tell him where the rocks are?"

- For the newly appointed pastor, know who your key support people are. Your key people will be your support as you move into ministry within the congregation and the community. Be cognizant of the community and the history of the church. You will gain a greater appreciation of the culture and an understanding of who the members are and from whence they have come. Be aware of community needs and do not be hesitant about seeking remedies from the local officials. (Do not chase drug dealers! Leave apprehending criminal offenders to the authorities.)

- Do not criticize individuals or families in the congregations because no doubt you will be speaking to a family member, and you do not want your comments boomeranging back to you and thereby straining your relationship(s) with members.
- Be certain to honor the senior members of the congregation and especially the matriarch and/or patriarch of the church. They are very influential and can influence the attitude of the members of the congregation. Dudley maintains, "Patriarchs and matriarchs are at the center of the church . . . they no longer sit on the official boards of the church . . . but they have one essential feature . . . (they) have lived through the historical moments of the church . . . their presence . . . carry the identity of the church."[20] Be open to the advice of older or retired pastors and allow them to participate and play a role in the ministry of the church.
- Learn nicknames and use with permission of the individuals. The significance of nicknames is they convey or describe an important aspect of a person's character or physical features about a person.[21] Some are pleased that you know their nicknames.
- Listen with a second ear on what is going on in the midst of the congregation and the community.

- Keep a keen eye open for those that are missing for a short period of time. Send an email, a written card or telephonic contact and express concern about their absence.
- Make certain that you maintain professional integrity by observing rule concerning boundaries in your ministry, and honor your Sabbath time.
- When members develop enough trust, they will welcome you into their homes not just as the absentee minister from the conference but as their Pastor. Rev, Dr. Calvin Morris put it this way: "When members invite you to their kitchen, you have become their pastor"[22]
- Learn what the special events are in the life of the church, show enthusiasm and support of the events.

Chapter 3

Interregnum

July 1993–July 2000

I spent the next seven years of my ministry in serving two urban congregations, located in Baltimore and Washington, DC. Significantly both Mount Zion and Ebenezer were declining program churches and in reality functioning as pastoral-size congregations. Each suffered from aging membership, crises, and changing neighborhoods. Both needed major repairs to their physical plants.

Mount Zion United Methodist Church

The Context

Mount Zion is located in northwest Baltimore City in the community known as Ashburton. The community during the 1950s and 1960s reputedly had a sizeable population of upper-middle-class

African Americans: attorneys, business entrepreneurs, college and secondary educators, industrial managers, professional athletes, prominent pastors, retired military officers, and mid- and upper-level federal and state employees. To live in Ashburton was a symbol of status and success and the aspiration of many other African Americans to be residents of this community. A very influential civic association served as gatekeeper of the community and its culture and social values. Mount Zion was a microcosm of the demographics and mosaic of Ashburton.

The physical structure of Mount Zion is very impressive. The building was constructed during the 1920s and reflective of English Gothic architecture. The entire structure is granite stone with a large tower. Stained glass windows are positioned on the eastern and southern sides of the cavernous sanctuary. Adjacent to the sanctuary is a Christian education wing with three large classrooms (each with an office), a sacristy, huge lounge, finance office, two restrooms, and storage rooms. Next to the choir loft is a choir room and on the other side of the choir loft was the pastor's Sunday morning office with a private restroom. The lower part of the church has a huge auditorium with a stage. A commercial kitchen is next to the auditorium. Office spaces, two classrooms each with their own office, five restrooms, and the sexton's closet were other spaces in the lower area of the church. In addition the basement has not only the furnace room but a recreation room with two bowling lanes and ping pong and pool tables. (From my office I could hear youngsters using the bowling lanes that were in need of repair.)

I found myself ecstatic on the first Sunday of July 1993. Finally, I arrived at my castle on the hill. I had a big church in Baltimore! Wow! I had a big office. I had a staff consisting of a secretary, a business manager, and a duty trustee. Wow! I was a big-time city pastor in a great community. Wow! I had a day care center. Wow! The image I had of urban ministry in a program church materialized, so I thought, on the first Sunday of July 1993. There was joy, joy, joy down in my heart! Shortly thereafter, reality, however, would set in.

The sanctuary was in dire need of air conditioning. A member commented, "We pray for a breeze to come through, Reverend." The organ, a Moeller, needed repair as soon as possible; periodically without warning, the organ sounded due to some malfunctioning within. (There was a joke that a ghost played the instrument.) A wooden door needed to be replaced on the street-side in the lower auditorium. The choir consisted of eight persons, two of whom were not members of the church but friends of the organist. A number of members were inactive but would consider reactivating their membership. The foregoing were just some of the issues that brought me back to reality. I would find myself spending the first part of conference year 1993–1994 on relationship building and gaining the trust of the members in addition to re-igniting the ministries that were defunct and initiating new ones.

Key Players

The daily operation of the church was carried out by a paid and volunteer staff. The late Robert Byrd, local pastor, was the business manager. Several secretaries served until Ms. Arlene Jones joined the staff and continues after nineteen years of continual faithful service; I will address the matter of the secretarial staff later. The late Francis Handy, volunteer, served as duty trustee; he would send notices for publication in the weekly bulletin and to various ministry areas. His notes became known as "Handygrams." (Mr. Handy, a retired Baltimore City firefighter, instituted his own rite of passage for each new pastor: to climb to the top of the tower and get a view of Baltimore City where, on a very clear day, the harbor could be seen.) Russell Young, chair of Staff Pastor Parish Relations Committee, stopped in daily. The late Lucille Allen Taylor, owner and operator of the daycare center, was well known for hosting and serving sumptuous meals to civic leaders and preachers on Thursday afternoons in the kitchen or in the auditorium. (I gained most of my weight during my tenure at Mount Zion because of "Mama Lou's" meals.) Mrs. Taylor, a very generous woman, passed during the summer 2013. There was standing room only at her funeral at Community Church of God where the Rev. Dr. Melvin Green eulogized her.

My secretarial situation in the beginning was not reliable. One secretary had to be fired while another abruptly left after an incident regarding a missing deposit for a wedding. Subsequently, the late Mrs. Elizabeth R. Washington, a member of the church volunteered to serve as the church's secretary on a part-time basis. She was a classic secretary with impeccable skills, a retired office administrator of the Baltimore County School system and in her mid-80s. Mrs. Washington spoiled me, having a cup of coffee ready for me at my arrival. With her skills in shorthand, she would prepare letters and memorandums for my signature. She scheduled my daily visitations to members, and she gave me directions and other pertinent information about my scheduled visits. Besides her professionalism, she was a quick-witted cut-up. After about nine months and the urging of her adult children, Mrs. Washington resigned from the position. She promised, to be always be on standby if needed. Mrs. Sarah Gross, a federal retiree, served as a receptionist on the days when Mrs. Washington was not in the office.

Ms. Arlene Jones was hired during the spring of 1995. As a young woman of the charismatic persuasion and with excellent administrative and clerical skills, Arlene is a blessing to Mount Zion. She exhibits the fruit of the Spirit along with her strong work ethic and time values. The office stabilized once again with her being on board. Ms. Jones continues to serve as office administrator at Mount Zion.

Two ladies played an integral role during the second half of conference year 1993–1994. Mrs. Carrie Staten, retired principal, and Mrs. Bessie Franklin were the owners of a travel agency called

The Wonderful Workers of Mount Zion. In the spring of 1994, they donated a sizeable financial gift to the church for the specific purpose of installation of two commercial air conditioning units into the sanctuary. Other donations were made by these women for carpeting the sanctuary and upholstering lounge and pulpit furniture. It is to be noted that Mrs. Staten was instrumental in the church hiring the late Mr. Gene Swain, minister of music, who deceased in December 2006.

The administrative council was effectively chaired by Dr. Ann Venture Young. A detailed agenda was provided, and the meetings started on time. Dr. Young facilitated the meetings and spent no more time than was necessary on each item of the agenda. Ministry area reports from responsible leaders provided an account of their ministries. Meetings typically concluded as scheduled.

The late Robert Byrd served as business manager and lay leader of the church. He was very committed to the church and its ministries. At one point I would have contended that he was omnipresent in so far as the ministries of the church were concerned. Bro. Bob Byrd served also as coordinator of the district-wide School of Christian Growth for the Baltimore Northwest District that was hosted at Mount Zion. He was a good man, rather loquacious, and periodically I had to hold the reins on him due to his high energy level. He later completed a license to preach and became my associate pastor.

Mrs. Audrey Wharton, retired educator and secondary school English department head, was a faithful attendant of Bible studies. She eventually became the church lay leader when Minister Byrd was licensed to preach. She, too, would become licensed to preach and serve on staff.

The late Mr. Charles Wells was a long-time member of Mount Zion. His family owned and operated the Wells Printing Company in Baltimore City and was renowned for the printing services for churches and other African American business enterprises throughout the city. He was also patriarch of Mount Zion. During administrative council meetings, charge conferences or informal gatherings, I could observe the movement of the group dynamics toward Mr. Wells, looking for Charlie approval. When Charlie Wells spoke, the people listened. Charlie Wells was another quick-witted and humorous member of Mount Zion. I recall an occasion when I blurted out, "Charlie Wells, you old sinner." With a gleam in his eye, he responded, "Saved by grace!" From that time on we greeted one another in the same manner with a chuckle. The Wells family were very strong supporters of Mount Zion.

Several members who were active in various ministries of the church were from Eastern Shore, Maryland. Betty Gaskins, Gloria Young, and Sylvia Dickerson, members of the choir, attended the council meetings and advocated for choir ministry. These ladies were upper-level state and federal employees who would take on leadership positions later during my ministry at Mount Zion.

Froni Cunningham served as worship chairperson and a member of the choir. Mrs. Cunningham was very committed to her area of ministry and wanted to make certain that the correct seasonal paraments adorned the altar area.

Mrs. Margaret Summerville-Gaskins was very active with the conference United Methodist Women and traveled on behalf of the conference. She, too, was a retired educator who eventually served with the conference Board of Ordained Ministry as secretary.

Mrs. Doris Countess served as president of the local unit of United Methodist Women and was very active with district affairs of the UMW. She served as lay member to the annual conference.

Catherine Blackmon, Col. William Jackson, Minnie Smoot, Lettie Stanley, and Elmo St. Clair were the committed and faithful members of the finance committee.

The foregoing key persons were connected to the various ministries of Mount Zion and routinely were present during the week as they carried out their responsibilities. Each used their gifts and graces within the area of their calling in the body of Christ.

I review the ministries of Mount Zion through Nurture, Outreach, and Witness.

Nurture

I utilized the traditional pattern of worship service as outlined in the United Methodist Hymnal and Book of Worship. My worship team consisted of the late Minister Robert Byrd; Audrey Wharton, Lay Leader and lay speaker who eventually would be licensed to preach; Hattie Green, liturgist, and Fronnie Cunningham, worship chair. On the Sundays the focus was on young people with Zeara Chambers, liturgist, and my nephew Dennis Omar DeFord, who served as scripture reader.

One of the highlights of my ministry at Mount Zion was the instituting of the Disciple Bible Study program. During my three years, I was able to schedule two sessions of Disciple Bible Study: mid-day and evening. Minister Audrey Wharton and Dr. Ann Venture Young served as facilitators of the noon-day Bible study. The evening sessions varied in attendance from eight to sixteen students. Moreover, until the mid-day was established, several persons from other Methodist congregations and other denominations attended our classes. Out of the Disciple Bible studies, the late Nathaniel Morehead, attorney, joined our church.

The intent of the Disciple Bible Study program was fulfilled, in my opinion, in the faithful members of the classes. Mrs. Staten, a case in point, disclosed that she would get up daily at 4: 00 a.m. and study the lesson for the day. Frequently, she questioned me about certain points that were unclear to her. Mrs. Staten, although a long-time member of the church, was categorically a seeker. Through the Disciple study, transformation was evident in her life. She would eventually become lay leader of the church. (Mrs. Staten now resides with her adult children in California.)

I frequently smiled to myself as I listened to their "scrappy" group discussions regarding the lesson of the evening. It was all good! They were becoming more biblically literate and deepening their spirituality. I am convinced Disciple Bible Study series contributed to the transformation of the following individuals:

- The late Robert Byrd was licensed to preach, aka "Reverend Byrd," and delivered sermons;
- Audrey Wharton was licensed to preach and delivered sermons;
- Dr. Ann V. Young became a lay speaker and delivered sermons;
- Carrie Staten became a certified lay speaker and lay leader;
- Faye Johnson became a certified lay speaker; and
- Fannie Perry became a lay speaker.

Each of the members allowed the Spirit of God to empower them for ministry within the body of Christ. (1 Corinthians 12:27–31)

Membership care is an important area of nurturing ministry. The membership secretary was the late Mabel Bailey, who vowed at her retirement luncheon that she would dedicate more time to serving the church. Mabel perfected our membership directory and routinely followed up on members. She kept me informed. She was very active with the usher board, especially working with the junior ushers among who was my niece Tamara. Ms. Bailey died suddenly, which stunned the entire church. At her funeral, my six- year-old niece wrote her own reflection of how Miss Bailey's death affected her; she received a standing ovation at the funeral! As a postscript, my niece died tragically in an auto accident in 2006.

Visitations with members of the church typically occurred on Wednesday or as needed during any other time of the week for hospital visits. I adopted the practice of having the secretary call in advance to see if the pastor's visit would be convenient for the homebound or sick member. Many of the older members during communion visitations enjoyed the Word and Service Table V for sick and homebound. One member wanted to sing various hymns out of the old Methodist Hymnal; I relied on family members who were present to sing. Generally visitation day took about six hours (10 a.m. to 4 p.m.), including travel time.

There was no significant difference in funeral services of the churches that I served (i.e., in the urban, suburban, and rural communities). At Mount Zion, however, there was usually a struggle getting the casket down the staircase from the sanctuary. On one such occasion, in my haste to help the pallbearers and funeral staff take the casket down the stairs to the first platform, I became sandwiched between the casket and the wall. There was some concern as to whether I hurt my ribs, but I was okay. From that point on, I learned to leave the handling of the casket to the funeral staff and pallbearers.

The day of the funeral was long and demanding. I met with the family between 9:00 and 9:30 a.m. for family prayer at their home.

Upon the family's arrival at church, I met with them in the narthex to lead them into the sanctuary where friends and neighbors could meet the family during the Family Hour; and at 11:00 a.m., I began the service. At the conclusion of the service between 12:30 p.m. and 1:00 p.m., the funeral procession to the cemetery began and once the body was committed, we returned to the church for the repast. The repast was a tribal feast, and it was imperative that the pastor sit with the family at the head table. Between 4:30 p.m. and 5:00 p.m., family members, friends, and neighbors were gone, the hospitality committee completed their task of clean-up, and I was exhausted and went home.

The next day I checked on the bereaved family to see how they were doing. Either at that time or on the following Sunday, I read a card or verbal expression from the family, thanking the church and the pastor and staff for their care to the family. I oftentimes thanked the Lord for having the opportunity to help families during such difficult and trying times along life's journey.

Outreach

Mount Zion conducted two outreach ministries that I feel were cynosures in the community. The Mount Zion Ex-offender Advocacy Program (MZEAP) and Science Is for Everyone, sponsored by the Community College of Baltimore City were two ministries that were signature ministries of the church. MZEAP continues since its inception in January 1995 as a vital ministry and supported by the United Methodist Women of Mount Zion. MZEAP originated from my project dissertation for my doctor of ministry degree. The United Methodist Women readily responded to participate in the project. The initial team members were: Rutha McCants, Margaret Summerville, Elizabeth Washington, Margaret Wells, and Gloria Young. Chaplain Larry Covin, department head of Religious Services, and Ms. Gwendolyn Oliver, Director of Inmate Activities, were instrumental to the ministry we conducted at the Baltimore City Detention Center. At the start of the prison ministry, we visited twice per week, Tuesday and Thursday. However, Thursday seemed to be the best day for the team and the staff of the detention center.

I facilitated the beginning of the ministry with the women residents by presenting an overview of what we hoped to accomplish through biblical studies and discussion of pertinent issues of their choice. After a few weeks, I saw that this approach was going nowhere. Margaret Summerville gave a powerful presentation on domestic violence; the women opened up, became animated in their sharing of personal stories of violence against them, and one woman disclosed because she assaulted her abuser, she was awaiting sentencing. From that point on, Margaret and the team members gave the presentations, and I took the backseat. From that experience, the attendance increased and more meaningful topics were presented and discussed.

Aftercare was offered to three women residents. One woman, pregnant with twins, anticipated probation but did not receive the same. She gave birth to the twins while incarcerated. The sister of the young woman took custody of the children. The United Methodist Women on a certain Sunday invited the aunt to bring the twins with her to our worship service. There was no fanfare about who she was and her reason for being present other than being a visitor. After service, the aunt of the twins gathered with the team members in the UMW's room where an abundance of infant items were given to her and the twins, a boy and girl. The children had grown and were rambunctious toddlers.

The other two women ex-offenders did not respond to our ministry. One woman, who was a regular participant in the Thursday meetings, did not stay too long in the community after her release from the detention center. The other young woman, according to her mother, did not follow her release plan by returning home and seeking meaningful employment but was back into her old habits of drug addiction. While the outcomes at that point were discouraging, the team members faithfully continued their ministry to the incarcerated women of the Baltimore City Detention Center. I completed my dissertation project: "The Local Church as a Resource for Ex-Offenders during Re-integration into the Community." On May 8, 1996, I was conferred with the Doctor of Ministry Degree.

"Science Is for Everyone" was a program sponsored by the local community college and normally took place on Saturday mornings.

Youngsters were introduced to the world of science and the careers associated with the scientific community. Mount Zion served as a host church for a presentation on physics. On such an occasion, the youngsters were wowed when they saw a banana placed into liquid (nitrogen, hydrogen, or oxygen) transformed in a solid that broke like glass. On another occasion, an African American female chemical engineer talked about her job in the field of chemical engineering. Many of our retired educators served as chaperones for the participants as we visited the Aquarium, located in downtown Baltimore's inner harbor. These were meaningful experiences to the young people who participated in the program.

Witness

Mount Zion provided meeting spaces for two community groups: a community civic association and a retired seniors group. Many of the members of the church were a part of both groups. While it is not clear why both groups opted out of Mount Zion, the church continued to offer its facility to the various groups, organizations, and individuals.

The Matter of Conflict

When I arrived, Mount Zion had emerged from a conflictive relationship with my predecessor, and from all indications, the church wanted to move ahead. There were relatively few conflicts during my tenure. Whenever reference was made regarding issues with my predecessor, my response was, "Let's flip the page and keep moving on. That's history." My mission was to rebuild trust and strengthen the pastor and laity partnership in ministry. This would be a challenge on occasions.

A year or more into my tenure, a situation occurred. A male member started a rumor that the pastor was secretly seeing a woman in the church. The rumor circulated, but I did not pick up on it. I was oblivious to the subtle comments. Finally Mrs. Washington, the secretary, explained to me what was being gossiped about. At first I thought it was a joke, but Bob Byrd and Mama Lou corroborated the issue. I went ballistic! Immediately, I called Handy, chair of the Staff-Pastor-Parish Relations Committee, who coincidentally wanted to speak with me about the matter. He already made some preliminary investigations and wanted to arrange a meeting. The meeting took place with the woman, her husband, my wife, and me and the chair of SPRC.

Some details were brought to light that we were unaware of and it was clear how and why the rumor started. The genesis of this issue pre-dated our appointment to Mount Zion. The woman and her husband apologized to both of us as to what had happened. It was a tremendous burden lifted, but I still questioned introspectively, "Why didn't somebody say something to me sooner?" I felt alienated, isolated, and betrayed. The passage of scripture came to my thoughts regarding Peter's denial of Jesus as recorded in Matthew 26:31–35 and the assurance our Lord offers in Matthew 28:20b: "And remember

I am with you always, to the end of the age" (NRSV). From this experience, it took some time for me to reconcile with the member who triggered the rumor. I struggle to recapture the essence of the true flavor of reconciliation reminiscent of my days at St. Mark's.

The inner conflict associated with itineracy that I experienced at St. Mark's was not prevalent at Mount Zion. Although my father joined but did not participate in the ministries of the church, my nephew Omar participated in youth ministries, served as youth liturgist and reader, and my younger sister and her two daughters were attending, I did not feel the pain of separation as much. We are Methodists, and we choose to follow the polity of the church. I began my appointment at Ebenezer United Methodist Church on July 1, 1996.

Lessons Learned

Reflectively, I enjoyed the opportunity of serving a prestigious congregation in Baltimore City where the people hungered to learn. It also presented its challenges in terms of the physical condition of the building and its aging membership. There some valuable lessons learned:

- It is very important to have the right administrative staff person to manage the day-to-day functions of the office. While it was good to have had a well-qualified member who knows the nuances and peculiarities of the congregation, a pastor fares better with a nonmember paid employee.

- It is very important to listen with a second ear what is happening within the church than to be caught off-guard. When persons are speaking cryptically about situations, ask them to explain what is being said.
- It is very important to deal with conflict immediately than to let it fester.
- It is very important to allow the funeral director and staff members handle the physical aspects and handling of casket(s) and flowers. The pastor is responsible for the worship service.
- It is important for the pastor to serve as coordinator for social justice ministries but allow the laity to facilitate the implementation of the said ministries. Moreover, do not become discouraged in your ministry at occasional negative outcomes.

Ebenezer United Methodist Church

The Context

Ebenezer United Methodist Church, located at 4th and D Streets, SE, Washington, DC, is a historical African American church on Capitol Hill. It is the site where the first public school for colored children of the District of Columbia was housed, according to the US Department of the Interior National Park Service: National Register of Historic Place Inventory Nomination Form. Like many black Methodist Churches of the 19th century, they grew out of mother churches. Ebenezer, the mother church, eventually changed its name to Trinity, currently Capitol Hill United Methodist Church, 5th and Seward Square, SE. In 1825, African American members outgrew the galleries which were reserved for them in the mother church. Property was purchased on April 27, 1838, and a new construction was erected that became known as "Little Ebenezer." "The term 'Little' was dropped and the church became known as Ebenezer M.E. Church."[1]

> In September 1896, a terrible storm swept over the city causing irreparable damage to [the church]. Rev. Mathew Clair began plans for a third church building, but he left in 1897 to become Presiding Elder, and Rev. John Griffin (1897–1903) who succeeded him, undertook and completed the building of the third and present church. Because of the richness of the heritage and program of the church, Trustee Daniel Webster often referred to the new church as "The Old Cream Jug."[2]

I was introduced to Rev. Alfonso J. Harrod in August 1979 while a senior seminarian at Howard University School of Religion. I served my internship at Ebenezer where Rev. Harrod was improving the quality of music and worship in addition to new ministries within the church. Under his leadership, I was able to train a group of youngsters to become acolytes, among whom was Kevin Smalls, his nephew. I joined Ebenezer in 1980 and began the process of candidacy in the United Methodist Church. In 1981, Rev. Harrod received his doctorate, and his dissertation was entitled, "Worship and Its Effectiveness in the Ebenezer United Methodist Church."[3] Dr. Harrod's reputation precedes him, and he is a mentor to many pastors including myself in the Baltimore-Washington Conference. It was not unusual for congressmen, the mayor of Washington, DC, or Congresswoman Eleanor Holmes Norton to drop in to worship at Ebenezer. Dr. Harrod enjoyed a fifteen-year pastorate at Ebenezer. He left a profound impression upon the history of this church.

Both congregations are situated on a square block, with Capitol Hill on the northwest corner and Ebenezer on the southwest corner. From Ebenezer's upstairs back kitchen windows, Capitol Hill is visible. For years, there have been talks about a merger. The "old timers" of Ebenezer spurn the notion; however, with the current trend of an aged membership and gentrification of the neighborhood, it is only a matter of time, in my opinion, that this historic church will close. Presently, the church is part of a cooperative parish configuration with Queen's Chapel United Methodist Church, Muirkirk, Maryland. Reverend B. Kevin Smalls, senior pastor, is a son of Ebenezer who feels called to serve also as pastor of this historic congregation and his home church.

The change in the surrounding neighborhood brings with it a different culture. Many of the members of Ebenezer travel in from the surrounding suburbs, namely: Montgomery and Prince George's Counties, while the immediate community is transforming into a predominantly white neighborhood. Double parking, especially during funerals, and emotive worship services that can be heard when the windows are raised do not bode well in the immediate community. It was not uncommon to get negative reactions from the current residents when large funerals were conducted. On one such occasion when nearly four hundred or more attendees were present; their double-parked cars were ticketed by the police. The funeral director had to intercede on behalf of the attendees to rescind the parking violations. Later that evening, I along with a few of the members of the leadership met the neighborhood Advisory Neighborhood Council and council representative. This was a contentious meeting where it was clear there were cultural differences. Sadly, during my tenure there would be an ongoing conflict between the church and the residents of the community. Ebenezer was not alone; several other African American congregations were experiencing similar issues, and their pastors were frustrated.

Ebenezer's infrastructure was deteriorating. A renovation campaign had been initiated by my predecessor, and I was given the baton to complete the project. The entire building had to be rewired; new flooring in the narthex and certain sections of the sanctuary had to be replaced due to termite infestation; new lighting fixtures were installed from contributions in memory of the late Ellsworth Colbert; the entire sanctuary plastered and repainted; a new slate roof was installed; handicapped accessible bathroom installed; lower fellowship hall and office spaces reconfigured; and carpeting of sanctuary along with upholstery of the pews were done. While the renovation was in process, some of the community residents regularly put their unwanted furniture and trash in the dumpster that was reserved for debris from the renovation project. Apparently, at night after the contractors left the church, the persons took the liberty to leave their personal discarded items in the dumpster. The said activity became a nuisance.

To add insult to injury, a neighbor's son was observed by one of our trustees taking some stone blocks from the church's retaining wall and putting them into his father's garden as decorative stone blocks. We confronted the parent, but he vehemently denied that his son would do such. About an hour later while in Bible study, there was a loud pounding on the door of the fellowship hall and a person cursing and telling us to take the (explicative) stones that were thrown on the steps of the church. I decided not to call the police. Two years later when the man and his family were relocating elsewhere, he came to me and apologized. I believe we reconciled.

In light of the above, Ebenezer United Methodist Church, a historical church, was caught in the throes of a rapidly changing community populated with people of different cultural backgrounds while the formerly indigenous members of the congregation were aging, declining and residing elsewhere. The congregation was thoroughly ensconced in its tradition, and a merger with Capitol Hill UMC would be contravening. This was the context within which I was appointed to minister to the people of Ebenezer. There would be some key people to partner with me in this ministry.

Key Players

My wife and I were enthusiastically received by the members of Ebenezer on July 1, 1996 and viewed as a son returning home. After fourteen years, many of the members had aged, were in declining health, and some were homebound and in nursing homes. Those that remained were vital to help me with the ministry.

Ms. Beverly Johnson, chair of Administrative Council and daughter of the late Dr. Richard Johnson former pastor and district superintendent, continued to be an active member of the church. She is also the matriarch of the Johnson Family and sister of the late Dr. Charles A. Johnson. The late Mrs. Julia Johnson, widow of Dr. Richard Johnson and former first lady, was the grand matriarch of the Johnson Family.

Mrs. Mildred G. Colbert, business manager and member of the United Methodist Women is the matriarch of the Greene Family. The late Ellsworth Colbert, "Corby" saxophonist, treasurer, trustee, jack of all trades, and husband of Mildred Colbert, was a fixture in the church.

The late Lawrence A. Trimmer, "Lonnie," lay leader for fifty years plus, patriarch of the church, was a faithful aide-de-camp to all pastors. There is a picture of him as a ten-year acolyte standing in the lower choir loft, circa 1912.

The late Lucy Kittrell Brown, retired educator and Sunday school superintendent, was a woman with an indomitable spirit as she worked with youth.

The late Philips Conway, lay speaker and worship leader, was noted for his elocution and flair for words. He was animated while projecting his voice.

Ms. Beverly Spencer-Rollins, chair of Staff Pastor Parish Relations Committee, educator, would later marry my fraternity brother and subsequent pastor to Ebenezer, Rev. Dr. Michael A. H. McKinney.

Mrs. Lorna C. Morgan, the sister of Ellsworth Colbert, was the recreation specialist and Christian educator.

Mr. Thomas Davis, "Tommy," chair of the Board of Trustees, was committed to keeping the property cleaned and noted for his providing Popeye's chicken for meetings in the annex.

Mr. James Gilchrist, Jr., youngest trustee, was committed to Ebenezer; he was also known as "Roomy." He erected scaffolding on the inside and outside of church during renovation.

The late Raymond Gray, Sr., retired union arbitrator and trustee, held dual membership with Ebenezer and Capitol Hill.

The late Manila H. Boyd, retired government employee, active with the District and Conference United Methodist Women, member of the Conference Board of Ordained Ministry, communion steward, sister of Dr. Alfonso J. Harrod, and grandmother of Rev. Dr. B. Kevin Smalls, was a dear friend of ours.

Mrs. Joan Askew, educator, sister of Beverly Johnson and Rev. Dr. Charles A. Johnson, and a member of Staff-Pastor-Parish Relations Committee, was a long-time member of Ebenezer and a very candid individual.

Mrs. Muriel S. Sweatt, retired Charles County, Maryland educator, worship chairperson, was my birthday mate.

Mrs. Marion Stroud, (aka Mitzi), secretary and sister of Mildred Colbert, was a retired federal government employee.

Mrs. June Robinson-Slonicki, a very confident outgoing person, served as a communion steward, trustee, and member of the Renovation Committee.

Miss Helen V. Dyson, long-time member and church historian, maintained the archives. She sent birthday cards to us until her health declined.

The late Erlease Burrell, long-time president of the communion stewards, was meticulous about dressing the pulpit and altar area. Mrs. Erlease Burrell Proctor, daughter of communion steward Burrell, was member of finance committee and board of trustees.

Mr. Ernest Green, affectionately known as Ernie and brother of Mildred Colbert, was business entrepreneur that was instrumental in having the late Maya Angelou to present an evening of poetry during the Homecoming Anniversary of 1999.

Mr. Frederick Ambush, a World War II member of the Buffalo Soldiers stationed at Ft. McNair, Virginia, is a very faithful usher and periodically calls me and my wife.

Mrs. Helen Lester, retired government employee, lay speaker, and choir member, with a Barnabas-type personality, sends birthday cards to us and periodically calls to chat with my wife.

Each of the foregoing members played significant roles in the overall ministry of Ebenezer United Methodist Church, "The Old Cream Jug."

Church Administration

Conference year 1996 through 1997 was a period of stabilizing the church secretary position. For a period of time, the late Jacquelyn Greene served as secretary on a part-time basis. Health reasons militated against her continuing as the church secretary. Ellsworth Colbert filled in as receptionist until we were able to hire Mrs. Yvonne Anderson. Mrs. Anderson served the church for approximately nine months until she relocated to Virginia. In the late spring, 1997, Mrs. Marion Stroud, a recent retiree from the federal government, assumed the secretary position on a part-time basis. At last the church secretarial position was stabilized.

The ongoing renovation within the church provided an opportunity for the administrative office to relocate in the church's fellowship hall, specifically in the newly renovated finance office. The old finance office was reconfigured with an adjoining doorway to the downsized old pastor's office. The archives room located on the second floor that had been the old pastor's office was returned to its original purpose. This triggered a conflict with the church historian and her committee until such time I was able to demonstrate the value of having the fellowship hall serve as archives with all its associated historical artifacts and display cabinets while having the same area serve as a meeting place. The remaining historical documents and files were placed in a newly constructed storage space in the basement. The members of the committee were very pleased with the decision. With the changes initiated, the hub of administrative operations resumed in the fellowship hall of the main church building.

A daily rhythm emerged that remained during the remainder of my tenure at Ebenezer. Mrs. Mildred Colbert became business manager, a volunteer position; she along with her sister, Mrs. Marion Stroud, "Mitzi," kept the flow of the day-to-day office routine. From 9:00 a.m. to 3:00 p.m., "the sisters" managed the office and kept me abreast on administrative matters. Ms. Mildred scrutinized requisitions for purchases of various supplies and Christian education materials. Mitzi prepared the weekly bulletins and scheduled my visitations. A certain number of bulletins were set aside for the sick and shut-ins. The office was running smoothly. Mr. Trimmer, like clock-work on Monday mornings, removed the previous Sunday's sermon title from the marquis and in similar fashion on Friday mornings placed the new sermon title or information on the board. Meanwhile, John Lowery, the sexton diligently went about his job of keeping the church clean while periodically Tommy, chair of the trustees, would drop in at unannounced times to check on John and see if Ms. Mildred needed any supplies to be picked up.

The newly decorated upstairs pastor's office gave me a sense of calm, comfort, and peace. My wife was the interior decorator of my office. It was my place of escape where I could get inspiration for weekly sermon preparation. My calls were screened by the secretary and very little traffic came upstairs. I thought I'd reached the height of my pastoral career. I was content to remain until my eligibility for retirement.

Church Council meetings were routinely conducted as scheduled. The primary focus was on the progress of the renovation project and the associated strain on the financial purse strings of the church. We fell behind on the payment of our apportionments, and it was suggested that we seek relief through Jubilee (suspension of apportionment payments for a designated period of time) while in the process of renovation. For a few months, the council convened at the annex due to the construction work in the main church building and fellowship hall. I proposed that we explore the possibility of using space at Capitol Hill UMC. The idea was vehemently rejected because some of the older members feared it would be a pathway toward the disestablishment of Ebenezer. As it turned out, we met at the annex, and when feasible we met in the sanctuary on the side that was not in the process of being painted and/or without scaffolding.

Tommy Davis continued to convene the Board of Trustees at the annex. At each meeting, Tommy provided an evening meal of Popeye's chicken and sides of French fries, soda, and biscuits. The meetings promptly began at 7 p.m. and concluded between 8:30 p.m. and 9:00 p.m. Typically, Ms. June Slonicki kept us informed on matters related to the renovation. Jimmy Gilchrist kept the trustees informed of the various activities of the Trustee Fellowship of Washington, DC, an ecumenical group of trustees. The trustees for the most part performed their duties in a faithful manner.

Normal conflict, comparatively speaking, was minimal during my administration. We were preoccupied with the renovation of the church and scheduling a special worship service for a certain family that wanted the entire service focused upon their family. Meanwhile, another dominant family wanted some time set aside for the baptism of their grandchild because there would be family members coming from out of town. What appeared to be a simple matter of including the family in the service became a major source of conflict with the two families. I was able to get the families to compromise on the matter of the special service and the baptism after meeting with them on several occasions. The outcome was a second brief service of baptism following the main special day service. While the foregoing conflictive situation appears to have been settled in several meetings, it took a longer time for the matriarchs to reconcile.

The administrative machinery of Ebenezer functioned appropriately for a pastoral-sized congregation although attitudinally and ideologically it was a program-sized church.

Nurture

The nurturing ministries of Ebenezer were the dominant areas of activity. Worship, Christian education, fellowship, and pastoral care were ministry areas that received primary attention.

Pertinent to worship, I conducted traditional pattern of worship services at Ebenezer similar to Mount Zion in Baltimore City. Mr. Gregory Crowe served as the minister of music; he is an exceptional pianist and organist. There were three choirs under his leadership: Sanctuary, Chorus, and Men's Chorus. Mr. Arttrus Fleming served as choir director and musician for the Ebenezer Ensemble, younger members who preferred more contemporary music resulting in my hiring a percussionist (drummer). Initially, there was some push-back from the older members and mixed reviews from the general body of the membership. The young adults loved it. Mr. Fleming was supportive of the inclusion of the drummer in the worship service. Later Rev. Charles Robinson, a young adult African Methodist Episcopal minister, became the choir director and musician due to the death of Mr. Fleming. Rev. Robinson was quite contemporaneous with the Ensembles.

Each choir had its notables. The late Odean Wilkerson was known for her unique soprano voice, and her signature was the very high notes that she could flawlessly reach on certain anthems and hymns. Samuel (Jack) Green has a deep bass voice and frequently sings at funerals. Patricia Milliard, young adult trained in music, often added to the quality of music among the Ebenezer Ensemble. Each used their gifts and graces on Sunday mornings and at other services to the glory of God.

I was accompanied in the pulpit by Mr. Lawrence Trimmer, lay leader and lay speaker, and Phillips C. Conway, lay speaker and liturgist. Mr. Conway typically gave the morning announcements with his bass voice and in his own way an elocutionist; he would read one of the Scripture lessons. Mr. Trimmer offered the morning prayer and served as a reader also of one of the lectionary readings for the day. Both faithfully met with me in the lower fellowship hall pastor's office for prayer prior to meeting with the choir.

My sermons were based upon the prescribed lectionary scriptures; however, I was not glued to the lectionary readings. During the time of the renovation, I was thematic in my sermons particularly based in the Nehemiah passages. I made certain that the kerygma is in the proclamation and continue to do so. There were occasions I was more emotive and less cerebral and vice versa. Overall, the goal was to get the message to the people with the hopes of bringing about transformation in their lives, becoming faithful followers of Jesus Christ with a deeper spiritual formation.

The communion stewards served under the leadership of Erlease Burrell who held the position for nineteen years. She was a very personable lady and a perfectionist. Each Saturday afternoon prior to the first Sunday, Mrs. Burrell guided the aging communion stewards as they painstakingly dressed the altar. After service on Sunday, the senior ladies "stripped" the altar of the communion furnishings and put in place the paraments reflective of the season of the Christian year. After several hospitalizations and weakening health, Mrs. Burrell relinquished her office. She was able, with her very personable and persuasive way, to convince the ladies to elect Lila, my wife, to serve as the chair of the communion stewards. My wife reluctantly accepted the position as chair.

Lila initiated a regular meeting schedule and established a schedule for the ladies who would serve on a given Sunday while others were seated on the second row center aisle, if not for ceremonialism's sake only. Subsequently, three younger women joined the communion stewards in addition to a teenager, the daughter of one of the new members. The younger women assumed the duties while the senior ladies enjoyed being a part of the ministry and being seated on Sunday mornings in their white communion uniforms. "We are important too, Reverend." was a comment from one of the very senior members of the communion stewards. One of the initiatives Lila started was honoring communion stewards on

World Communion Sunday in October and expressing appreciation to the members for their commitment to their ministry area. The service by the ladies who served at the altar was part of the mosaic of the nurturing ministries of Ebenezer.

Ushering in the African American church is a very important aspect of the worship service. In some churches, there is pageantry in ushering and an expectation that the ushers will "do their march." Some churches are noted for their outstanding usher boards and their esprit de corps. Mr. Raymond Gray, Sr. was president of the International Ushers Union, a consortium of local and national usher boards. As president of the said organization, Mr. Gray made certain that the ushers of Ebenezer reflected the training and skills of ushering. By the time of my appointment to Ebenezer in 1996, some of the members of the usher board had either died or health reasons prevented them from being active participants. The remaining few proudly carried out their ushering duties with dignity and pride. Mr. Gray eventually stepped down due to aging and having relocated in Montgomery County, Maryland. The board diminished to approximately ten or less members. I could readily depend on Freddie Ambush (Buffalo Soldier), Mattie Coates, the late John Harper, Mary McCoy, George Saunders, Celbrough Terry (Sarge), and Valerie Wheeler to serve as gatekeepers to the sanctuary.

Annual days and special worship services were events that drew worshipers to Ebenezer. Such occasions gave a glimpse of the church's heyday when it was not uncommon for the sanctuary to be full both on the main floor and in the gallery. The homecoming event of September 1999 was chaired by Ernest "Ernie" Green, who orchestrated a series of weekend activities: picnic in the church yard where a huge tent was erected; instrumental musical concert by four teenage cellists among whom was our own Kulan Brown; an evening program with a full house that featured the late Dr. Maya Angelou; and a concluding Sunday worship service with lunch in the churchyard. For weeks after the special homecoming, members continued to bask in the memory of the event.

Funerals at Ebenezer were always very special times and opportunities for the church to express care and empathy to the bereaved families. From the earliest notification of death to the interment, my mission was to walk beside the families throughout the experience and follow up with them in subsequent days. On the day of the funeral, the lower sanctuary was normally full, but on occasion, the gallery would have some occupants. The two largest funerals that I officiated were for the late Ellsworth "Corby" Colbert in June 1997 and Julia Johnson in 1998. For Corby, the gallery was full to capacity while there were worshipers standing around in the sanctuary and fellowship hall. For Mrs. Johnson, a number of preachers were in attendance who gave words of comfort; and Rev. Dr. Charles A. Johnson, who despite his stroke condition, spoke on behalf of the family. Once the interment was completed, the family and friends returned to the church for repast in the fellowship hall. The foods for the repast were completely donated by various members of the church.

The positive outcome of some funeral services was certain members re-affirming their faith and becoming active with the ministries of the church. Another positive outcome was the son of a shut-in member, who had passed, joined the church. Joe Freeman expressed his faith in Christ, attended new membership class, and was read into membership. Joe became a faithful member who participated in various ministries of the church until his death.

The downside to funerals at Ebenezer was the cultural differences between the growing new white residents and few remaining African Americans in the community. On one such an occasion, an irate white resident on D Street, SE, went to the church office where she complained and wanted the cars immediately moved, despite the fact that the funeral service was in process. There was a verbal exchange with an office staff member, subsequent to which the irate woman left the fellowship hall. Not long after the incident, the police were ticketing a number of the double-parked vehicles. The funeral director requested all of the drivers of the ticketed cars give him the tickets because the funeral home would take care of them. Through the joint efforts of funeral directors and the church, we were able to have no parking signs posted on 4th and D Streets, SE, with the hours 9 a.m. to 1 p.m. This incident did not bode well in terms of the church's intent to be hospitable toward our immediate neighbors.

I initiated a Friday intercessory prayer group. The prayer group gathered in the old choir loft on the main floor of the sanctuary. We began by singing a selected hymn of the morning followed by opening prayer by Mr. Trimmer. Each member brought a concern, a petition from members or nonmembers. Each of us prayed for the concerns cited. Prayers of thanksgiving were also prayed. Each week the attendance varied, but Mr. Trimmer and Mrs. Louise Washington were steady in their attendance. In all, the intercessory prayer group provided a general catharsis not only for its members but for those who just did not want to share openly in the congregation their various struggles in life.

Worship ministry was central to the lives of the aging congregation at 4th and D Streets, SE. It provided not only an opportunity to express their faith in God but in a given existential moment to experience the presence of God through various aspects of the worship ministry such as singing on the choir, serving as a member of the communion stewards, ushering, and assisting the pastor in pulpit. The members felt a sense of self-esteem through participation in some aspect of the nurturing character of the worship ministry.

Christian education ministry was under the co-leadership of the late Lucy Kittrell Brown and Lorna C. Morgan. Both headed up the Sunday school classes conducted in the annex on Sunday mornings. A member of Capitol Hill United Methodist Church with her young people joined with the ladies in the annex where Sunday school classes for the youth were conducted from 9:30 a.m. to 10:30

a.m. Meanwhile, Mr. Trimmer and Mrs. Louise Washington were co-teachers of the adult class that met in the old choir loft on main floor of the sanctuary.

The Disciple Bible study series was a boon to the Ebenezer congregation. Two sessions were offered, one in the afternoon and the other in the evening. During my tenure, we were able to cover all three segments of the Disciple series in addition to the Christian Believer series. At one point, three Bible study opportunities were offered, with my wife and Lucy K. Brown facilitating the other classes while I conducted Christian Believer lessons. Participants were encouraging other members to enroll. Mrs. Lucy K. Brown continued to facilitate Disciple Bible studies after I was appointed to Metropolitan UMC.

Fellowship and hospitality were key features of the nurturing ministry at Ebenezer. Each Sunday after worship service members gathered in the fellowship hall where volunteers provided an assortment of pastries, salads, and sandwiches. Coffee, tea, and juices were also available. Pre-meeting discussions were conducted, as well as debriefing on my sermon by various persons. Occasionally, I would hear the comment, "I always wanted to know what that meant in the Bible." The chatter, laughter, and periodic chastisement by parents of children romping in and out of the fellowship hall into the church yard could be heard. It was not uncommon for members to linger up to an hour or more after service, although there was not a meeting upstairs. I attribute that to the fact many of the members no longer lived in the immediate community or walking distance from the church. The fellowship hour provided opportunity for the congregants, especially the very senior members, to have social interaction that was so important to them.

Mrs. Lucy and Lorna, both were active with youth ministries and, through their nurturing efforts, touched the life of a would-be-at-risk youngster. Kenny Hoover, a short stocky kid and leader among the youth, was like a grandson to Mrs. Lucy, who would transport him and his siblings to and from church in a nearby marginalized section of Southeast Washington, DC. Lorna could depend upon Kenny to invite classmates and friends to youth activities. In his own affable way, he was quite evangelistic and could persuade some of his neighborhood friends to come to youth meetings and worship services.

Kenny organized a group of several youths in the church and during a youth Sunday worship began singing a popular selection by Kirk Franklin, "I Sing because I Am Happy" and another popular song by Rance Allen, "Something about That Name Jesus." Initially I had mixed emotions about what he did, but then, the Spirit spoke to me, "This kid has a gift." At ROCK, a powerful Christian fun-filled weekend in Ocean City, Maryland, in January 1999, Kenny and his group did a rendition of "Something about That Name Jesus."[5] The kids received a standing ovation from the youth at ROCK. Mrs. Lucy and I felt very proud of our youngsters. Kenny learned mime and now is serving as a youth minister in a cooperative parish in Washington, DC.

Pastoral care was a high priority for this congregation. The sick and shut-in list was extensive, requiring visitations in each quadrant of the city. By the time I completed the visits at the end of the month, the cycle was in readiness to begin again. Fortunately, Mr. Trimmer, lay leader, and Mrs. Mildred Colbert, lay speaker, shared some of the burden by visitation of members in their quadrant of Washington, DC thereby reducing the load upon me. My visitations normally began mid-morning and concluded by late afternoon, just prior to evening traffic. Visits with very senior members were coordinated with their adult children or caregivers. I tried to be as close to the scheduled time as possible. Hospital and nursing home visitations were often longer and could throw me off schedule due to other patients, nonmembers, wanting prayer. (I recalled my days when doing clinical pastoral education (CPE).) The homebound members wanted to hear of the activities happening at the church or to inform me of what they heard. They simply wanted corroboration of the information received from their friends from the church. Somehow, hearing it from the pastor authenticated what they heard from member friends.

It was also important for the homebound members to receive a most recent copy of the bulletin. Once they glanced through the bulletin, they were ready for the sacrament of Holy Communion. Amazingly, some of the members regardless of their age and apparent hints of dementia were able to quote verbatim the communion ritual. At the conclusion of the communion service, I offered prayer for any specific concerns the members disclosed. As I prepared to leave, I would hear, "Reverend, I know you are a very busy man and you have to see other members, but please come again and stay a while, you and Mrs. DeFord." Leaving was difficult because of their hunger for company and a sense of tangible connection with the church. I would hear the echo, "Reverend, we are important, too." The visiting days were exhausting both physically and emotionally, but there was always a sense of satisfaction because this is what God called me to do and I was striving to be faithful in carrying out the assignment.

Nurture in whatever aspect is the giving of oneself to benefit others in their experience of the presence of God in their lives and God working through the nurturer to help perfect the potential of the gift of God's grace within one's life. By doing such, the nurturer is an instrument of God's love being made a reality in the life of the receiver. This is the thrust of nurturing ministries.

Outreach

Two signature programs under the auspices of two ministerial coalitions operated at Ebenezer. A summer camp program sponsored by an African American ecumenical clergy group, Wednesday Clergy Fellowship headed by the Reverend Dr. Frank Tucker, First

Baptist Church, Washington, DC, provided educational and supervised recreational activities during the summer for the participating churches and their youths. During the fall and winter, the same group sponsored tutorials for community children. Staff members were paid a stipend for their services. We utilized our annex during the summer and provided the regulated meals as stipulated by the US Department of Agriculture.

The other program focused upon providing shelter for homeless families for a month. Ebenezer fortunately availed the annex that had four bedrooms, affording privacy to our homeless guests. The late Gretchen Kimbo, a long-time trustee, provided meals without cost to the church. She tragically was killed in an auto accident. We named the outreach ministry in her honor, Gretchen Kimbo Outreach Ministry to the Homeless. The ministry to the homeless had its bright spots in addition to some troubling situations. Several of our young adult women took the young teenage girls of the homeless families just before Easter to a beauty salon for hairdos and shopping for new clothes. The families joined us for Easter worship service.

On another occasion during our second year in the program, a meal was provided for the families on a Sunday afternoon, but the families never showed up for the meal in the annex. We later learned that the guests went to McDonald's for the Sunday afternoon meal and did not want to receive a handout from the church. (This was a communication problem.) We encountered a situation of an abusive boyfriend that we had the police to remove from the premises only to learn not long after the woman opened the window where the fire escaped was located and brought him back into her room. We did not let the problems of our guests deter us from continuing the ministry to homeless persons.

The foregoing ministries continued after my appointment to Metropolitan United Methodist Church in 2000.

Witness

Ebenezer is a historical church that stood the test of time while being a testimony to the enduring strength of a faithful people of the Lord Jesus Christ. Its documented history discloses explicitly the will of the people to build and maintain a house of worship in southeast Washington, DC. Miss Helen Dyson, church historian, articulates the history of the church when tourists on Capitol Hill visited the church. On one such an occasion, a tour guide from the United Kingdom took pictures of the stained glass windows in the church for purposes of updating an earlier tour guide book in which Ebenezer was listed as a tour site. News channel Fox 5 did a segment on Ebenezer as one of the historical African American churches in the District of Columbia and public school for children of color. The theme of faith of the people and their love for Christ was the spiritual glue that held them together over the years. The late

Raymond Gray, Sr. often commented, "Here I raise my Ebenezer;" as a testimony to his faith in God and faithfulness to this local church. [4]

The local unit of the United Methodist Women was a very vital ministry area within Ebenezer. The unit met faithfully the second Sunday of each month after morning worship. The women gathered in the upper fellowship hall and followed the protocol of the UMW.

Ebenezer's witness in the immediate community was hampered, however, due to the changing demographics and the church's mixed feeling toward diversity and inclusion. The situation was conflictive due to a clash of cultures, in my opinion. Members seeking parking spaces on Sunday mornings double parked, resulting in the ire of white residents. Further, and as alluded to early on, funerals conducted during the weekdays exacerbated the negativity toward the church. Some members, on the other hand, were suspicious of white visitors during worship services. In some instances, some of the members felt that white neighbors were snooping.

Hindsight is a great teacher; looking back as the servant leader of Ebenezer the latter part of the 1990s, I would have taken a different approach. The core issue was hospitality. I would have attempted to cultivate an attitude of hospitality and inclusion of all God's people. With a more welcoming spirit, Ebenezer may have been a more attractive model for a diverse worship experience. I have profound regrets for not giving the leadership that was needed in this particular area.

Leaving the Urban Context

The proverbial "call" came to me on a Monday evening in March 2000. The Reverend Mary Jane Coleman, District Superintendent of the Washington East District, informed me of my new appointment to Metropolitan United Methodist Church, Indian Head, Maryland. I was livid. I did not receive a vision of anyone from Indian Head beckoning to me to come over and help them. I was contented regardless of the occasional conflictive situations with some of the neighbors on Capitol Hill. Did I really have to leave Ebenezer? Maybe I could be "Jonah-like," but that would not really help. Finally, it occurred to me that I did take a vow at my ordination to itinerate. The shock wore off, and I prepared myself and my wife for our eventual move to the new appointment in Indian Head, Maryland. We would leave Capitol Hill for what we perceived as a rural community in the western part of Charles County, Southern Maryland.

My seminary classmate and friend the Reverend Harold W. Watson was the pastor of Metropolitan, and he was retiring after twenty-four years of ordained ministry in the United Methodist Church. He thoroughly enjoyed his ministry at Metropolitan and was retiring on a high note. My transition conversations with him took place in the office and as we traveled around the community. It was obvious as we met various parishioners in the community that many of them and nonmembers were saddened to see him leave. I did not feel at all adequate or desirous to serve this community. But God works in mysterious ways!

Lessons Learned

The experience of serving Ebenezer United Methodist Church on Capitol Hill, Washington, DC taught me a few lessons. The congregation attitudinally viewed themselves as an urban program church while in actuality, the church was a pastoral-sized congregation. Further, the demographics were rapidly changing in the neighborhood, and minimal preparation was made to address the shift that was taking place in the neighborhood that was once predominantly African American. I learned:

- It is important to affirm the historical significance of the church and its role in the community at large.
- It is important to work with key leaders in preparation for needed changes within the church.
- It is important to begin to cultivate a realistic view of the church in its existential circumstances and its effectiveness in ministry to the community.
- It is important to work in concert with the trustees pertinent to the requirements of the physical structure.
- It is important to work with members when conflict arises to reach a just outcome and reconciliation.

- It is important to develop a ministry of radical hospitality that welcomes all to the worship of God.
- It is important to look for new and creative ways of dealing with neighborhood parking during service times.

Chapter 4

Exurbia: the New Rural Community

Metropolitan United Methodist Church

The Context

I officially began my new administration on July 1, 2000, with Metropolitan United Methodist Church, located in western Charles County, Maryland. It is within the boundaries of the township of Indian Head, but the members of the immediate and surrounding communities of the church have affinity with Bryans Road, census-designated place (CDP) and Pomonkey, an unincorporated community [1]. Bryans Road serves as a bedroom community for the many residents who work in metropolitan Washington, DC, Northern Virginia, and the nearby Indian Head Naval Surface Weapons Center. I would soon discover the significance of this local church and its valuable role in the community.

Metropolitan United Methodist Church was established 146 years ago as an outgrowth of prayer meetings in the homes of twenty people. Under the leadership of Henry Datcher and Coates Slater, land was purchased for the purpose of having a "meeting place," according to MUMC's *A Snapshot of Our Church History*. The Washington Conference of the Methodist Episcopal Church appointed the Reverend Charles Wheeler in 1869 to serve as the first pastor of the congregation. Records reflect that Reverend Wheeler served for three years. Under the pastorate of the Reverend Charles Price, the congregation was named Price Chapel with a membership of 304. The congregation would eventually become designated as the Pomonkey Charge. Reverend L. E. S. Nash served from 1901 to 1906, during which time a new church was built and named Metropolitan Methodist Episcopal Church. The said structure would serve the congregation until 1975 during the administration of the late Reverend Edwin Williams (1969–1979), when the church was razed to clear the ground for the new worship center. The church was constructed in 1976, and the mortgage of $145,000 was paid off in 1977. The church entered into another building program for an addition under the pastorate of the Reverend Harold W. Watson (1996–2000) and completed during my administration in 20003. The new addition was consecrated on June 29, 2003 by Bishop Felton E. May.

Metropolitan United Methodist Church is a predominantly African American senior pastoral-sized congregation that enjoys the reputation of being the church where many of Charles County's local educators have held their membership. A nearby dormitory, years ago, housed some of the single women teachers who regularly attended worship services and some later joined into full membership. Such noted local late educators as Annie Kennedy Barbour, Pearl Fury, Aaron and Sarah Kane, Bertha Key, Joseph and Havannah Morton, Mary B. Neale (former school supervisor and for whom a school was named in her honor), Joseph Christopher "J.C." Parks (former supervisor of Colored Schools of Charles County with a school named in his honor), Inez Schoolfield, James and Muriel Sweatt (Mr. Sweatt was principal of Bel Alton High School), Mercedes Upshaw, and James and Suzy Washington, to name a few, were very active and influential members of the congregation. Metropolitan as a result became an unintentional magnet for those with affinitive educational backgrounds and aspirants thereof. On the other hand, neighboring African American congregations viewed the church as being sort of snooty and not as emotive as other churches. As of this writing, there continues to be a significant number of active and retired educators who volunteer with local schools. Dr. Edith Patterson, college administrator and first African American Charles County Commissioner, holds her membership at Metropolitan UMC. This congregation continues to be the shining example of leadership of African American United Methodist Churches in Western Charles County.

The immediate community setting of Metropolitan UMC is a zone of transition from rural to suburbia.

> The suburban fringe church is reached by leaving the metro area, traveling through the suburbs and reaching the fringe are without passing through any great expanse of sparsely populated land . . . The suburban fringe church is characterized by transition . . . streets are widened, fields give way to concrete. [2]

The above describes the semirural situation of the area surrounding Metropolitan. Metropolitan Church Road is slightly over a half mile long and has less than twelve homes of which one is a trailer. The homes consist of several wood-framed structures, and the others are all brick ramblers. Several new homes have been built off of Metropolitan Church Road; the said homes appear to be in the upper $300 to mid-$400 value. Part of the old Pomonkey High School auditorium/gym remains as a historical site that is owned by the Pomonkey Alumni Association. A relatively new development off of Metropolitan Church Road is Brawners' Estates that was constructed for upper-low to low-middle income residents and sponsored by the US Department of Agriculture. The homeowners helped to defray the cost of the building of their houses by doing some of the construction work on the houses. (The said area has provided a pool of youngsters who attend the church.) What is unique about the community setting is some homeowners along Metropolitan Church Road periodically have Garrett Marbury, a member of the church, use his round baler farming equipment to roll bales of hay on their properties. Round bales of hay can be seen during late spring and early fall of the year on some of the homeowners' properties. So, what a person would see once they turned into the community would be aspects of both rural and suburban-like living. It is exurbia, a semirural community.

Metropolitan's physical structure is relatively new with the multipurpose center having been completed in 2003. Some still grieved the razing of the old church building in 1975, however. The narthex contains plaques honoring previous pastors and ushers. Seasonal motifs are displayed. A wall is dedicated to members and families who contributed to the construction of the multipurpose center. The current worship center can comfortably seat between 150 and 200 worshipers with the old fellowship hall serving as an overflow seating area. With the multipurpose center, completed in June 2003, additional people can be accommodated, especially during large funerals, and the service viewed on a big screen television set.

There is a split chancel with two pulpit chairs made by Amish cabinet makers. The pulpit area is slightly crowded with a Leslie speaker, large cross with fish figurines, dorsal curtain, and communion table. At floor level, there is an organ and a piano. The walls of the sanctuary consist of multicolored translucent glass windows and seasonal banners. The rear of the sanctuary has two large glass windows that separate the old fellowship hall from the main sanctuary. The old fellowship hall, while serving as overflow space, also has the media center. It is to be noted that the narthex, fellowship hall, and sanctuary are kept meticulously clean due to the efforts of the trustees and Vernon Myers, sexton, in addition to two newcomers who take pride in keeping the church clean.

The multipurpose center of Metropolitan consists of three office spaces: finance office, pastor's office, and church administrative office. In addition to the office spaces, there is a large commercial kitchen, mechanical rooms, and restrooms. The church has made available use of the facility to Lifestyles, a social justice ministry in Charles County for housing homeless families for a week, civic and community groups, bread ministry, and other church groups. In fact, the Morgan State University Southern Maryland Alumni Chapter was established in this very same multipurpose center in October 2005 and thrives today as a well-known historically black college and university alumni group in Southern Maryland. In this aspect, Metropolitan is quite missional.

Key Players

My first official day at the office began with Mrs. Violet Simmons, a retired Charles County school office administrator and native of Charles County. Mrs. Simmons, a matronly Roman Catholic, is assertive, personable, and well-known as an activist in the community. She is very active with civic associations, Pomonkey High School Alumni Association, and is an associate member of the Morgan State University Southern Maryland Alumni Chapter. She is very supportive of the church's fundraisers and uses her entrepreneurial skills to secure orders, especially when the fall fruit sale takes place. Mrs. Simmons was able to get the county to install larger signage on Route 210 to indicate the turn onto Metropolitan Church Road. She gave me a briefing on the community and location of members in the community. In a manner of speaking, Mrs. Simmons reminded me of the late Sister Elizabeth Washington, who was my secretary in Mount Zion in Baltimore City. Mrs. Simmons was of inestimable value to me during my earlier days of ministry at Metropolitan.

Girard Myers, long-time member and son of the late Reverend Frederick Myers and current patriarch of Metropolitan, is ever present at the church. He is "Mr. Fix-it," who is owner and operator of Myers' Fix-it Service. Girard was very helpful in getting me settled in the office and taking me around the community where I was introduced to various members that were homebound. Girard served in just about every area of ministry within the church with the exception of preaching. Typically, Girard and Junior Clark could be found attending to some of the simple electrical issues, and with the more complicated electrical matters, the late Clarence White, former industrial arts teacher and owner of an electrical installation and repair service, would guide them as he sat in his wheelchair . (Mr. White was disabled, but his wife Anna White operated the company.) Needless to say, Girard is totally committed to Metropolitan and the Lord.

The late Joseph "Joe" Morton was the other patriarch of Metropolitan. He, too, like Girard, assisted me in getting settled, and when Girard was not available, he took me around and introduced to parishioners. Joe was a retired educator and staff member of the Maryland Department of Education. I had heard of Joe Morton while I was pastor of Mount Zion United Methodist Church in Baltimore City. The late Larry Custis of Mount Zion frequently talked about Joe and when absent from worship, Larry would be visiting Joe at Metropolitan. When I met Joe, I said, "Finally, I have met you. Larry talked about you so much." Joe would be very instrumental as we worked through the building program for the multipurpose center. He, too, like Girard, served in just about every area of ministry with the exception of preaching.

The late James Washington was lay leader and retired mathematics educator. He was in his own way a sort of laid-back gentleman who offered his encouragement to me during my first couple of years at Metropolitan. He oftentimes gave affirmation to me regarding my sermons. Ms. Lillian V. Parks, eventual lay leader, served as lay member to the Annual conference and educator with Prince George's County School System. She is the daughter of the late J. C. Parks for whom the nearby elementary school is named in his honor. Ms. Parks has been a long-time member of Metropolitan where she served as a Sunday school teacher. She volunteers with the Board of Child Care Auxiliary, Board of Ordained Ministry (BOM) and District Committee on Ordained Ministry (DCOM). In later years, she suffered a debilitating stroke but manages to continue being active with the BOM and DCOM. The Metropolitan Church family is her family.

Edith Myers, the wife of Girard, serves in various ministries of the church. She was very active as the coordinator of outreach ministries, especially with the Red Cross that trained her as a member of the disaster response team. Edith worked with the Share food program.

Merton Myers, Sr., is the son of Girard and Edith Myers and a US Marine veteran. He serves as the treasurer of the church and keeps meticulous records. Merton is very dependable in addition serves as a committed and faithful usher. Kathy, his wife, serves with the worship team and a member of the usher board. Vernon Myers, brother of Merton, serves as the sexton for Metropolitan where he faithfully carries out his responsibilities daily after work. He has been the church sexton for forty years! Sheila Myers is the sister of Merton and Vernon. She is the youngest of the siblings and serves as the church administrator. Her administrative skills are impeccable.

The late Havannah Morton, wife of Joe Morton, was a retired music educator who directed and played for the Choraleers, the men's choir. She was a very articulate woman. Ava Morton, daughter of the late Joe and Havannah Morton, serves as choir director and member of the worship team. Moreover, she is a trained singer who graduated from Hampton University. Ava demonstrated leadership skills among the young adults of the church where she organized a liturgical dance group, Sisters-in-the-Spirit. Marcia Gutrick, sister of Ava Morton, is an educator in Charles County and is a graduate of Salisbury State University. Marcia is gifted in stage choreography and plays. She enthusiastically presented the children's moment each Sunday.

Drs. Sanford and Mildred Wilson were not indigenous to the community. Dr. Sanford Wilson, known as Sandy, was a retired US Army colonel who brought his leadership skills to serve as the chair of the administrative council. Both he and his wife worked for the Charles County School System. Sandy was very helpful to me in organizing and editing the policies and procedure manual for Metropolitan.

Mrs. Anna White was the long-term secretary for the administrative council and the wife of Clarence White, owner and operator of a small electrical installation and repair business. Mrs. White was noted for the copious notes that she took during meetings.

The late Robert "Bob" and Mabel Bailey served respectively as chair of the Staff Parish Relations Committee and chair of the Finance Committee. Bob Bailey, a Tuskegee Airman and lawyer by profession, was also a certified lay speaker.

Mrs. Eva Chesley, a retired educator, served as president of the United Methodist Women and noted for her commitment to serving as a tutor to children in the local elementary schools. In the community she enjoyed serving in leadership capacities for her sorority, Alpha Kappa Alpha, Inc. Nu Zeta Omega Chapter. Mrs.

Chesley extended acts of kindness toward us, especially to my wife Lila, and was very supportive of our ministry.

Alvin Marbray, nephew of Joe Morton, and retired educator and vice principal in the Prince George's County public school system, served as president of the United Methodist Men for over a decade. He was the understudy of his Uncle Joe in terms of serving as lead trustee. Al eventually was selected to serve on the Baltimore-Washington Conference Board of Trustees.

Thomas "Tommy" Datcher, is a lifelong member of Metropolitan. He is a retired educator and department head who served in various ministries of the church. He willingly uses his gifts and graces. Tommy, a graduate of Morgan State University, was of significant help to me in organizing the Morgan State University Southern Maryland Alumni Chapter in October 2004, chartered in May 2005.

The late Mercedes Upshaw, a retired educator, was reputed for her generosity to the church. She was instrumental in having the marquis installed on the campus of the church.

The late Thelery Thomas, sister of Joe Morton, gave leadership to cooking for various events and reading the church paper during funeral services. She oftentimes brought produce from her gardens.

There were other members that played vital roles in the overall ministries of Metropolitan that helped under gird its ministry within and without in the community.

Church Administration

The day-to-day administrative activity at Metropolitan was constant. There was an unspoken expectation that there would always be someone at the church: the pastor, a secretary, or a trustee. Mrs. Simmons personified the always-present staff member at Metropolitan. To paraphrase Proverbs 31:10, "A committed, faithful, and efficient secretary who can find? She is worth far more than her salary." She proved to be an immense help to my ministry by her excellent administrative skills and attention to details. One of my first tasks for Mrs. Simmons was publicizing my schedule: Monday was my Sabbath, Tuesday and Thursday were my office days, while Wednesday was my visitation day, and Friday was my preparation day for the following Sunday's sermon. Without a problem she picked up on my rhythm and would have my bulletin draft completed on Thursday and my final copy ready on Friday while Girard Myers would put the sermon title on the marquis. Mrs. Simmons signed for all deliveries and when she was not available, Girard cared for the matter. Mrs. Simmons retired as secretary for Metropolitan in December 2003 due to reaching her 70th birthday and wanting to spend more time with family and other activities. It was very difficult to fill her position.

Sheila Myers served on a part-time basis until securing full-time employment with the University of Maryland in 2005. For a short time, Ava Morton covered the administrative duties until a permanent secretary was hired in the person of Ms. Deloris Warder, a retired administrative person from the nearby Stump Neck Naval Facility. Dee, as she preferred to be called, worked nearly a year for us until such time she resigned in anticipation of getting remarried. We finally hired in 2006 Mrs. Cynthia Rodgers who remained with us until my joining the Baltimore-Washington Conference staff as a regional guide in July 2008. A lesson I learned from Dr. Alfonzo J. Harrod was always have a good and reliable secretary.

Dr. Sandy Wilson served as chairperson of the Church Council. He conducted said meetings on Tuesday evenings and kept on task and to the points of the agenda. The major item during the meetings was the construction of the new multipurpose center. Strategies for re-applying for building permits and construction loan from the conference were the focal points of the discussion.

Questions emerged during the church council meetings regarding policies and procedures and the need to update the same. I suggested that a committee or task group be organized for that purpose. Sandy was very helpful in assisting me gathering a task group for the purpose of developing a policies and procedures manual. The Metropolitan policies and procedures manual were completed on April 3, 2002. (Significantly, other congregations have used Metropolitan's policies and procedures manual as a model.)

The church council meetings were well attended by the membership. Typically each ministry area leader gave their report on their specific ministry. Some gave very thorough reports while others reported on their intentions to complete that which they were supposed to have completed in preparation for the current meeting. Mrs. White, secretary for the church council, took very copious minutes and requested copies of the reports from the ministry area leaders. The meetings generally lasted between one and a half to two hours. The meeting concluded with the saying of the "watch-word" (Genesis 31:49).[3] I explained that the saying was not appropriate for the benediction or sending forth. There were few contentious meetings, I recall.

Nurture

The ministry category of Nurture branches off into three main ministry areas: Worship, Membership Care, and Christian Education.

Worship Ministry

Worship ministry is very important to the Metropolitan Church family. Upon my arrival in 2000, there were five choirs: Gospel Choir, Combined Choir, A. C. Kane Choir, Choraleer's Men's Choir, and Celestial Children's Choir. Each choir had its own musician. Eventually, I was able to hire a drummer who played for us on the second Sunday of the month. Initially, some of the members were not supportive of the idea but eventually came around, seeing that it was a progressive move for the church.

Bro. Jacques Banks and I discussed the possibility of having a prayer service once a month on Friday evening. After the 9/11 tragedy, I moved ahead to have *Sweet Hour of Prayer* every Sunday morning beginning at 6 a.m. Like most new initiatives, there was a strong turn-out, but eventually it dwindled down to less than ten each morning. Jacques faithfully led the service with the attendance of Girard Myers, Kelvin Jordan, Earl Jordan, David Collins, Lillian Parks, and me. Periodically, others would attend, depending upon their joys and concerns. Earl Jordan, the reticent stammerer, father of Kelvin, and faithful attendant of the prayer service came out of his shell with confidence and flawlessly read in my presence a passage of scripture. The next Sunday morning, Earl did the same in the midst of the congregation; needless to say, there were shouts of "Hallelujahs." Prayer changes things!

A second service, casual in nature, was initiated as an early morning worship service. The said service lasted one hour and began at 8:00 a.m. Newcomers attended the early morning service and subsequently joined into full membership. Some members attended the early worship service on occasion in order to visit with friends in other churches or attend sorority functions. The early worship attracted a number of new members, especially several biracial couples and three white persons. One of the long-time members privately asked me whether the persons that joined the early morning service were legitimately members of the church. I cited the persons that joined the early morning service "fulfilled all righteousness" by attending the new members' class that I conducted, took their membership vows, and had offering envelopes with assigned numbers. Further, one of our new members was enrolled in Wesley Seminary. It occurred to me that this type of thinking amiss was prevalent among some of the members. Ava Morton suggested during worship team meeting that the fifth Sunday be utilized as a unity Sunday to bring to the two worshiping groups together. It was a great idea. The fifth Sunday would be the unity service.

The early morning worship service provided opportunity for diversity. Two of the biracial couples joined due to the convenience of the hour, the informal conduct of the worship experience, and genuine hospitality. Three white persons, two women and a disabled man became regular attendants of whom two joined. The white gentleman who was evangelized by Girard Myers died a year later. Of the remaining two women, one relocated to Eastern Shore while the other subsequently migrated to an Eastern religious community of faith. The early morning worship service was attractive to persons of diverse ethnic backgrounds. (More will be said about diversity in Metropolitan UMC.)

The early morning worship service attracted a group of youngsters from Brawner's Estates. A blended family of five or six youngsters began coming to the early morning service. They had a few rough edges, but some of our ladies began to work with them. Before long, the youngsters became interested in ushering and serving as acolytes. I was eventually able to get the older youngsters into confirmation class and confirm them. Their parents periodically attended the early morning service. Two of the boys would join with several other youngsters under the guidance of Mr. Samuel Bryant to form the Christian Rappers 4 Christ.

Metropolitan has a very strong choir ministry and staff of trained musicians. Each of the choirs is served by very able and well-trained musicians with capabilities of playing both piano and organ. Further, Ava Morton, trained singer and director, augmented the choirs. The late Havannah Morton, retired music educator, played for the Choraleers for a number of years until her health began to decline. The late Inez Schoolfield, retired music educator, played for Metropolitan and other churches and was the first musician who played for the early morning worship service. Mrs. Vivian Lewis and Mr. Samuel Bryant both bring an emotive and spirited worship experiences as they serve at the instruments. Mrs. Joy Hinton, music educator, musician for the youth choir, assumed responsibility, along with Mr. Samuel Bryant, for the music ministry for the early morning worship service subsequent to the sudden death of Mrs. Schoolfield.

The choirs of Metropolitan are very capable in the sense that they sing contemporary and traditional gospel music in addition to the great traditional hymns of the church. It is not uncommon for the Holy Spirit to break out in the choir and upon the musicians.

During funeral services, the giftedness of both choirs and musician is evident. Such services are very moving.

Ushering in the African American tradition is highly significant. The late Jackie Jordan, wife of Kelvin Jordan, set the pace for ushering at Metropolitan. She became thoroughly assimilated into the life and ministry of the church. I appointed her president of the ushers. With her skills as a retired Army veteran, she skillfully organized the ushers and pursued training with the Interdenominational Ushers Union. The ushers were trained as a result of her efforts. Ushers learned their signals, positioned themselves as required, and carried out their ushering duties with dignity. Jackie was instrumental in taking a youngster with Downs Syndrome, training her, and giving her meaningful duties. Her impact upon the ushering ministry at Metropolitan will long be remembered.

The worship services were recorded each Sunday. Aaron Kane and Kelvin "Kelly" Jordan taped each service that was made available to the sick and shut-ins with televisions equipped with VCRs.' The taping of the services served as a means of connecting the shut-ins with the church.

Lay speakers are tremendous help to the pastor. Jacques and Cindy Banks, Kelly Jordan, Reginald Guererrio, Robert Gutrick, and the late Robert (Bob) Bailey served regularly as lay speakers during the morning worship services. Jacque and Cindy would eventually become local pastors in neighboring churches. The lay speakers served during the pastor's vacation or on scheduled Sundays. The lay speakers play an integral role in the worship and training aspects of the ministry at Metropolitan.

Worship team meetings were conducted typically on the Saturday morning before the first Sunday. During the team meeting, we debriefed on the previous month's worship experiences and offered suggestions as to how to improve upon the overall worship experience. Kelly Jordan prepared the agenda as based upon the worship guidelines of our denomination. Ava usually brought in new ideas that would enhance the service and took an objective view of what we were doing. Planning for special services usually was cared for during the team meeting. Overall, I believe the work of the worship team contributed to the effective worship ministry of Metropolitan UMC.

Membership Care

The visitation of sick and shut-ins was a very important part of my ministry. Since my visiting day was on Wednesdays, the secretary telephoned the homebound members the preceding day to schedule my time with them if convenient. I usually began about 10 a.m. on Wednesday morning in a route that would lead me toward the church where I would stop by to check in and get messages and so forth. I continued on until my last visit, normally during late afternoon.

I was greeted with a warm smile and an invitation to take a seat. Most of the shut-ins wanted to hear the news of what was happening at church. Some would say, "I heard you had a good one on Sunday." The interpretation is the worship service was quite spirited and the sermon was good. Each wanted a copy of the Sunday bulletin. Somewhere in the conversation, there would be inquiry about a certain member and/or my wife. Then there would be the talk about their various ailments, illnesses, and scheduled doctors' appointments. For the widows, occasional references would be made about their deceased spouses and their lives together. Eventually, I would read a passage of Scripture and give an abbreviated version of my most recent sermon to the congregation. Following, I gave the sacrament of Holy Communion. Holy Communion is very important to the shut-ins and connects them with the church and, of course, with the Christ our Lord.

Visiting hospitalized members and those residing in nursing homes usually took more time while expecting the unexpected. I would have to consider whether they were being seen by the medical staff, in physical therapy, receiving their meals, or in the best of disposition. For the member-patient or -resident it is affirming to have their pastor visit with them. There was one occasion I visited with a member in the assisted living area of a certain nursing home. While I was visiting with the resident, a nurse came into the room for the purpose of attending to my member. The nurse flippantly said, "I am going have this guy step out for a moment, honey." Why did the nurse say that?

My member went off; she angrily and vociferously stated, "That not just a guy! This is my pastor, the Reverend Doctor George De Ford . . ." The nurse quickly and profusely apologized to my member and me. I told the nurse not to be upset. I lovingly and quietly chided my member, who was known for her outspokenness. I told her that she was a representative of our church, and we wanted to have a good representation. The member responded," She doesn't talk to my pastor like that!" (The pastor in the African American church is held in high esteem, and respect is expected from all.)

Membership care is also expressed during the times of deaths. A certain set of dynamics initiate when death occurs, particularly in the African American rural community. Telephone calls by various members to others initiate the process. It can be expected if the pastor was not with the family at the time of the death that someone other than a family member will call the pastor to inform him or her. Typically, the pastor will initiate a visit to the bereaved family as soon as possible while somberness pervades over the community. Telephone calls, emails, and texting regarding the deceased member is the main subject. Next the question of when the service will take place emerges. A call usually comes from the local funeral director for purposes of notification of the death and/or coordinating with pastor's and church's availability for the service.

Once coordination of services is confirmed, the local newspaper is contacted. Meanwhile the administrative machinery of the church begins its course of action: scheduling the funeral, the bulletin preparation, members of the choirs that will be present, visiting clergy, the repast, the availability of grave space, and the trustee on duty. Typically, Thornton Funeral Home is one of the most patronized service; Mr. Leon Thornton is a member of the community and very well known for his service to the community. The membership care and nurturing aspects of Metropolitan are seen in the manner in which funeral services are conducted. Compassionate and spirit-filled services best described what takes place along with invitation to Christian discipleship. Most interments take place in the church cemetery.

After the funeral services are completed, some of the members of the choir transition and don aprons, assume positions behind the buffet line, and serve the families and friends in attendance. Special seating arrangements are made for the immediate family while hosts and hostesses serve them. There tends to be a super-abundance of food. A "preacher's pack" consisting of additional plates of food to be taken home is prepared for the pastor and other clergy after having dined with the members and bereaved family. This kind of care is part of the culture of the African American Church.

The funeral service for a recent white member, an amputee, was an awkward experience. I was called on a Sunday evening in late fall by the local sheriff; the member died in his wheelchair in the yard. My business card was in his possession. When Girard and I responded to the home, I sensed that some of the family was surprised to see an African American pastor. Once his body was removed, I had prayer with some of the immediate family. Later in an attempt to schedule an interview with the family, I was not successful. (I speculated on various reasons.) Eventually, I was able to speak with a family member by telephone that gave me scanty information about the decedent a widower.

The funeral service was conducted at local mortuary in La Plata, Maryland; the service was awkward for both the few members from the church and the decedent's family. The sermon was very short and ended with a prayer. I was later informed by the daughter that when her mother died, the presiding clergy said, "a few words and gave the Lord's Prayer and that was it . . . you did more than he did . . . thank you very much" to use her words. At the entombment, I gave the committal and informed the family I would meet them at the church for the repast. Nearly two hours later, some of the family members straggled in to the church for the repast.

The family explained one of their relatives suffered some distress and was transported to the local hospital after the committal. Moreover, they were very surprised that the church provided a meal after the service! The family expressed appreciation for the hospitality and caring for their ailing father. I made a perfunctory call sometime later to the family, but I confess I did not follow up with them. This was a missed opportunity! Looking back over that experience, I conclude that I should have been more astute pertinent to the cultural idiosyncrasies. Had I been more understanding, the probability of evangelizing that family could have been very positive. Killen states, "Funerals take place in a cultural context. It is a good idea to inquire about local funeral customs (and) talk with the local funeral director . . ." [4] My own biases bedeviled with me, I confess.

Celebrating special occasions in the lives of members is very important, particularly in the African American church. Baptisms, birthdays, weddings, and wedding anniversaries are moments for pause and to affirm the members. Baptisms of infants typically bring a lot of family members to the church. So as it is with weddings; there are many who come out for such occasions. This also provides opportunities for evangelizing; however, the unchurched attendees typically come for the celebration and are not seen again despite follow-up.

The Matter of Diversity

The matter of diversity in Metropolitan United Methodist Church is a reflection of the Baltimore-Washington Conference of the United Methodist Church. It is not uncommon for United Methodist local churches to be a microcosm of multiculturalism of the annual conference. Metropolitan UMC is no exception.

I began my new appointment on July 1, 2000 at Metropolitan. The week preceding my assuming the pastorate, while being briefed by Reverend Watson, a young white woman in nursing garb drove up. She was visibly distraught and wanted to speak with my colleague. Later that afternoon, my colleague informed me that the young white woman came from the doctor's office where she was employed. The office had been subject to an armed robbery. The young woman, Cindy, was the wife of Jacques, and both were active members of the congregation. There was also another biracial couple with children, the Reid Family. Joe, a Caucasian, was married to Carol, who grew up in Metropolitan. The young children were active in Sunday school. Joe due to his work schedule occasionally attended worship services.

The Banks made an appointment with me. Jacques expressed during our meeting his desire to participate in the worship ministry; both he and Cindy became certified lay speakers. Each delivered sermons especially, when I initiated 8:00 a.m. early morning worship service. In 2007, Jacques and Cindy were hired to serve as local pastors of Indian Head UMC, a predominantly white congregation. I referred to them, as "Aquila and Priscilla" protégés of the Apostle Paul (Act 18:18). Eventually, Cindy became the pastor of Shiloh UMC while Jacques continued as pastor of Indian Head UMC.

The Guerreros joined during my ministry. Reginald, a Pacific Islander, and Michelle, African America, joined by way of the 8:00 a.m. worship service. Both were contract employees of the nearby naval weapons facility in Indian Head, Maryland. Reg, a part-time student at Wesley Theological Seminary, would routinely deliver sermons that were reflective of his biblical and theological training. Michelle, his wife, became a committed member of Staff-Parish Relations Committee. Both actively participated in the Discipleship Bible Study series; Reg contributed to the study with information learned in seminary. I learned subsequent to my appointment as regional guide with the conference staff that the Guerreros eventually left the area.

Another biracial couple joined our congregation. Jesse and Lynn, a retired military couple, visited on several occasion during the early morning service. Jesse expressed a desire to join the church but was hesitant due to being in a biracial marriage. To dismiss his apprehensions, I referred him to Jacques who was able to quell Jesse's uneasiness because of the con-naturalness of experiences. Jesse and Lynn joined after new members' orientation. Jesse was active in the ministries of the church. I learned that the couple relocated to Kentucky due to employment change.

Metropolitan embraces diversity as shown through the adoption of biracial couples and families that fully participated in the various ministries of the church. Moreover, I am convinced partly because of the welcoming attitude of the church, Indian Head UMC, a predominantly white congregation desired to enter into a cooperative parish arrangement in 2007 with Metropolitan serving as the lead congregation. More will be said about this.

The Matter of Accessibility

The Americans with Disabilities Act (ADA) has been in existence for more than twenty years. [5] Metropolitan UMC puts into practice the principles of that legislation: "adapting facilities, new and existing such as church sanctuaries, educational buildings . . ."[6] Early on I cited Ms. Lillian V. Parks, lay member to the annual conference and lay leader of the church who suffered a debilitating stroke. Ms. Parks, an independent and resolute spirit, continues in active ministries with the local church and district and conference boards of ordained ministries.

Vernon Myers is mentally disabled but serves as a member of the choir, ushers, and is long-time sexton of the church. He is very personable Christian gentleman with an infectious smile and gleam in his eyes. I alluded to the late Jackie Jordan, president of the usher board. Jackie and her sister-in-law Deborah Jordan, were key to enlisting Shannah, a Downs Syndrome teenager to serve on the usher board. She was noted for her eagerness and faithfulness to serve as an usher. Sadly, the teenager died in 2010 as a result of disease. There was also an autistic young woman who occasionally attended services with her parents. While her behavior was sometimes unpredictable, members of Metropolitan were compassionately understanding of her circumstances. Her parents were encouraged to continue to bring her to worship services.

Accessibility to Metropolitan is facilitated by the sanctuary, and multipurpose center being on one level. Further, seating is commodious for disabled, one row on both sides of the sanctuary aisles were removed in order to accommodate wheelchair-bound worshipers. The restroom facilities of course are ADA compliant. Overall, this local church is hospitable to those with physical challenges.

The Matter of Conflict

My journey with Metropolitan was not free from normal conflicts. Generally, whatever the source of the conflict, we dealt with the issue and moved on. However, on one occasion a very senior member of the congregation died while I was on a three-month Sabbath leave.[7] Rev. Harold Watson, who was covering for me, cared for the arrangements. Feeling that I just had to make a brief appearance, I went in casual attire to pay my respects to the family. During my brief visit, Rev. Watson who knew the family very well assured me that everything was moving along smoothly and I need not worry. Upon my return from Sabbath leave, a member of the decedent's family filed a complaint with Staff Pastor Parish Relations Committee that it was inconsiderate of me not to have stayed for the funeral service to honor the oldest member of the church and give some pastoral words of comfort to the family. The chair of the Staff Parish Relations Committee felt I went beyond the call of duty to come in while on Sabbath leave to greet the family, however, briefly.

On another occasion, a written complaint was forwarded to Staff Pastor Parish Relations Committee regarding my failure to participate in an early gathering after Sunday worship service at the waterfront home of members of Indian Head United Methodist Church. What actually took place was that my wife and I arrived later in the evening at the Indian Head UMC member's waterfront home to watch the beautiful breath-taking sunset over the Potomac River. Again, Staff Pastor Parish Relations Committee minimized the complaint but wanted me to be cognizant of what had transpired. I expressed my appreciation to the committee for their support and put the matter behind me.

The Matter of Sabbath and Self-care

Sabbath time and self-care are very important to pastors and their families. Caring and shepherding God's people is very draining, and as our Lord took time to get away for rest and revitalization, the same applies to clergy. I refer to my wife Lila as "my girlfriend and wife who is one and the same." Once a member of the MSU Southern Maryland Alumni Chapter teasingly asked, "Who's your mistress?" Pausing to respond, I replied, "The Church!" The church can become the mistress of a pastor if allowed; the church can become the idol of a pastor's ministry. Moreover, when that happens, the pastor becomes less effective and a candidate for burn-out.

I recall a Baptist pastor who commented about an occasion when he became sick and had to be hospitalized. While hospitalized he was worried about his church, and the head of his deacon board visited him. The deacon told him that things at the church were going on very well. The deacon said, "Pastor, things are going on so very well; in fact we got some new members. Don't worry about getting back to the church too soon." The church will take care of itself. That is the reason it is so important to keep one's Sabbath; be with family and give attention to self-care.

Taking time for family is a necessity. Whether the pastor is in early stages of his/her ministry, mid-point, or winding down, it is crucial to devote time to family in order to have a wholesome life. If we were not shopping at the commissary or stopping to get something to eat, we were together and devoting time to each other. It was an expression of love by taking time to be and focus on her.

Pertinent to self-care also are eating the proper foods, getting enough rest, and participating in some form of exercise and recreational activities to add to one's health and vitality. I am a swimmer who maintained a weekly regime of swimming at the local county recreation center, and the benefits were lower blood pressure, loss of weight, and good muscle tone. John Coleman, a PGA golf instructor, military retiree, and member of the congregation introduced me to the game of golf. Playing golf with my fraternity brother Rev. Dr. Michael A. H. McKinney was always therapeutic for the both of us as we discussed various matters and bounced ideas for sermons off of one another. Each time out on the course, we tried to perfect our game and talk "trash" about our scores. It was a revitalizing time.

Christian Education

The worship services move the soul and spirit while Christian education helps nurture the mind of the members. Bible studies were conducted on Thursday afternoon and evenings. All of the Disciple Bible Study series including the Christian Believer course were taught during my pastorate. Several short-term Bible studies were provided and listed under the heading, "Summer Breeze Bible Study." The late Rev. Dr. Shirlimarie McAroy-Gray and I conducted a joint Bible study during my first summer at Metropolitan.

Mrs. Marcia Gutrick served as church school superintendent and presenter of the Children's Moment during worship service. Church school met each Sunday morning with an average attendance of ten adults and seven youngsters. The adult class met in the sanctuary and operated on "automatic pilot"; that is to say, each morning either the late Fred Richardson or his nephew Vernon Myers distributed the Sunday School Adult books and a member of the class would begin reading and have open discussion on the subject matter of the morning. Initially, I stepped in to give leadership to the class of ten members or more. Jacques Banks subsequently served as the class teacher until such time his employment conflicted with his presence. My wife eventually assumed the role as teacher for a period of time while I conducted confirmation class. Upon completion of confirmation, I resumed the role as teacher. At the conclusion of the adult class, Vernon collected the books and Fred received the Sunday school offering.

Marcia readily organized Vacation Bible School (VBS) yearly. On several occasions especially during the construction of the multipurpose center, Shiloh UMC of Bryans Road, Maryland made available their facilities for us to conduct the VBS. It is significant to note that Marcia brought passion to her ministry with the youngsters on Sunday mornings during the Children's Moment. She presented meaningful object lessons were presented. But her forte was creating plays and costumes.

Mrs. Gutrick conducted plays and created costumes for the young people. Especially during the Lenten season, she used her skills to do makeup for the cast of characters in the plays. On one such occasion, Marcia had Dwayne, a tall youngster, portray Jesus. His makeup was very authentic, including the beard designed by Marcia. Her enthusiasm for this ministry was infectious.

The role of biblical characters of African descent is significant, especially in the black church. Each February, which is designated African American History month, I made it a point to devote a series of sermons pertinent to the role and presence of persons of African heritage in the Bible. Two Sundays would be devoted to the Old Testament while on the remaining Sundays, emphasis would be on the New Testament. Typically after service, the comment was made, "I never knew that, Reverend."

Each March I highlighted the role of women in the life of the church and in the Holy Scriptures. Bulletin covers, blurbs, and facts about women were means of educating women and affirming their contributions in the life of the church. Dr. Edith Patterson, member, made history when she became the first African American woman who was sworn in as county commissioner in Charles County, Maryland in 2005. Encouragement to young girls and young women to maximize their academic potentials was my ongoing refrain while pointing opportunities for them.

Ministry area leaders and interested members were encouraged to participate in conference and district-wide training events. Typically, members of Metropolitan readily responded to training opportunities for sharpening their skills in their areas of ministry. My mantra to the leadership of the church was, "How can you lead me if you have not been trained?" I was very pleased with the members for taking advantage of the training opportunities. Christian education at Metropolitan continues to be a vital part of the overall ministry.

Outreach

Reverend Harold Watson, Sr., my predecessor, organized the Bread Ministry as a means of outreach to the community. Several of the men twice a week journeyed to Washington, DC, where they obtained bread, English muffins, and pastries from Bread for the City warehouse. The products were brought to the church and stored in the fellowship hall where members, members of neighboring churches, and needy persons could select the items that they wanted free of charge. A diverse group of needy persons from the community regularly received the benefit of the free breads, muffins, and pastries. It was not uncommon for some of the individuals to seek additional help in terms of financial assistance to pay for their utilities bills and/or rent. Our connection with Neighbors Eager to Serve (NETS) allowed us to refer the persons to the said social justice ministry, organized at Indian Head United Methodist Church. Occasionally some of the individuals seeking help became belligerent due to our not providing financial support. We were compassionate but firm as to why cash was not given to anyone.

The signature ministry of Metropolitan, in my opinion, is Safe Nights, sponsored by Lifestyles, Inc. During late fall to early spring, Lifestyles engages community churches to house homeless persons. Metropolitan opened its doors for one week to show hospitality to the homeless persons. The number varied from night to night; however, over the years during my pastorate, the number of guests ranged from fifteen to forty. The church provided a hot meal for homeless persons and a place to sleep until the next morning. Various ministry areas took responsibility to provide the nightly meal and morning breakfast. Neighboring congregations dispatched their members to prepare the evening or morning meal. This situation fostered a sense of collegiality among the neighboring church members.

Metropolitan makes its facilities available to a cancer-awareness program, churches, community groups, and families. A cancer-awareness program, sponsored by the University of Maryland Medical School, conducted periodic information sessions. Other congregations have used Metropolitan's facilities for training and retreat planning sessions. The Pomonkey High School Alumni Association periodically holds their meetings and special gatherings in the multipurpose center. The Morgan State University Southern Maryland Alumni Chapter also periodically meets in the facility; the said alumni chapter was organized in Metropolitan, and I became the founding president in 2004, although it was chartered in 2005.

What has become an annual event is the prayer breakfast for the Ministers' Alliance of Charles County and Vicinity. Each second Saturday for over ten years, the Ministers Alliance conducts their prayer breakfast. Mrs. Everdeen Jordan and her family prepare the meal for the assembled ministers. She is like a fixture for this event. The Alpha Kappa Alpha Sorority, Inc., Nu Zeta Omega Chapter, of Charles County conducts their tea for debutants as a fundraiser. On each occasion there is a full house. Individual families have utilized the multipurpose center for special occasions such as birthday celebrations, wedding receptions, and anniversaries.

My opinion is that Metropolitan plays a dynamic and vital role in outreach to a community that was once rural in its orientation but has transitioned into an exurbia context. The level of activity in outreach such as hosting health initiatives, community groups, churches, and families for their particular events while also serving as host for social justice ministries is indicative of a church serving in a suburban context.

Witness

The United Methodist Men and United Methodist Women units were very strong ministries in Metropolitan United Methodist Church. Both groups met regularly, and it was not uncommon to have a minimum of twenty or a maximum of thirty attendees. The men's group under the leadership of Al Marbray typically met every fourth Sunday from 7:00 a.m. to 9:00 a.m. for breakfast by scheduled cooks; Al served as president for ten years. Ms. Parks, the lay leader, would be the only woman in attendance at the meeting. The men sponsored youth attending ROCK, an annual gathering in Ocean City, Maryland. The women meanwhile typically met after church service on the second Sunday. Both the UMM and UMW are still very strong units.

Reverend Mel Grover and I immediately became friends in 2000. He was a retired Senior Chief like my-self, and both of us had ties to the submarine community. During one of our conversations, the idea of doing a joint Lenten service emerged. I contacted Shiloh UMC, Grace UMC, Smith Chapel, and Alexandria Chapel UMCs and organized a series of worship services on Wednesday evening. The pastors agreed to serve as guest preachers, and the sermons would be centered upon a particular theme. The offerings received were designated to specific social justice ministries in the community, such as Catherine Pregnancy Center, Christmas in April, Lifestyles, and Neighbors Eager to Serve (NETS). From the initial service in 2001 the number of participating United Methodist Churches increased with the following: Faith, Providence-Forth Washington, St. Paul, Corkran Memorial, Church of the Redeemer, Asbury, and later Oxon Hill UMCs. We called ourselves the Route 210 Corridor of Churches. While the Lenten series of services continue, most of the original pastors that began in 2001 have moved on to other appointments or have retired or died. The significance of the Lenten services has resulted in several bishops, district superintendents, and other conference level persons starting the series of services on Ash Wednesdays.

The Route 210 Corridor of Churches conducted a joint evangelism campaign in 2005. With emphasis on our diversity as Christians, we organized four groups with each group having a representative from the participating churches. Armed with flyers containing locations of the churches and service times and ministries, we set out on visitations to communities along Maryland Route 210 (Indian Head Highway). We began at 9:00 a.m. on a Saturday morning. Visits were made and flyers distributed until we exhausted them. Our campaign concluded at about 12 noon. We were excited about what had been accomplished; however, based on my recollection, the results were minimal to nil. We were using the attraction model with the hopes people would come to us. I confess that I was very disappointed.

Reflectively, I believe since the inception of the Route 210 Corridor of Churches a stronger sense of connection among the participating churches evolved and continue until the present. It is not uncommon for members of the participating churches to feel a sense of familiarity and anticipation of the next year's event. More significantly, however, there was opportunity for multicultural experiences and a greater appreciation for the manner each group worship God in Spirit and in truth.

The Multipurpose Center

Over the years I learned that in each church that I served there was some form of a capital improvement program. Whether it was renovation of the current worship facility and/or adding an addition to the current structure, some form of physical improvement was in the making. For Metropolitan, it was the adding on of an education center that was postponed during the 1970s when the current worship center was built. Some steps were taken to achieve the goal of constructing the education center: a building committee was in place, building permits were filed with Charles County, and an application for a loan was approved by the conference. Both the district superintendent and my predecessor emphasized that the construction of the education center was a top priority.

The major item for my administration was to re-energize the building program that began on July 10, 1996 under the leadership of Rev. Harold W. Watson, Sr. Shortly, after my arrival, Joe Morton and Anna White gave me a briefing on the building campaign and their progress to date. The building permit expired, the anticipated loan from the annual conference in the amount of $50,000 expired due to non-activity by the church, and no bids had gone out. Reality set in. Succinctly, through fundraisers, increase in financial giving from families, and special donations, we were able to apply for a commercial loan from a local bank, reactivated our loan application from the annual conference, obtained a new building permit and received bids on our construction project. The late Joe Morton and Anna White, along with Alvin Marbray served in leadership capacities for the building committee. Baker-Cooper and Associates, P.C., of Washington, DC, was the architectural firm that prepared the specification document for the multipurpose center on May 23, 2000. The specification document was reviewed again with eagerness in anticipation that the building of the multipurpose center would become a reality in the not-too-distant future.

A reactivated building campaign began with a donation tree which members and families purchased rocks, acorns, and leaves for specific amounts of money. Again we would have to go before the District Committee on Building and Loans in order to secure approval from the said committee to move ahead for seeking a contractor and to construct the educational facility. The BWC approved a loan in the amount of $75,000. Community Bank of Tri-County agreed to grant us a loan in the amount of $400,000 with an adjustable rate of between 7.25 to 8.25 percent. Joe Morton, Alvin Marbray, and I went to settlement with the BWC CFO James H. Knowles-Tuell on November 6, 2001. Bids would go out, but only three prospective contractors responded. On the day bids were taken, one contractor pulled out, and another's bid was extremely high. We selected a minority construction firm out of Prince George's County, Maryland who we felt would do us a good job. After months of tedious preparation, a groundbreaking ceremony was conducted on November 11, 2001 at 3:00 p.m. The construction began early on in 2002 but with a series of unexpected delays.

The county changed certain building codes that nullified previously approved permits. The one-thousand-gallon grease trap tank approval was overridden due the church having a commercial kitchen. This required the church to obtain a two-thousand-gallon grease trap that delayed the construction project. On the occasion of attempting to secure the required permit, the county engineer was out of the country in excess of a month. Other issues of construction delays caused the contractor to take another construction project and pull out the heavy equipment. For several months, work was at a stand-still. The biweekly meetings reduced to once a month and subsequently none at all. Tempers began to flair; as a result I wrote a letter to the Bishop's office, requesting a meeting with conference officials, construction managers, and the lead architect.

The outcome of the meeting brought clarity for parties concerned. Our change orders, the county engineer's office delay in authorizing certain phases of the project, and the idle heavy equipment with accumulating rental fees were the issues negatively impacting the situation. Fortunately, the late Joe Morton, who was an instructor in the building trades industry, navigated us through this conflictive matter. Construction resumed. We were 200-plus days behind our completion date. In the late spring 2003, the punch-out list was completed. On June 29, 2003 Bishop Felton E. May consecrated the multipurpose center. The project at its completion would cost over $850,000.

The multipurpose center as previously alluded to, has been a blessing not only to the church but to the community as it is available for usage by other congregations, community groups and families.

Metropolitan-Indian Head
United Methodist Churches Cooperative Parish

The Book of Discipline 2004 provides for the cooperative parish arrangement among congregations. Such arrangements are beneficial in order for ministries to operate effectively with congregations and in the community. Pastor Mel Grover in 2007 received notification that he would be appointed as a clergy staff member of Lexington Park United Methodist Church, Lexington Park, Maryland. Consequently, a new pastor was needed for Indian Head UMC. Plans were in effect for Indian Head UMC to be placed in a cooperative parish arrangement with another white congregation. The leadership of Indian Head UMC strongly objected and expressed a desire to be in cooperative parish ministry with Metropolitan UMC. The reasons for their desire were: [1] hospitality extended by Metropolitan; [2] worshiping together during 210 Corridor Lenten Services; [3] bonds of friendships that developed as a result of the Lenten Services; and [4] the leadership style of the pastor of Metropolitan UMC. On the Sunday afternoon of our introduction to the leadership as the incoming pastor and wife, with assisting ministers Jacques and Cindy Banks who would serve as district superintendent hires (DS Hires), we were well received. Jacques and Cindy would serve under my pastoral leadership. Some of the basic information was shared such as how we would implement the ministry and my sacramental responsibilities to both congregations.

The Rev. Dr. Ianther Mills, Team Leader and District Superintendent Washington East District, guided us through the arrangement of the parish. Upon the conclusion of the meeting prayer was offered and subsequent meetings scheduled for purposes of implementing the new ministry.

The roles of the pastoral staff were clarified in preparation for implementing cooperative parish. I further explained that I would consecrate the elements while Jacques or Cindy would distribute the same during worship services either at Metropolitan or Indian Head. I scheduled an alternating rhythm of preaching the first Sundays at each church and celebrating communion. At the early morning service at Metropolitan, I consecrated elements for both services so that Jacques or Cindy could distribute the same during the 11:00 a.m. worship while I was serving Indian Head UMC. This method worked very satisfactorily.

The administrative machinery of the churches operated without any serious issues. Cindy morphed into Jacques's administrative right arm while he did most of the preaching. Each of us was present for the church council meetings at both churches. The monthly meetings at Indian Head became somewhat perfunctory at this point; therefore, I delegated to Jacques to brief me on some of the meetings in my absence. Most of the meetings centered upon recapitulations of activities engaged upon during the month and the financial standing of the church. Overall, the church council meetings at Indian Head UMC were uneventful.

Joint worship services for special occasions proved very beneficial. Thanksgiving Eve and Christmas morning services provided opportunities for meaningful worship experiences as a cooperative parish. Participants from both churches and combined choirs afforded the members to use their gifts and graces to the glory of God. The Christmas Cantata of December 2007 amplified the value of joint worship experiences appreciated by all in attendance and the collaborative work of the musicians: Ms. Frye and Mrs. Vivian Lewis. Reflectively, the 210 Corridor Lenten Services, in my opinion, the handiwork of God making available the opportunity for two congregations to join together in a spirit of connection and cooperation to form a Cooperative Parish for effective ministry for Jesus Christ. More significantly, the Indian Head congregation, from the community standpoint, was no longer viewed as "that white church" but as a blended church with a propensity to multiculturalism.

My successor was the Rev. George E. Hackey, Jr. He had served as pastor of Sharp Street UMC, Sandy Spring, Maryland, for twelve years. Rev. Hackey and his wife Dory would bring their gifts and graces to Metropolitan that would take the church to a higher level of ministry, particularly in evangelism. The third Sunday of June, 2008, would be my last Sunday as the lead pastor of Metropolitan–Indian Head UMC Cooperative Parish. Both congregations would join in for a farewell service as I prepared to join in the Adventure Guide extension ministry with the Baltimore-Washington Annual Conference, effective July 1, 2008. The transition was seamless with all particulars addressed and keys turned over to Rev. Hackey. I said to myself, "Hit the road Jack, and don't go back!"

Lessons Learned

The Spirit of God does move in the midst of the Cabinetthat is composed of the bishop and district superintendents who make recommendations for pastors to itinerate to churches in our denomination. Admittedly, I was very upset upon learning that I was to be appointed to Metropolitan United Methodist Church, Indian Head, Maryland. To use the expression, "I was going kicking and screaming." However, I did not comprehend the blessing that God had in store for my ministry. I learned:

- It is important to trust the process that we as United Methodist clergy have benefit of and our vow serving as itinerate ministers.
- It is important to remember that God blesses the faithful labor of hand in new areas of ministry.
- It is important to learn the history and the culture of the community where our new appointment is located.
- It is important to recognize God inspires new ministry opportunities.
- It is important to rely on your key people to assist you in navigating within and beyond the local church.

- It is important to get to know the local businesses, civic groups, ministerial associations, social justice ministries, and political leaders.
- It is important to take whatever leave time and/or Sabbath you are entitled to and have a colleague to cover for the church.
- It is important to be mindful that there will be conflict, but one can survive.

Chapter 5

We Are Out of Sight and Out of Mind

I was appointed by Bishop John R. Schol to serve as a Discipleship Adventure Guide in the Baltimore Washington Conference, Annapolis Southern Region (ASR) in 2008. I succeeded the Rev. Dr. Rodney T. Smothers, my colleague and friend. The ASR staff was comprised of the Rev. Dr. Ianther M. Mills, District Superintendent of Washington East District and Team Leader; the Rev. Chris Holmes, District Superintendent of Annapolis District; the Rev. Susan Kern-Kester, Adventure Guide; the Rev. Clarence Davis, Jr., Adventure Guide; Pam Niedig, Regional Administrator; Sharon Fleet, Assistant Regional Administrator; and me as an Adventure Guide. Later the Rev. Victoria (Vicky) Starnes would fill the slot vacated by Rev. Kern-Kester due to her relocation to Indiana. The adventure guides were commonly referred to as "the guides." Each district superintendent cared for the pastors in their districts while the guides were responsible for pastors in both districts. The guide ministry provided opportunities for pastors of local churches to be coached and assisted by conference staffers in a variety of ways, such as conflict resolution, fill-ins while pastors were away from their pulpits, and small group facilitators, director of the Discipleship Academy, the position I succeeded the Rev. Dr. Helen Flemming in, to name a few. At one point, I was responsible for a total of thirty-seven pastors located in both the Annapolis and Washington East districts. The churches assigned to my care spanned from Glen Burnie, Maryland, northeast quadrant of ASR to Scotland, Maryland, to the southeast tip of Southern, Maryland, not far from Point Lookout where the Potomac River flows into the Chesapeake Bay. Periodic visitations and routine telephone coaching calls were scheduled with the pastors. This ministry was very meaningful and rewarding to both guide and local pastors. Although a minority number of the pastors were not as enthused. I viewed the extension ministry of the adventure guide as that of an assistant district superintendent, although this is not the language of the Book of Discipline.

Monthly small group meetings known as "Discipler Groups" were occasions that guides served as facilitators. Each month certain topics of discussion were presented to help perfect the spiritual and leadership skills of the pastors. The attitudinal responses of the pastors span the spectrum: another unnecessary meeting on the pastor's calendar; there is nothing that the guides can tell me; an opportunity to share what is happening in my congregation; can I get some help with my unique problem; a time to get away from the ranch and be with colleagues; and a time to share the problems that I am having with the lead pastor. I observed that the small groups situated in suburban communities were less enthusiastic about attending while, to the contrary, the group members from rural congregations appeared most enthusiastic and maintained a higher attendance level. In conjunction with the rural group members, the white female clergy were more apt, at least in my group, to share about their issues within the church while the African American women clergy tended to be reticent. Admittedly, I welcomed working with the rural disciple group as opposed to the suburban groups.

A series of topics were addressed during the Discipler Group meetings. The topic that generated most discussion was the matter of conflict and its impact upon the congregation and its pastor. It was during the discussion on the said matter that the African American women clergy became much more participatory by sharing experiences when they were initially introduced to their congregations. Further, resistance to them came from both men and women. Some of the experiences shared by the female clergy women of color were unbelievable. My later telephone coaching calls with the women clergy revealed to me some of the issues that hampered them in their ministries: obstructing and recalcitrant members. I scheduled visits with the pastors to observe them in their worship settings and give them feedback after service.

I conducted visitations to certain churches pastored by African American women, and found that there was no monolithic example of ministry. At one church there was a sparse attendance, and the pastor was apologetic for the few worshipers. She spoke of members who left because they could not have their way. At another church, the sanctuary was filled and the members were quite enthusiastic and spontaneous with talk-back during the service. Still at a third congregation, there were about thirty members in attendance. The male choir obviously led by an elderly man tended to dominate the singing by the choir. The pastor had just stood behind the pulpit with a few words of introduction and was about to deliver the message when the old gentleman started singing again and leading the choir! He interrupted the pastor by high-jacking the service. After the service, she pointed out that the old gentleman was one of the thorns in her side. This item became a coaching issue with the pastor: being more assertive and exercising her authority as the pastor.

In light of the challenges and concerns some of the African American women colleagues encountered, I will present an excursus in Chapter 6 pertinent to the role of clergy women of color in the Baltimore-Washington Annual Conference.

The guide ministry provided an opportunity to confirm of some of the notions I had in reference to the small membership minority church. While many of the issues related to small-membership churches in both white and African American congregations were similar, there were some unique characteristics peculiar to the African American churches. For example, current descendants of the organizers of the church, raising money for support of the pastor and ministries of the church, fundraising activities were more prevalent in the minority congregations. While the end result was to raise monies by the sales of dinners and various types of rallies to meet the church's obligation to pay conference benevolences and ministerial support, the process provided opportunities for the members to have fellowship, an intrinsic value. Melvin Amerson in his book, *Stewardship in African American Churches: A New Paradigm* offers the advice, "the church needs a paradigm shift for it to remain relevant and viable to the communities it serves."[1] From my observations, there still lingers among some of the rural churches the attitude of fundraising by selling dinners to support the ministries of the church plus the fellowship. I turn my attention to three rural churches in the southern most area of the Washington East District.

Three Historical African American Rural Churches in St. Mary's County, Maryland

Three small historical African American rural congregations formerly part of the Saint Mary's Parish, were established during the antebellum and post-Civil War eras. Two of the churches were part of my regional responsibility as a conference guide. As I reflect upon my tenure as a conference staffer, the churches stand out in my memory. Saint Luke, Ridge (Scotland), Maryland; Mount Zion,

Saint Inigoes, Maryland; and Bethesda, Valley Lee, Maryland were my southern-most local churches with pastors that were part-time local pastors, and lay hire: Pastor L. Boldley, Reverend A. Statesman, and Pastor I. Beverly. Each congregation has a significant history in St. Mary's County.

Bethesda United Methodist Church, located St. George's Church Road, Valley Lee, Maryland is the reputed oldest African American Methodist church in southern St. Mary's County. The church was founded by Rev. Benjamin Tippet as Bethesda Methodist Episcopal Church circa July 10, 1830, a white congregation and passed into African American use on May 27, 1866. The church was erected on the site in 1870 and replaced in 1911. That structure remains until this day. I made my initial visit with Pastor Beverly on August 15, 2008. His church was first of three stops in southern St. Mary's County on a Wednesday morning. He recapped the ministry of the church when the late Pastor Harvey Custis, who recruited him to be his successor. Pastor Beverly was hired in 2000 and has effectively led the congregation. The congregation averaged forty-two worshipers per Sunday in 2000. Worship service typically began at 10 a.m.

He proudly shared that the narthex with restrooms was added in 2003. The worship space was quite neat and evidenced being well cared for although there was concern for termite infestation at the door leading to an adjacent parking lot. He took me on a tour of the church and across the parking lot where the fellowship hall was located. In the fellowship hall, the administrative and pastor's office, food pantry, thrift shop, and new kitchen were housed. Pastor Beverly reflectively alluded to a late member who donated funds for the kitchen to be constructed at the cost of $10,000. At the conclusion of my visit, he said, "I'm glad you came because we don't get visits from the conference. It is like the conference doesn't know that we exist. We are like out of sight and out of mind. Thank you for coming."

Pastor Beverly, servant of the Bethesda United Methodist Church, is in his fourteenth year as lay pastor of this congregation. He sees himself as an old school Methodist that prefers traditional worship experience. However, he recognizes that balancing his approach to sermonizing and music is an ongoing issue for him. He patiently worked with this congregation to institute some policy changes that were obstructions to the growth and development of the congregation. As a result, the average worship attendance increased to where it stands at seventy-five.

Pastor Boldley serves St. Luke United Methodist Church, located on Point Lookout Road, Ridge, Maryland. According to county records, this congregation was founded by US colored troop veterans. The documents reflect that church members conducted worship meetings in their homes until 1886, when the congregants were able to purchase the old St. Mary's Chapel in Ridge. In 1887, it is reported that the church burned, and a new edifice was constructed. Initially, the congregation was known as Lowentown congregation, but eventually became St. Luke Methodist Episcopal Church. The church in 1968 became part of the United Methodist Church. Currently, St. Luke reports an average worship attendance of sixty-four. [2]

Pastor Boldley began his ministry with St. Luke in 2002 as a part-time local pastor having pastored Mt. Zion United Methodist Church, St. Inigoes, Maryland from 1989 to 2002. My visit with Pastor Boldley on August 15, 2008, was the second stop on my itinerary for the morning. The purpose of my visit was to get familiar with the location and hear about the pastor's ministry with the people of St. Luke. The pastor arrived early in preparation for my visit; he later told me that a trustee told him, "The conference man was not here yet." The pastor gave me a tour of the sanctuary and the fellowship hall where pictures chronicled the various ministries of the church; he was especially proud of the young people who went on to college and a well-known professional basketball coach who was connected to the congregation. He further mentioned that some of his congregants traveled from King George, Virginia and Prince George's County, Maryland, to worship there each Sunday. Upon the conclusion of our meeting, I scheduled to visit the church during worship service but would not be there for the entire service as I needed to visit another church, as well.

My last stop was Mt. Zion United Methodist Church, located on Mt. Zion Church Road, St. Inigoes, Maryland. According to tradition, the congregation was organized during the late 18th century.

A slave named Isaac Braxton became a Methodist preacher and founder who preached to his fellow slaves. In 1872, the church was constructed on an acre of donated land. The said edifice was burned and replaced by the current structure built in 1908. Recent conference statistics reflect an average worship attendance of thirty-five. Reverend Statesman, an associate member with thirty-three years of active service retired in 2002 and was hired by the district superintendent to serve Mt. Zion United Methodist Church. After eight years as a district superintendent's hire, he returned to full retirement. The congregation's present pastor is Derrick Walton, a newly appointed part-time local pastor (PTL) in the pursuit of completing requirements for local pastor certification.

I met with Rev. Statesman subsequent to my visit with Pastor Boldley on the Wednesday before the scheduled Sunday visit. The pastor took me on a tour of the church where in the fellowship hall a new counter was being installed as part of renovation project. He expressed hopes of constructing a narthex as an addition with restroom facilities on both sides. We concluded our meeting, and I looked forward to my visit with the church on Sunday morning.

Sunday Visitations

My wife and I began our 118-mile trek from Prince George's County to St. Mary's County on August 19, 2008, at 6 a.m. Bethesda was our first visit on that Sunday morning. The pews were completely occupied. Pastor's Beverly's worship leadership style was very spirited and reminiscent of the flavor of "old time church." He lined out the songs a cappella fashion with the choir and congregation following. Midway during the service the musician came in, played a few selections, and just before the pastor stood up to preach, the musician abruptly left. (The pastor later informed me that the musician played for several other churches during the morning and was on his way to the next church.) The preaching was in the traditional black preaching: call and response—talk-back. At times the pastor touched upon experiences and human conditions in the African American context. There was an occasional laughter, but his point was well taken with a shout, "Amen, Pastor!" At the conclusion of the sermon, the invitation to Christian discipleship was given in addition to an altar call. As we prepared to leave, Pastor Beverly indicated his appreciation for our visit with his congregation. His statement was, "It makes me feel good that the conference would send someone here. We are so far down here that we are out of sight and out of mind." We left to journey to St. Luke's in Ridge, Maryland.

Our next visit was St. Luke United Methodist Church, the southern-most African American United Methodist Church in St. Mary's County, Maryland. The trip was 17.6 miles to St. Luke. Upon our arrival at St. Luke, parking was at a premium. I intentionally parked on the road so that it would not be difficult to leave the parking lot from which we would drive four miles to Mt. Zion. My wife and I experienced what I would describe as "radical hospitality." The sanctuary was filled to capacity with worshipers responding enthusiastically to the ministry of the praise team. After the praise ministry, Pastor Boldley expressed gratitude for the conference sending me to visit St. Luke. Using his words, "I am glad the conference was interested enough to send someone way down here to see us." I was given a welcome package with a ballpoint pen, and I in turn gave words of greeting from the Bishop. Further, I gave words of appreciation and offered my encouragement to people of St. Luke. As the service progressed, I could feel an authentic spiritual fervor among the members. I regretted having to leave so soon, but the next visit was to be made at Mt. Zion.

This Sunday morning at Mt. Zion would be a surprise for me. I was delayed about fifteen minutes while traveling the four miles from St. Luke in Ridge to Mt. Zion in St. Inigoes. At our arrival, an usher escorted us to a seat. There was a sparse attendance with several young children with adults. The lay leader hurriedly came and informed me that the pastor was waiting for me in the study to have prayer before I preached! Lay Leader Greene, who serves as church administrator and worship leader, took me to the pastor's office. Rev. Statesman apologized for the misunderstanding, presuming my visit was for the purpose of preaching. (I learned years ago from an old pastor: "Always have a sermon in your pocket"—be ready to preach.) The pastor introduced me to the congregation as the conference representative and apologized on the miscommunication regarding my being the guest speaker. Nevertheless, I preached and received a lot of talk-back from the thirty or forty worshipers. God was gracious!

After service, we were treated to a delicious meal with sumptuous deserts and fellowship with the members of the congregation. Rev. Statesman and his wife expressed appreciation for our visit as we began our journey back home, where we arrived at 4 p.m. Based upon my experiences on that August Sunday in 2008, I conclude it was unusual for the small rural African American United Methodist congregations in southern St. Mary's County to receive visits from conference officials. The churches welcomed us, and I believed it signified to them that the conference was indeed interested in their wellbeing as a church and the progress of their respective ministries within their local communities. Moreover, while each pastor expressed appreciation for the writer's visit, there was a sense that the pastors felt affirmed by the conference because of the vital ministries conducted in their particular settings.

Profile of the Pastors

The pastors of the three rural African American historical churches in St. Mary's County are typically older married men who are bi-vocational or retired. They are not seminary trained but have taken training provided by the United Methodist Church, such as the Course of Study, a five-year curriculum designed by the Board of Higher Education and Ministry, or they have taken lay speakers' courses (lay servant ministry courses). John Bennett cites, "It is evident that the predominant form of pastoral leadership for the rural church will be that of licensed, commissioned, or bi-vocational clergy."[3] The pastor of St. Luke, for example, is a professional commuter bus driver who is not totally dependent upon his pastoral compensation. Pastor Beverly is a retired federal government employee, also not completely dependent upon his clergy salary. Rev. Statesman is a retired associate member with thirty-three years of active ministry whose part-time service was of tremendous help to a struggling congregation, and he was not totally dependent upon the compensation plan provided by the local church, either. "For hundreds of small churches, when benefits are measured against costs, the most attractive alternative . . . will be to seek an officially retired minister who is interested in a three to seven-year pastorate in a small church . . ." is the comment by Lyle E. Schaller [4] Further, retired ministers are often sought to serve small membership congregations because of their experience and the non-obligation to provide health and pension benefits. [5] Moreover, the assigned pastors live within the twenty-five mile radius of the congregations. Each of the pastors had no less than fourteen years and as many as thirty-six years of pastoral ministry. Each of the pastors is married with adult children. Each pastor was not present on a daily basis at the church office. Each pastor felt that he was adequately compensated by their church. "Given the part time nature of their ministry, many rural pastors are satisfactorily supported by their churches economically." says Lincoln. [6] A characteristic trait of the said pastors was their commitment and faithfulness to the ministry of Jesus Christ for the transformation of the world. Each was motivated to use their gifts and graces to the glory of God.

Representative Example of a Key Layperson in the Rural Church

Lay leaders play a very important role in the life of the rural church context due to the nature of its ministry. Pastors typically do not live in the immediate community resulting in the lay leader serving in the absence of the pastor. Lincoln comments:

> The absentee nature of rural pastoral leadership means that church members are more independent and must develop their own networks of spiritual care and nurture. Lay leaders take active roles in mid-week services . . . (due to) absentee and itinerant nature of the rural ministry. Lay leaders have developed a strong sense of ownership of their churches and the pastor is often regarded as a necessary but an occasional visitor . . . the sense of possessiveness, pride, and power are unparalleled in other phases of African American life . . . but they often speak of "my church."[7]

From my observations over the years, the rural church is typically administered by a dedicated lay leader that was indigenous to both community and church. The lay leader, usually a woman, functioned in multiple areas of ministry. Lay Leader Delores Greene who is a life-time member of Mt. Zion UMC, St. Inigoes, Maryland, is representative of the dedicated, baptized lay servant who served in such areas as lay member to the annual conference, church council chairperson, Sunday school teacher, and aide-de-camp to the pastor. Further, her ministry involved serving as the church administrator that prepared the charge conference reports each year. Lay Leader Greene was surveyed and gave her views of her local church, Mt. Zion UMC. She comments, "Mt. Zion continues to bea rural church idealogically but is situated in a moder growing suburban-like community."[8]

The demographics of the community have not significantly changed although there have been a few newcomers and new homes of new employees of the Patuxent Naval Air Station and adjacent and satellite facilities. The ministries of the church remain traditional in nature with such yearly events as annual revival meetings, homecoming, and various anniversary days of ministry groups (choirs and ushers). Weekly prayers were routinely conducted. Lay leader Greene said former pastors were noted for their being readily available to members of the church and their strong financial support. The current minister Pastor Walton is described as a young, energetic leader who conducts Bible studies and leadership development and has an overall impressive agenda for ministry.

The comments offered by the lay leader, from my perspective, are not atypical of what other lay leaders or persons in leadership in other rural congregations would proffer. In addition the reflection upon the ministries of the church tends to be nostalgic and wanting to return to the days of yesteryear. In a manner of speaking, the lay leader is the culture embodiment and keeper of the corporate history of the church. Each church has such a person and Lay Leader Greene is representative of the key layperson that plays an invaluable role to each pastor appointed to the African American rural congregation.

Tips for the Newly Assigned Pastors

- Become familiar with the historical setting of the churches, their communities, and the descendants that make up the small-membership congregation to which one is appointed by the Bishop or hired by the District Superintendent;
- Be mindful that one may have to serve as a bi-vocational pastor due to the inability of the small-membership church to provide a compensation package that will meet the needs of the pastor;
- Be aware that there is not an expectation for the pastor to be present daily in the church office but only when needed;

- Be aware that there will be a member of the laity who will be on the forefront as leader and administrator of the affairs of the church. Typically, this person will have a long history with the church;
- Be aware that conference staffers are available for coaching, preaching, and facilitating overall support;
- Be certain that when expecting or inviting conference official(s) to your church, there is a clear understanding of what role the said individual(s) will play during the worship service(s);
- Be aware that pastors are not left alone in a foreign and distant land—you are not out of sight and out of mind.

Chapter 6

Excursus: Some Observations of African American Women Clergy

The matter of women serving as preachers and pastors has been an issue in the African American church but has changed somewhat. There is still a remnant of conservative-thinking church folks who believe women should not be preachers, let alone serve in pastoral leadership in the church. That sort of thinking is amplified in some African American small churches in rural settings. Dr. Cain Hope Felder in his seminal work, *Troubling Biblical Waters: Race, Class, and Family,* addresses the matter of female church leaders and in particular accepting the unique role black women ministers bring in God's family. Felder contends:

Male church leadership has no exclusive right to this challenge that Revelation also extends to female church leadership. Women are part of the family . . . they give rise to the Church family and sustain it sometimes even when men disbelieve or otherwise falter.

The Bible shows a remarkable, progressive spirit in improving the social position of women and human rights . . ." [1].

An elderly gentleman commented to me as he was walking out of the sanctuary after worship service in which the speaker was one of our women certified lay servant ministers. He said, "Reverend, let me know the next time you are not preaching. I don't believe in women preachers!" His attitude was reflective of the conservative thinking relative to women preachers that continues to linger in some of our churches. I am the grandson of a woman preacher, the late Sallie Ann Peterson Hayes. While there are no extant records of her ordination, some of my grandmother's biblical study books were signed:

- Mrs. Sallie Hayes—Evangelist, Minister, November 4, 1941
- Mrs. Sallie Hayes—Evangelist, Minister, September 4, 1942
- Rev. Mrs. Sallie Hayes, 1944
- Rev. S. A. Hayes, January 17, 1945

Evidently between the years 1942 and 1944, there was some elevation in her status from evangelist minister to reverend. My earliest recollection of attending worship services was at various churches with my grandmother during summer months. Some of the churches were what were described as "store-fronts." (These were buildings previously used for commercial purposes but converted into worship centers.) The said store-fronts were typically pastored by clergy not trained in traditional seminaries or were trained in noncertified local religious schools. Woman pastors typically served these small urban membership churches.

I further recall my grandmother's very strong influence upon the family especially by encouraging my mother to have my late sister and me attending Enon Baptist Church in Baltimore City, and not Sharp Street Memorial Methodist Episcopal Church. As I grew older, it was apparent to me that my grandmother did not have the status of sitting in the pulpit with the male ministers and senior pastor. She sat in the pew section with the deaconesses. On communion Sundays, she wore a white outfit with a white hat. Mama Hayes, as we called her, was quite emotive during worship services and/or at home during devotional times. I still recall during a communion service that seemed to last forever, being awakened from my nap on her lap. Suddenly, her legs were rapidly going up and down as if she were peddling a bicycle. She was slapping her hands together as she was caught up in the spirit. As I grew older, I would become embarrassed when my Sunday school chums ridiculed me about my grandmother getting "happy." My rationalization was "That's what old people do in church." That helped to handle some of the comments from the guys. Meanwhile, I managed to drift away from Mama Hayes and hang out with the guys in my Sunday school class in the gallery of the sanctuary. Nevertheless, during worship service, my grandmother continued to worship the Lord in spirit and in truth.

There were several things that fascinated me that belonged to my grandmother. They were her religious books and handwritten manuscripts. Oftentimes, I thumbed through the pages of the books and looked at the pictures of biblical characters. There was her old black three-ringed binder notebook that contained her sermons, written in ink and occasionally in pencil. Her Bible, notebook binder, and other papers were kept in a brown leather briefcase with two straps that securely fastened the outside flap with brass buckles. (How I wish that I had those old documents now!) As a consolation, I have the following old books: *The Desire of the Ages: The Conflict of the Ages Illustrated in the Life of Christ* by Ellen G. White; *The Story of Patriarchs and Prophets* by Ellen G. White; *The Great Controversy: The Conflict of the Ages in the Christian Dispensation*; and *Bible Readings for the Home: A Topical Study in Question-and-Answer Form.* The said books are treasures and linkage to my grandmother.

My grandmother always said to me that I was called to be a preacher. According to my late mother, a certain Baptist preached prophesied about my being called to become a preacher. Mama Hayes maintained this understanding about me until her death in 1955.

Looking back, my grandmother, Reverend Sallie Hayes, was among a small population of African American women during the 1940s and 1950s who sensed a call upon their lives to preach the Gospel of Jesus Christ. Yet certain mainline denominations were not ready to receive such women on a par with their male counterparts. The women had opportunities to establish their own congregations that typically assembled in what were known as store-fronts: churches with minimally trained clergy women that were given some degree of recognition as clergy, such as the apparent circumstance with my grandmother. Still, the privilege to sit in the pulpit with her male colleagues and/or administer the sacrament was not available to her. The attitude that prevailed during my grandmother's era still persists today in some mainline denominations. In some other communities of faith where women are on par with clergy, there is still evidence of congregations not being receptive to women clergy.

Rev. Sallie Peterson Hayes January 23, 1945

A Trail-blazer

The late Rev Dr. Emma Pinkney Burrell was one of the few African American women clergy who was a trail-blazer in a mainline denomination, the Methodist Church. Official conference records exhibit:

> (She) was ordained Deacon [in] 1953 . . . admitted into the Conference . . . 1956 . . . ordained Elder 1959 and became the first woman to obtain full clerical rights on the level with men with all rights and privileges pertaining thereto: Washington and Baltimore Conference. [2].

The Rev. Dr. Burrell served as assistant to the pastor at three churches: Ritchie Methodist Church, Ritchie, Maryland; and St. Mary's Larger Parish and Asbury Methodist Church in Washington, DC. Subsequent to serving at Asbury, she was appointed to Jackson-St. Luke Methodist Church, Forrestville, Maryland, 1956–1961. Dr. Burrell would later serve Mt. Vernon Methodist Episcopal Church for a period of seven years (1962–1969) in Ivy City, a community in northeast Washington, DC. Her appointment to Brightwood Park United Methodist Church, Northwest Washington, DC was brief in 1970–1971; subsequent to which, she would serve Good Hope Union United Methodist Church, Silver Spring, Maryland for eight years, 1972–1980. Prior to her retirement, Dr. Burrell served

Community United Methodist Church, in northeast Washington, from 1981 to 1982.

I met the Rev. Dr. Burrell in the fall of 1980 while I served as an assistant to the Rev. Dr. Alfonso J. Harrod, senior pastor of Ebenezer United Methodist Church, Capitol Hill area of Southeast Washington, DC. My initial impression of Dr. Burrell was she was a confident, direct no-nonsense, outspoken, and aging woman pastor. I soon learned that she was a member of the conference Board of Ordained Ministry. Our conversation during this initial informal meeting centered on my aspirations of becoming an ordained Elder and full member of the Baltimore Annual Conference. She briefly outlined the requirements I needed to meet to become a certified candidate. I felt a bit intimidated during our talk but was quite relieved when Dr. Harrod arrived in preparation for going into worship service. In later years, the Rev. Dr. Burrell was a friend to me and during her retirement years often filled in for me at St. Mark's UMC, Laurel, Maryland during my vacation periods.

The Rev. Dr. Emma P. Burrell's significance and legacy in the history of the Baltimore-Washington Conference is she was the first African American woman ordained as Elder in the former Washington Conference. As a college-educated woman who was a daughter of clergy parents: the Rev. Florence P. Simms, local pastor, and the Rev. Dr. William Simms, Emma Burrell found a meaningful pastoral career in the United Methodist Church, where she served family to pastoral-sized congregations. Her legacy is that she became a mentor to incoming clergy women and in a manner of speaking broke the stained glass ceiling in the church for opportunities for women. The Reverends Katherine Butler Luckett (sister of Dr. Burrell), Pearlena L. Woolridge, Mamie A. Williams, Kay Albury, Alfreda Wiggins, Mary Brown Oliver, Barbara Sands, and lanther Mills would be beneficiaries of her trail-blazing in ordained ministry in the Baltimore-Washington Conference of the United Methodist Church.

The Rev. Dr. Burrell maintained her charge conference affiliation with Ebenezer United Methodist Church, Southeast Washington, DC until her death on February 26, 1989. A room is named in her honor in the Baltimore-Washington Conference Mission Center, Fulton, Maryland. The impact of the Rev. Dr. Emma P. Burrell is analogous to a stone thrown into the lake of the Baltimore-Washington Conference creating a ripple in the 1970s, a rush through the 1980s, with a surge in the 1990s, and a continual after-effect with millennials in 2000s. The Rev. Katherine B. Luckett was received on probation in 1969 and ordained elder in 1973.The Rev. Pearlena Lewis Woolridge was received on probation in 1970 and ordained elder in 1973, along with Rev. Luckett. Later during the 1970s, the Reverends Mamie A. Williams and Kay Albury would be the two clergy women of color received on probation, respectively in 1976 and 1979, and admitted into full membership in 1979 and 1981, respectively.

The number of African American clergy women increased significantly in the 1980s. Rev. Mamie Williams describes this period as the "rush." [3] Sixteen African American women during the decade of the '80s would be admitted on probation and eventually become full members of the annual conference. Such noted clergy women with reputations that preceded them are: the Rev. Dr. Alfreda Wiggins (Dean of Women "Pulpiteers" and nationally known); the Rev. Mary Brown Oliver, first African American Woman District Superintendent in the Baltimore-Washington Conference; two clergy women whose fathers served in the old Washington Conference, including the late Rev. Cornelia Lake-Smith (the late Rev. Moses Lake) and the Rev. Dr. LaReesa Smith-Horne (the late Rev. James Smith). The Rev. Drs. Barbara Sands and Douglas Sands were a clergy couple during this decade. Rev. Dorothea B. Stroman is noted for her long pastorates, and Rev. Joan Carter-Rimbach is the first African American woman senior pastor of First Church Hyattsville UMC; she is the wife of the Rev. David Carter-Rimbach (Retired Elder). Some of the clergy women continue to be in active status while others have retired. The foregoing was a sampling of clergy women admitted into the annual conference during the 1980s.

The 1990s would be a time of what I refer to as the "surge." A perusal of the *2014 Official Journal Baltimore-Washington Conference of The United Methodist Church* shows that thirty-six African American clergy women were admitted on probation in the annual conference. Of those admitted on probation during the

1990s and eventually to full membership was the Rev. Dr. Ianther M. Mills who became District Superintendent of the Washington East District, Team Leader for the Annapolis-Southern Region, and Dean of the Cabinet, 2005–2013. Many of these women are still serving churches as active and as retired clergy persons. Several of the women would die in later years, namely the Rev. Dr. Shirlimarie McAroy-Gray and Carol Sloan.

The millennial clergy women, those during the twenty-first century, numbered about nineteen who were on provisional status and later fifteen ordained as elders. I notes that of the fourteen women who were admitted into probationary membership, some would eventually become full member of the annual conference. The Rev. Patricia Allen is an example of a millennial clergy woman who is actively engaged in ministry beyond the local church and one of the organizers of our annual conference worship services.

A striking point of interest is the African American clergy women who serve as pastors in the Baltimore-Washington Conference are either bi-vocational or second-career professionals. While the predominant professionals were educators, there were others who transitioned from such careers as attorneys at law, correctional administrator, district court commissioner, registered nurse, social worker, and software engineers. The clergy women of color bring with them an impressive diversity of gifts in addition to being academically well qualified to serve the churches in this annual conference.

Interviews with Selected African American Women Clergy in BWC

I conducted a series of surveys through written and telephone interviews with African American women clergy that I served with at conference, district, and community levels over the year The selected clergy women are representative of the decades of the 1970s, 1980s, 1990s and 2000s.

1970s First Ripples

The Reverend Mamie Alethia Williams is an elder who was received on probation in 1976 and ordained as an elder in 1979. She is among the few clergy women who entered full-time ministry upon completing her seminary training. The Rev. Williams served a variety of congregations situated in urban and suburban settings such as in Washington, DC, Baltimore City, and Anne Arundel and Montgomery Counties in Maryland. She served as the second African American woman District Superintendent from 1998–2005. "Exciting, challenging, and empowering" is the description she gives relative to her career in ministry.

The Rev. Williams set a number of firsts in her career as a clergy woman. She was the first woman pastor to serve Calvary UMC, Washington, DC; Centennial-Caroline UMC, Baltimore, Maryland; and Hughes Memorial UMC, Washington, DC. Further, she was the first African American woman to serve as District Superintendent of the Annapolis District, BWC. While setting a number of firsts, reactions to her ministry were both positive and negative. Interestingly, push-back came from the suburban congregations with one congregation in particular that had a small group of women who were the instigators. Nevertheless, Rev. Williams strove to be pastoral to her antagonists.

Pertinent to worship, The Rev. Williams views herself as a "liturgical preacher" whose style of preaching is between cerebral and emotive, not a "whooper." Characteristic of her worship is hymns of the church while in some of the churches, there was a preference for gospel music. The matter of the hymns of the church versus gospel music was a point of tension with one particular congregation. Throughout her career, the average worship attendance ranged from 40 to 312 persons; however, her average attendance was 170. Of course, during special worship services, such as funerals, there would be an increase in attendance among those who were former or inactive members. Occasionally during the special services, some of the former and inactive members renewed their membership vows. Overall, Rev. Williams feels that her worship leadership was in conformity with the general church, although challenged at points to keep congregations focused on their heritage as worshipers of the Methodist persuasion.

Salary equity and leadership style were areas the Rev. Williams reflected upon. She believes because of her gender, it factored in her not being on par with her male colleagues, for the most part. While serving as a district superintendent, her salary was on par with the other colleagues. However, her service on behalf of Jesus Christ was more rewarding and of value than being equal in pay with her male colleagues. The disparity gap between male and female clergy is closing. As for her leadership style, Rev. Williams believes the most effective way to lead is through the process of participatory leadership. She prefers to work with the leadership of the church rather than to be dictatorial.

Besides ministry within the boundaries of the local church, Rev. Williams was active in the community. In Washington, DC, she was an active member of the Washington Inner City Self Help; the group advocated for renters in the community. As a clergy advisor, she along with other clergy worked on social issues with the late Marion Barry, former mayor of the District of Columbia. B.U.I.L.D. was a social justice ministry that she worked with in Baltimore City. While serving as district superintendent, Rev. Williams was connected with R.E.S.P.E.C.T. another advocacy group for the marginalized and poor in the Annapolis area. Rev. Williams' ministry indeed conformed to the principle of John Wesley: "The world is my parish."

The Reverend Kay Francis Albury is an ordained elder in the Baltimore-Washington Conference. She was admitted on probation in 1979 and ordained at the Baltimore Annual Conference in 1981. Rev. Albury has served in congregations located in urban and sub-urban communities. Her longest appointment was with Ames UMC,

Baltimore, Maryland, 1985–2005. Ames is located in the historic community of Sand Town, northwest Baltimore City. In five of six churches she served, Rev. Albury was the first woman pastor. In some of the congregations, there was excitement in having her as their pastor, and as expected there was some push-back from those who preferred not having a woman pastor. There were members who left because of her gender while others had been inactive rejoined and reaffirmed their membership vows. According to Rev. Albury, her average worship attendance during her career was eighty-nine.

Rev. Albury's circumstance pertinent to pay equity was similar to that of her colleague Rev. Williams. There was, however, a slight twist; because she was married at the time, the church felt that she should not receive a pay increase that would put her on par with other clergy, namely male colleagues. The conference was able to grant her an equitable salary assistance package. "At times I felt that I would have gotten a salary increase if I were male" was her comment.

Rev. Albury describes her leadership style as a pastor who encourages and teaches her congregants with the end result of empowering them for leadership in ministry. She admits that each church is unique unto itself, and therefore she had to adjust her pastoral leadership style. At times, she contends, this thwarted her creativity. The accomplishments of Rev. Albury over the years are reflected in her having effectively trained laity for leadership in the local church by engaging them in Bible studies and volunteerism beyond the church. Every church she pastored consistently paid their apportionments in full. Further, she is proud of the fact while serving a certain congregation, an educational wing was added on to the church.

For a two year period, Rev. Albury served as an Adventure Guide for the Baltimore Region. Her experience as a seasoned pastor afforded her the opportunity to serve in the said extension ministry where her expertise was utilized to assist other pastors in the Baltimore Region. Currently, Rev. Albury is serving St. Matthews UMC, Dundalk, Maryland.

Both Reverends Williams and Albury are seasoned African American women clergy who began their ministerial careers during the latter part of the 1970s. Each has served in urban and suburban communities in the Baltimore-Washington Conference where they experienced the friction of resistance to women serving as pastors. The resistance was expressed through such means as obstruction to compensating the clergy women with salaries on par with male colleagues. Moreover, some of the members of the church pushed back because of their gender; however, push-back comes to all clergy as they are going about their ministry—nothing new under the sun. It is to be noted that both women served on the Conference Board of Ordained Ministry. The two women set examples for other African American clergy women who would come after them in the next decade.

1980s The Rush

Sixteen African American women would be admitted on probation in the Baltimore Annual Conference. Among the growing population of women clergy in the Baltimore Conference, several African American women clergy would become nationally known and history-making ministers.

The Reverend Dr. Alfreda L. Wiggins is a former District Court Commissioner and retired elder who was received on probation in 1981 and ordained elder during the 1985 Annual Conference. Dr. Wiggins is a nationally and internationally known preacher who has preached at such events as the black Methodist for Church Renewal (BMCR) and Hampton's Ministers Conference. Moreover, her reputation precedes her as a charismatic revivalist who is in demand. The annual conference of 2004 was blessed to be the recipient of Dr. Wiggins's powerful sermon, "Burn, Baby, Burn!" As her sermon drew to its climax, the kinetics in the auditorium was at fever-pitch as she challenged the conference to be on fire with the Holy Spirit. (I have since referred to her as "The Dean of Women Preachers.") Anecdotally, Dr. Wiggins served on the Conference Board of Ordained Ministry where she chaired the Sermon Review Committee and Conference Relations Committee.

My conversation with Dr. Wiggins revealed her feelings about her ministry. She said her gift is preaching and her position is that if clergy is to be successful in the black Church context, he or she must be able to preach. She describes her ministry as being very successful and had no difficulty in serving her appointments. She asserts, "The churches I served were accepting, cordial and receptive to my being appointed to them" The members of her first appointment were very nurturing since she was young to the ministry. A few members reaffirmed their membership vows during her tenure at her first appointment, Hereford Charge; the attendance at the several churches ranged from twenty to thirty in worship.

Concerning pastoral compensation and support, Dr. Wiggins at the time of her first appointment was not cognizant of her male colleagues' salaries. Her salary remained the same as her predecessor while at the first appointment. In later years her salary would be on par with her male colleagues.

Dr. Wiggins primarily exercised a democratic leadership but could be become authoritarian when needed. At her last appointment her style of leadership was more authoritarian. One could attribute her leadership style to her previous career as a district court commissioner.

The accomplishments made by Dr. Wiggins are significant with one being history making. She built an office at Gough United Methodist Church (Hereford Charge), Cockeysville, Maryland. Her most significant achievement was to become the first woman pastor at John Wesley United Methodist Church, Baltimore City. She served the said congregation from January 1, 1995, until her retirement in 2011. Her retirement was brief; in 2012, she became pastor of St. Luke UMC in Sand Town, Baltimore City.

The Reverend Mary Brown Oliver is a former educator from the District of Columbia Public School System and retired elder who made history in the Baltimore Conference by being appointed by Bishop Joseph Yeakel to serve as the first African American female District Superintendent of the Washington Central District. The 2014 Official Journal Baltimore-Washington Conference shows Rev. Oliver was received on probation in 1983 and ordained elder in 1985. She pastored Westphalia UMC in suburban Prince George's County Maryland and Northwood-Appold, Baltimore City. Significantly, Northwood-Appold was a multicultural appointment where initially there was some push-back, but because of her love for people, she was able to bond with the congregants. In fact, two men who initially did not want her at the church became her strongest supporters. Her words of wisdom are: "Love them, but don't let them rule you."

Rev. Oliver was appointed to the Washington Central District in 1990; subsequently the said district's name was changed in 1994 to Washington-Columbia District, to reflect the boundary changes that extended to parts of Columbia, Maryland. As she assumed additional responsibilities for other churches, Rev. Oliver's skills as an administrator aided her in being selected by Bishop Yeakel to become the Dean of the Cabinet. (This was another first for Rev. Mary Brown Oliver—MBO.) She served with distinction.

The late Charles Oliver, her husband, was Rev. Oliver's strong moral support throughout her ministry. Charles, a professional chef, prepared culinary delights at district gatherings and other special occasions. He was a visible presence at many functions that his wife was a part.

Rev. Oliver feels for the most part her salary was on par with many of her male counterparts. Upon completing an extended term as a district superintendent, she was appointed to St. Paul UMC, Oxon Hill, Maryland. After five years of pastoring at St. Paul, she retired in 2003. She comments, "It's been a good journey!"

The Reverend Dr. LaReesa Smith-Horn, daughter of the late Rev. James Smith and former educator, is in her 28th year of pastoral ministry. She was received on probation in 1987 and ordained elder in 1989. Dr. Smith-Horn is serving Christ UMC in East Baltimore City where she has been for the past eight years. In each of her three appointments, she was the first woman pastor. The first assignment was a rural setting with a two-point charge in Sykesville, Maryland: St. Luke–Mt. Gregory–White Rock Charge. She makes the comment: "Based on rumors, the people at the first appointment did not want a woman even though it was the church where my father was the associate pastor . . . for a few years . . . they did not care whose daughter she was . . ."[3] The attitudes of the antagonists changed. Subsequent appointments were ready to receive her with open arms. It is important to note that at her current appointment, her predecessor did a very fine job in preparing the congregation to receive a woman pastor.

Reflecting on her second appointment, Dr. Smith-Horn felt that she was seasoned enough to pastor for the next fourteen years the rural assignment in Severn, Maryland. She was stronger, confident, competent, and a more effective leader. The average worship attendance ranged from 95 to 100 attendees in this said congregation. She lived in the parsonage and describes the experience from good to great. While serving this appointment, she was a member of the Conference Board of Ordained Ministry. Her next appointment would be in the urban setting, and there would be a life-changing event.

Dr. Smith-Horn was appointed to serve Christ UMC beginning July 2006. The said congregation is located in East Baltimore. It was at this church where she met and married the Rev. Norman Horn, his family's home church. Her husband is very supportive of her ministry and may be regularly seen at her side. The ministry at Christ UMC bodes well for Dr. Smith-Horn. Her worship attendance ranges from 125 to 140. "High praise" is the description she gives and enthusiastically reports along with the great music that there is an orchestra that plays on the third and fifth Sundays. [4] Moreover, she is among African American women clergy who can "really preach the Gospel." Dr. Smith-Horn at the Annual Conference of 2004 preached the sermon "When Noah Got Drunk," the focus was upon when we put aside our Christian principles and let our minds and hearts become influenced by worldly thinking. Without a doubt the sermon was quite powerful.

Christian education is a priority of Dr. Smith-Horn. She reports having five "well-attended" adult Bible study classes. As for youngsters, on Sunday mornings they are permitted to leave the general worship service to attend church school classes. While this is not her preference, it appears to be the most effective way to meet the needs of the families in attendance. The church school staff is praised for the sacrifice they make to conduct the church school classes while the main worship service is in progress.

A significant feature of Dr. LaReesa Smith-Horn's ministry is the longevity that she has enjoyed over the years. At her first appointment, Sykesville: St. Luke–Mt. Gregory–White Rock Charge (rural churches), she served five years. Her next appointment was in Severn: Metropolitan, where she pastored fourteen years. Currently, Dr. Smith-Horn is in her ninth year at Christ UMC in Baltimore City where change is taking place. The community around the church is rapidly changing, both physically and culturally due to the influences of the expansion of Johns Hopkins Hospital complex; there is strong evidence of gentrification in the immediate community. Christ UMC will soon have to adjust its ministry approach in the community.

In my opinion, Dr. Smith-Horn is very much like her father, the late Rev. James Smith who enjoyed his ministry and did not want to stop. The old adage says, "The fruit does not fall far from the tree."

1990s The Surge

The African American women clergy surge is characterized by women who answered the call to ordained ministry in the United Methodist Church while employed in traditional professional and in some instances, in nontraditional professional careers. The Reverend Dr. Ianther M. Mills is an example of such a clergy woman of this era. Dr. Mills was employed as a software engineer who graduated from Georgetown University. She is among the numerous preachers nurtured at A.P. Shaw United Methodist Church that was pastored for over forty years by the late Rev. Everett Stevenson, Sr. (nephew of the Rev. Dr. William B. Simms, father of the Late Dr. Emma P. Burrell). Her seminary training was at Wesley Theological Seminary, Washington, DC.

The Rev. Dr. Mills was received on probation in 1997 and ordained elder in 2000. At her first appointment, Catonsville UMC, in the suburbs of Baltimore City, she was the first African American associate pastor. The average worship attendance at the said church was 400 with an emphasis on high church service in addition to contemporary flavor of worship. "The initial response at Catonsville UMC was some mild hints of racism. However, the congregation came to accept and respect me within a year" is the comment by Dr. Mills. [6]

Dr. Mills' next appointment was Good Hope Union, Silver Spring, Maryland; the late Dr. Emma Burrell served this congregation for eight years (1972–80). Some of the membership was concerned about her youthfulness. This would soon change. The average worship attendance was 160. For the five years that she served this congregation, new members increased yearly that ranged from ten to fifteen persons per year. The ministry at Good Hope Union was very fruitful, resulting in the church undertaking to build an addition to the church, a fellowship hall.

Pertinent to financial support, Dr. Mills felt that her compensation was sufficient at all her appointments. She said, "My salary was comparable to male colleagues and my male predecessors."[7] A housing allowance was not necessary as she and her husband resided in the parsonage at Good Hope Union and the Washington East District parsonage, while a District Superintendent.

Meanwhile serving the local church, Dr. Mills chaired the Washington West District Committee on Ordained Ministry (DCOM) and served as a member of the Conference Board of Ordained Ministry (BOM). I observed the leadership style of Dr. Mills, which was collaborative in nature during the examination retreats of candidates for ordination. Her demeanor was mild as she carried out her duties and responsibilities of leadership. The same practice of leadership ministry would be evident in her role as District Superintendent.

Bishop John R. Schol was looking for the best and the brightest to give leadership in the Baltimore-Washington Conference. In light of this, he chose some of the younger clergy to serve in vital leadership roles. The Rev. Dr. Ianther Mills proved well qualified as one of the younger leaders and was thereby selected in 2005 to serve in the district superintendent's ministry. While there rumblings about some of the younger clergy not "paying their dues," Dr. Mills proceeded on to make history in the Baltimore-Washington Conference to become the first African American woman clergy to serve as District Superintendent of the Washington East District. On January 1, 2007, she was appointed to serve as District Superintendent and Team Leader of the Annapolis-Southern Region. Meanwhile she was supported by her colleagues in the Cabinet to serve as the Dean of the Cabinet for two terms. Dr. Mills represented the Baltimore-Washington Conference as a member on the General Board of Higher Education and Ministry. Further, she traveled as a representative of the annual conference in foreign nations such Korea, Russia, and South Africa, where she preached and taught pastors. Needless to say, her ministry with the Baltimore-Washington Conference was extensive and rewarding.

Upon completing a term of eight years with the Cabinet in 2013, Dr. Mills made another historical first. She was appointed the first woman to serve as the Senior Pastor of the historic Asbury United Methodist Church, Washington, DC. Asbury is known for its very traditional worship style that is reflective of congregational profile: middle- and upper-middle income and well-educated African Americans. The worship attendance ranges from 250 to 300 per Sunday. In response to her worship ministry, ten new members joined during her appointment year 2015. The worship team is working to initiate a new worship service that will be attractive to a different demographic. [8]

The initial presumption that Asbury UMC would have a negative response to its first woman pastor is not supported. There have been women clergy on staff for years such as the Rev. Kay Albury who was an associate pastor (1980–82), the Rev. Pauline Wilkins, associate pastor (1994–96) and Min. Irene Pierce, retired local pastor. "[T]he congregation has been very open . . ." to use the words of Dr. Mills pertaining to the response of the congregation to her appointment. With her collaborative leadership style, she should be able to make great strides with the historic Asbury UMC, Washington, DC.

With attention to family support, Hilton Mills, her husband, has supported his wife's ministry throughout the years. On the occasions of District Christmas parties or Epiphany dinner parties Mr. Mills has always been present. He visited with her at various congregations throughout the Washington East District. I have found Mr. Mills a very personable man who is very supportive of his wife's ministry. He, too, is an engineer by profession.

Pastor Joan Jones is a retired educator in Calvert County. She was appointed to St. Edmonds UMC, a rural congregation in 1999; this has been her only appointment. While her description of her ministry is in conformity with the Book of Discipline, Para 340, there is an emphasis upon a teaching motif.

Pastor Jones is the first and only female pastor to serve the St. Edmonds United Methodist Church, Chesapeake Beach, Maryland. Many of the congregants knew her due to being in a nearby community. Push-back eventually came, and it was from one of the oldest founding members, a senior man, of the congregation and other males who preferred a male pastor. The older male member derogatorily referred to Pastor Jones as "Little Girl" and oftentimes took inappropriate moments during the worship service to make comments. Eventually because he could not intimidate her, the older man backed down from his foolishness and respected her authority as pastor. There were other men of the congregation and some women in leadership roles, particularly for long tenure, who also pushed back. The focal point of the push-back was the woman pastor's authority and not the preaching ability of the pastor.

With attention to Pastor Jones' worship ministry, the congregation has grown over the years in the rural setting. At her arrival in 1999, the average worship attendance was forty persons, but now it has grown to 110 each Sunday. The church grew from a family-sized congregation to a pastoral-sized church. "There were also many inactive persons who joined because I was a female and my reputation as being a no-nonsense person with integrity . . ." is her comment relative to membership growth of this rural congregation.[9] Further the pastor felt because of her evangelistic calling, others joined as a result of the changed atmosphere and climate in the church. [18]

One of the issues concerning small rural congregations is adequate compensation for the pastor. Pastor Jones was a seminary student and employed with the Calvert County School System when appointed to St. Edmonds UMC. Her salary was based upon quarter-time service; however, after retirement from school system, the church raised her salary to 50 percent of the equitable compensation formula. Currently, the pastor receives 75 percent of full-time compensation in addition to a housing allowance, reimbursement fund, and medical and pension benefits. [11] She makes no comment relative to comparable salary circumstances of her male colleagues.

Ask anyone, clergy or laity, in Washington East District about Pastor Joan Jones: more than likely the comment will be, "She is in charge of lay speakers' training." She comes from the ranks of certified lay speakers and taught lay speaking for a number of years. Pastor Jones is also noted for her high energy and enthusiasm for Christian education as reflected in her ongoing participation with the Discipleship Academy and Washington East District leadership training events. She served as the Associate Dean of the Washington East District Discipleship Academy; the responsibility was hers for caring for such details as registration and preparing certificates for the participants. Christian education is a part of Pastor Jones' DNA and has been very beneficial for the district.

A final comment by the pastor is, "I can now begin to see the fruit of my labor. It is refreshing to know that the congregation has come to know you . . . the feeling of trust have developed through these years of being together." Pastor Joan Jones is in her sixteenth year at St. Edmonds UMC.

The 1990s was a period of time in the Baltimore-Washington Annual Conference that a high number of African American women answered God's call to ordained ministry, some of whom were in lucrative professional careers. The Rev. Dr. Ianther Mills is an example of an African American clergy woman who was a part of the surge during the 1990s. Pastor Joan Jones is another example of a clergy woman of color who migrated from the public school system to preach and teach in the local church. These clergy women came into ordained ministry with very impressive professional credentials and are using their gifts and graces to the glory of God. I turn my attention to clergy women of the millennial era.

2000s The Millennials

The Baltimore-Washington Annual Conference would continue to witness a steady flow of African American women answering the call of God to ordained ministry. The women were bi-vocational and retirees from the professional ranks of local and state government and some from private industry. There was no indication of women of color who entered ministry immediately after undergraduate and/or seminary training, referring to the African American women clergy that entered during the 2000s as millennials.

Pastor Eloise Newman was a supervisory social worker for the District of Columbia for over twenty-six years. She was nurtured in the Christian faith at A. P. Shaw United Methodist Church, where the late Rev. Everett Stevenson was pastor for over forty years. She was received on probation in 2003 and retired on June 30, 2011. She is a widow with adult children who are very affirmative and proud of her as a pastor.

Wards United Methodist Church is located in Chesapeake Beach, Maryland. The community is rural and Pastor Newman opines, "My ministry setting is . . . rural. It is a family-oriented congregation . . . One of my problems is, so much of what is going on in the family ends up in the church, in terms of attitudes." [12] This is not an unusual occurrence in the small church for it serves as a place where the extended family can be expressive of its feelings. Author Steve Willis contends, "Feeling is the heart and soul of small-church life. Small-church folk experience Sunday morning through a combination of feeling, memory, and intuition. This openness to feeling gives people a deep and tenacious sense of belonging, both to one another and God." [13] Pastor Newman's congregation is not unique from the typical small rural membership church.

Pastor Newman has enjoyed eight years of longevity with the Wards congregation. Prior to her appointment to Wards UMC, she served for six years Bradbury Heights UMC, Washington, DC. While her appointment to Wards was very positive, there were elements in the congregation that continued to retain a negative attitude toward the former pastor, a woman, and subsequently left the church. However, many inactive members reaffirmed their membership vows, became active in the ministries of the church in addition to new members joining the congregation. The average worship attendance is approximately sixty-five. One of the contributory reasons for the increase in worship attendance is the vibrancy of the worship experience.

Pastor Newman's leadership style is hands-on partnership in ministry. She is of the opinion that method of leadership allowed the members to trust her more and feel a sense of self-worth and actual contribution to the ministry of the church. I noticed the attitudinal shift while I served as the Adventure Guide in ministry with Wards UMC from 2009 to 2011. Moreover, Pastor Newman's affect is maternal, and I suspect this is another reason for this congregation's affirmative response to her ministry style.

The vibrancy of worship is of course attributed to the presence of the Spirit of God in connection with Pastor Newman's spiritual formation and nurturing at A. P. Shaw UMC, Washington, DC. The children of the congregation are not excluded from the very lively teaching ministry for all ages. In conjunction with the vibrant worship is an active women's ministry: Women Anointed for Righteousness (W.A.R.) "There has been eight new converts, six new members, two returning members in addition to one affiliate member . . ." comments Pastor Newman. [14] Her accomplishments are impressive.

The Reverend Dr. Sonia L. King prior to responding to God's call to ordained ministry was employed as a Certified Therapeutic Recreation Specialist for sixteen years with the State of Maryland. Dr. King was received on probation in 2005 and ordained elder in 2008. She was appointed to several congregations: Asbury UMC, Jessup, Maryland; Mt. Zion UMC, Pasadena, Maryland; and St. Mark's UMC, Laurel, Maryland. Each of the foregoing churches is located in suburban communities. Rev. Dr. King was the third woman pastor at Asbury and St. Mark's UMCs, while she was the second female pastor at Mt. Zion UMC. Her initial experience at Mt. Zion was fraught with some resistance, which will be reflected upon.

Rev. Dr. King was initially assigned on an interim basis at Mt. Zion due to the appointed pastor being on voluntary military deployment. Meanwhile the retired pastor was delegated to serve along with the lay leader in the interim while the pastor was on military duty; however, the appropriate manner in handling the situation should have been to have the district superintendent make the decision on the pastoral care of the church in the absence of the appointed pastor. The retired pastor became quite disappointed upon being advised by the guide that Dr. King would serve in the appointed pastor's absence. This did not bode well. There was significant push-back, according to Rev. King, until there was some subsidence of the resistance. Displaced aggression was manifested through the refusal to bring her salary up to a level consistent with her predecessor and time in service. Despite the apparent negativity, Dr. King continued to strive to: " . . . love the hell out of them," using her words.[15]

The worship experiences have been spirited for the most part. While she found Asbury to be more of a traditional church, the other two congregations have benefitted from very spirited and uplifting worship experiences. In addition, one congregation had praise dancers that augmented the worship services. Black churches for the most part want to encounter the presence of the Lord with an enthusiastic, charismatic flavor of worship while having the message of the music speak to their daily life circumstances and conditions. To have a musician with the capability of reading music in addition to playing by ear while playing a deep-throated Hammond B-3 organ backed-up with a piano player and percussionist makes for an electrifying experience of worship. Thus, Dr. King could describe worship services at Mt. Zion and/or St. Mark's as: "lively, engaging, dynamic, wonderful choirs and musicians." [16]

Churches readily respond to leadership styles of its leaders. Dr. King describes her leadership style as democratic. She welcomes input from members of the team prior to making a decision. Additionally, the pastor avers, "I delegate responsibility and expect those in leadership to do their job" is her comment. [17] However contrary to her statement, I recall from my military days that one delegates authority but not responsibility. Further, Tom Berlin and Lovett H. Weems, Jr. offer, "Delegate tasks, not responsibility . . . the ability to delegate tasks while retaining responsibility is critical to fruitful leadership . . . delegation is an art to cultivate but not abuse . . . You continue to give oversight because you cannot shed the ultimate responsibility for the ministry . . ."[18] It is my assumption that the pastor really delegated some authority in order to accomplish certain tasks within the ministry of the church because some of the reported accomplishments clearly is indicative of persons using the authority delegated to them, such as renovation and expansion of the fellowship hall.

Rev. Dr. Sonia King is a pragmatist who reports learning valuable lessons from each church. From each of her appointments, she attempts to apply what was learned in order to hone her skills in pursuit of becoming a better pastor. She is deeply appreciative of the experiences in the several churches and love for the people.

> The Baltimore-Washington Annual Conference is noted for its receptiveness to clergy women of other denominations that desire to become a part of our community of faith. To this end there are several African American clergy women that served in the BWC as pastor and co-pastor who were part of my interview and survey. Both women clergy are Doctors of Ministry and served congregations but with contrasting experiences.

The Reverend Dr. Diana L. Parker is a retired elder of the African Methodist Episcopal Church and who was a mid-level manager in the federal government. I first met her during the early 1980s while

I was pastor at St. Mark's UMC, Laurel, Maryland. She along with two other clergy women was featured in the *Laurel Leader* in a story about the rise of women pastors in mainline denominations. Rev. Dr. Parker at that time served the Faith AME for a period of two years. Subsequently, Dr. Parker's judicatory appointed her to St. James AME Church, Frederick, Maryland, where she pastored for nine years. She finally joined with her husband, the Rev. Conrad D. Parker, and served in a co-pastor status with him at Grace UMC, Fort Washington, Maryland. After fourteen years of ministry at Grace UMC, both of them retired in 2011. Significantly, the Parkers are active in missions in Ghana, West Africa.

Dr. Parker describes her experiences in the three churches as very affirming and supportive. She reports no occasion of losing members from her congregations because of her gender, and the financial compensation was sufficient. She points out that the worship services in each church were spirit-filled and dynamic.

My ministry experiences with the Parkers were during special occasions such as annual revivals, women's day and Lenten services. I refer to them as the "Dynamic Duo" who support each other during preaching services. It is characteristic of the Parkers if one preaches, the other prays during the invitational moment. Moreover, both bring a charismatic flavor of worship in conjunction with a teaching ministry. Each Lenten season, congregations of the Route 210 Corridor looked forward with anticipation of how the Parkers would minister for the particular season. Dr.

Parker's description of ministry is equipping the saints for the work of ministry.

The Reverend Dr. Priscilla Boswell, a widow, is an elder in the African Methodist Episcopal Church. For a period of thirty years, she was a business consultant specializing in workforce development with clients in federal and local government agencies and private business organizations. She has a vast array of professional experiences, including working on the executive staff of President Jimmie Carter. [19]

Rev. Dr. Boswell made history by being the first woman pastor appointed to a certain rural church in the Washington East District in 2006, but the said congregation was not prepared for a female clergy person. The un-readiness of congregation for such a change resulted in a tremendous push-back by a small but very influential group of members from several prominent families. One of the members who desired to remain anonymous of the said congregation comments:

> [The church] has always had issues with change and pastors before Dr. Boswell's tenure, which could make it seem as though the pastor is the problem . . . there have been problems with pastors before her . . . like some other rural churches do not accept change very well and have issues with a woman as pastor. [20]

The picture the anonymous member paints is one of obstructionism and resistance to working with the pastor. According to Dr. Boswell, there was a small highly influential group of members who were very disruptive to the ministry. In his book, G. Lloyd Rediger contends, "An empowered but untrained laity is a contextual factor . . . that encourages the development of clergy killers . . ." [21] At the root cause is deterioration of spiritual health. Moreover, to dramatize the disrespect toward Dr. Boswell as pastor, a new Sunday school class was started without informing her. A list of other impertinencies was alluded to by the former pastor and ongoing conflicts that contributed to her eventual change of appointment.

The second appointment Dr. Boswell served was a multicultural congregation that was part of a cooperative parish setting in the suburbs of Prince George's County, Maryland, and there were some nuances related to the ministry. She was the second woman pastor and did not experience the degree of push-back as with the first congregation. She was serving as an associate pastor. The worship style at the second church was restrained and structured. Her compensation was less. Rev. Boswell was assisted by her daughter at the suburban church and comments, "She [her daughter] was acutely aware of and dismayed by the stresses and challenges" of pastoral ministry. Dr. Boswell served one year at the second appointment; "I occasionally feel deep sorrow, disappointment, and pain . . . have come to realize that every time I thought I was being rejected from something good, I was actually being redirected to something better" is her reflection on the experiences in the United Methodist Church.[22] At the end of conference year 2010–2011, Rev. Dr. Boswell returned to the African Methodist Episcopal Church.

Pastor Sandra was a former legal secretary in private industry and the current part time local pastor in her ninth year of pastoral ministry. She was nurtured in Methodism since a child and pastors a rural, fifty-three-member church that is predominantly African American with one white member. The church is located in Calvert County, Maryland, while the pastor's residence is thirty-one miles away in neighboring Charles County, Maryland.

Pastor Sandra was the second female pastor to serve the rural congregation. Early on the members of the congregation were quite specific that they preferred a male pastor. Upon her arrival, she was warmly received by the entire congregation while others took a wait-and-see attitude during the first year of her ministry with them. The only significant push-back was to the pastor's proposal of starting a liturgical dance group. Resistance came from a couple of older women congregants who felt there should be no dancing in the church. She appealed to them that nothing would be done that is not in conformity within the parameters of the Holy Scriptures, tradition of the United Methodist Church, and the Book of Discipline. As a result, the single liturgical dancer participated in worship services approximately for one year. She stopped due to getting married, and no one stepped forward to take up the said ministry.

There was growth in the membership and average worship attendance during her pastorate. Rather than attrition in the membership, several members returned who had left during her predecessor's administration. Five inactive members reaffirmed their faith. The range of attendance for worship service was thirty-five to forty per Sunday. "High-spirited" is the description she gave regarding the music for worship, although there was no talk-back or verbal response to her sermons. It was my impression during the visitation that the worshipers were attentive and reflective about the message. In addition, Pastor Sandra in her delivery of the message is not charismatic but, I suggest, cerebral.

Family and spouse support are key to a pastor's ministry whether male or female. Pastor Sandra disclosed that she did not receive her husband's support of her ministry. The main reason she cited was the number of occasions that she was required to be at the church during the week besides Sunday, Wednesday evenings, and occasionally Tuesday evening once a quarter. Her spouse became less visible at the church until his nonattendance. This played heavily upon her while serving the local church. The church provided less than minimal financial compensation for Pastor Sandra. She continues to receive less than the quarter-time financial support stipulated by the annual conference. A male colleague in similar circumstances received approximately $2,000 more than what her church pays. Nevertheless, the church has allotted educational funds that help her yearly as she matriculates in the Course of Study at Wesley Theological Seminary.

Pastor Sandra viewed her leadership style as a pastor-teacher. In commenting on her description of leadership style, the pastor stated, "I . . . lead by example . . . a team player . . . encourage others . . . to spread their wings . . ." She does not hesitate to use authority when required and has an open ear to hear matters before making an appropriate decision. I noticed in the pastor's comments on the interview form that she considers herself personable and approachable but not necessarily charismatic. I contend this also speaks to her worship style.

Engaging the church beyond the walls and into the community is a significant accomplishment by Pastor Sandra. Such social justice ministries serving the homeless sheltered in Project Echo Homeless Shelter, participating with the Calvert County's Safe Night project, and the American Cancer Society's Relay for Life are examples of ministry beyond the walls of the church. Pastor Sandra continues to faithfully carry out her pastoral ministry in a rural context in Calvert County.

Pastor Patricia Berry, a retired educator and former law student, benefits from a Master of Divinity degree. She narrated experiences in two churches at opposite poles in terms of response to her leadership as pastor. Church No. 1, located in the suburban community of Waldorf, Maryland, was pastored by a woman for a number of years. Her ministry at Church No. 1 flourished with a plethora of ministries within and beyond the local church. One of its signature ministries was a ministry to men with substance-abuse issues and same was reported in the conference newsletter in 2012. Further, Church No. 1 was listed as an Acts II church continuously for five years.

Church No. 2 was described as insular and the ministry was not relevant to the surrounding community. The pastor cited various instances in which there were missed opportunities to be the church in the community. She cites, "They opposed Warm Nights and the homeless guests that arrived, by trying to impose a 'dress code' on the homeless visitors before they would be allowed into the church."[59] Hospitality to the marginalized did not exist, based upon other occasions in which the church could have expressed the love of Jesus Christ, in her opinion. The comments were extensive in the interview form pertinent to the negative experience with this said congregation.

Pastor Berry succeeded a woman pastor that served Church No. 1 for many years. She was warmly received by the congregation and was strongly supported by them. However, in Church No. 2, there was a hostile atmosphere with a tremendous push-back. A couple of male members left prior to her officially assuming the pastoral leadership of the church and subsequently within a few weeks two families left. The pastor reports, despite those members who left, a greater number joined than those who left.

The worship experience at Church No. 1 was vibrant, wholesome, interactive, and Spirit-led. The average worship attendance was reflective of the church's vitality. At the start of Pastor Berry's ministry at Church No. 1, the average attendance was twenty persons. During her five-year appointment with Church No. 1, an early service was initiated and the average attendance increased to seventy persons per Sunday. Musicians were volunteers who enjoyed using their gifts and graces to the glory of God. A liturgical dance ministry was initiated with enthusiasm. Electronic equipment was purchased in order that worship services could be duplicated onto CDs that were given to anyone who wanted a copy. The growth at Church No. 1 was impressive, based upon the clergy talk around the Washington East District. Pastor Berry concluded by saying, "I was thoroughly invigorated and uplifted by the worship in this little church."

By contrast, Church No. 2's worship service was agonizing for the pastor. The worship team neglected to meet with Pastor Berry for purposes of discussing musical selections that would support the sermon themes. Her description of the worship ministry was summarized as chaos and disorder among the communion stewards and ushers. Attitudinally, the pastor interpreted the behavior of the musicians as well-paid professionals who felt they owed the congregation a performance over worship. The attendance fluctuated between eighty and one hundred worshipers. The worship experience for the pastor was draining and unfulfilling.

The forty-three-mile drive home after service left her fatigued and discouraged.

The conflict that Pastor Berry experienced at Church No. 2 was unnatural. In his work on pastors and congregations under attack, Rediger cites three types of conflict: normal, abnormal and spiritual. He comments:

> The third type of conflict, spiritual conflict, differs from normal and abnormal conflict in that the instigators have an intentionally unhealthy agenda, they resort to sinful tactics without remorse, and have a persistent energy for their nefarious causes that wears good people down. [23]

Pastor Berry obviously encountered spiritual conflict to the level that eventually led to her premature appointment change from Church No. 2 in September 2012. She commented:

> I would have blamed it on being a woman. I've been in physical, spiritual, and emotional recovery from the experience at Church #2 for nearly two years . . . I don't believe that being a woman has everything to do with the success (or failure) of an appointment . . . I believe that when women receive appointments—whether or not the appointments are considered desirable or equal to those of men—God's favor rests on us when we go in Jesus' name. [24]

There are some sobering comments that come from Pastor Berry:

> It is my opinion that there are considerations that have nothing to do with gender that make appointments viable, not the least of which is the support of the conference in truthfully revealing, addressing, and alleviating those external factors, hindrances, and hurdles that would derail the best prepared spiritual leader. The main concern of the conference in supporting a pastor in a new appointment should not be gender but, rather, making sure that a pastor does not face overwhelming externals that overshadow the main thing—becoming Christ's Church . . . I don't see my three-year tenure as failure, but as seed-planting mission. [25]

Pastor Berry is not serving an appointment as of this writing.

Two women colleagues are representative of later millennials pastors who are professionals from second careers. Each has brought their skills and integrated them into their calling as clergy-women.

The Rev. Patricia Allen former Assistant Commissioner for the State of Maryland Division of Corrections is an elder who served for the past eight years in the Annapolis-Southern Region, specifically in the suburban community of Glen Burnie, Maryland. Rev. Allen was appointed to Hall UMC where she was the first woman to serve the 137-year-old African American family church. There were several men who voiced their disapproval of her appointment and went to such extremes as to refuse to sit at the same table during meetings. Moreover, there were independent caucuses called to meet with church leaders without the pastor's knowledge. Rev. Allen describes the initial years as "very challenging."

In addressing the matter of push-back, Rev. Allen contends that she encountered the same and to some degree outright obstructionism. Countervailing the obstructionism was evidence of overall affirmation of her ministry. The push-back and obstructionism continues, even now. In spite of the negatives, very few parishioners left the church or became inactive members. New members joined and some once-inactive members reaffirmed their membership." What was meant for evil, God intended it for good" (Genesis 50:20b).

The worship services at Hall UMC are well attended. The pastor reports a range from 123 to 126 per Sunday. This falls within the category of a pastoral-sized congregation. I had the opportunity to preach at Hall UMC a few years ago, and what I observed was the congregation was quite spirited in the traditional sense of the black Church. A significant challenge for Hall UMC was the rebuilding the fellowship hall that collapsed during a snowstorm in 2003. Such disappointments as lack of approval of a bank loan, denial of permits from the county, and the associated issues connected with building confronted the congregation. After twelve years, the congregation is now in the process of constructing the fellowship hall at a cost of nearly a million dollars.

Rev. Allen made some accomplishments in her ministry at Hall UMC. With her gift of administration, she was able to initiate electronic giving, installed a check-clearing machine so that checks are immediately deducted from the members' checking accounts. A financial policies and procedures document was initiated during her tenure. A church bus was obtained. These were just a few examples of her accomplishments.

Pertinent to outreach and social justice, the pastor organized a ministry to meet the needs of the marginalized in the community. Soulful Slumber is a ministry that provides pillows for the unsheltered. Volunteers from the church serve at the local Boys and Girls Club. Here again, these are just a sampling of the vital ministry that Hall UMC conducts under the leadership of Rev. Allen.

Rev. Allen's family is very supportive of her ministry, especially her husband. Mr. Allen is an active participant in the choir ministry and men's ministry and attends Christian Education classes sponsored by the church.

Rev. Allen described her leadership style: "I am a pastor/teacher with gifts in administration . . . my primary leadership style initially was to direct, because there was no order/structure . . ." is her comment. [63] With leadership development and Bible studies that affirmed the gifts and graces of individuals, the members grew to a point where they are transitioning from a pastor-centered style of leadership. Her leadership helped to empower the members of Hall UMC. The vitality of Pastor Allen's Christian Education ministry is seen through the three adult Bible Studies in addition to a men's Bible study group. Moreover, two disciple groups were started.

For all that Rev. Allen does, the church saw fit to compensate her above minimum salary stipulated by the annual conference. Interestingly enough, her predecessor saw a reduction in his salary, housing, travel, and reimbursement allocation.

Rev. Allen, effective 1 July 2015 began her new appointment as the senior pastor of Oxon Hill UMC, Prince Georges' County, Maryland. She is the first African American woman to serve as senior pastor of this historic congregation.

The Rev. Johnsie Cogman was ordained in the Baptist Church of the General State Convention of North Carolina. Her husband is a retired military veteran. She is the mother of twin boys currently enrolled in college. Rev. Cogman is an educator by profession. At the 231st Annual Conference of the Baltimore-Washington Conference, Rev. Cogman's ordination orders were accepted, and now she enjoys the privileges as an elder in full connection with the annual conference.

Rev. Cogman serves in a unique situation with her two churches that are part of a cooperative parish configuration situated in two districts: the Greater Washington and the Washington East districts. Bells UMC is a predominantly white church, located in a changing demographic in Camp Springs, Prince George's County, Maryland, while Mt. Zion UMC, a historic African American church, is situated in northwest Washington, DC, specifically Georgetown. She was the first African American female pastor at both churches. Bells UMC wanted a white male pastor while Mt. Zion UMC was more accepting of her. She cites, "On my first Sunday as the new pastor of Bells, a Caucasian woman and her sister accosted me in the pulpit and outside of my office. The police had to be called."[26] The pastor did not press charges. Both women stopped attending the church; however, the older sister two years later apologized for her unchrist-like behavior. At Mt. Zion, several members left to follow the former pastor, and several members of Bells left due to the early time change in the worship service. A few inactive members returned, and two new members joined Mt. Zion. At Bells, several new members joined the church.

The worship services are different. Worship service begins at 9 a.m. with a traditional flavor of worship. During the one-hour worship, the music ministry has a five-member choir among whom are three members from Mt. Zion. One hymn and two selections are sung subsequent to which the sermon is preached by Rev. Cogman. At the end of the service, the pastor drives to Mt. Zion in northwest Washington, DC. The worship service begins with praise and worship at 10:45 a.m.; at 11 a.m. the contemporary service begins. There is a twelve-member choir accompanied with a variety of instruments: piano, organ, drums, and tambourines. The service typically ends around 12 noon or slightly thereafter.

The average worship attendance at Bells is thirty-two while at Mt. Zion the average is seventy-three. She keeps the same steady pace each Sunday.

Rev. Cogman has a very supportive husband and sons. Both sons are active in the ministries of the church. Her son, Jacob Cogman, is a lay servant minister and speaks on a regular basis both while home from college and while away in college.

Pertinent to financial compensation, Rev. Cogman believes she is on par with her male colleagues in terms of salary. However, she feels that because of her gender, she did not receive an increase in salary.

The pastor describes her leadership style: "My leadership style is democratic. I work diligently with my laity as well as various members of the congregation to set and accomplish goals."[27] Accomplishments at the churches revolve around social justice ministries. SHARE Food program, the Shelter Challenged, and connecting with neighboring public schools were some of the outreach ministries of both churches. Further, the congregations have changed somewhat in that they are more focused on missions, making disciples for Jesus Christ, and being more inclusive. Admittedly, Rev. Cogman acknowledges they are not where they need to be but are traveling in the same direction.

The focus of my excursus has been on the issues of African American female clergypersons in the Baltimore-Washington Conference of the United Methodist Church, the Southern Region in particular. I deviate now to share my conversation with a woman colleague that is a member of the Ministers Alliance of Charles County and vicinity; the colleague is a retired elder in the African Methodist Episcopal Church who was the founding pastor of the Mount Sinai AME church, Waldorf, Maryland. In her professional career she was the Assistant Branch Chief, Department of Labor, Data Processing Bureau of Labor Statistics.

The Rev. Beatrice Edwards, the founder of the Mount Sinai AME church, established the congregation in June 1993 in La Plata, Maryland. She described her church as a traditional Methodist congregation of seventy-five persons, ranging in age from nineteen to sixty. Currently, there are families with small children. In the past, new members of a transient nature joined the congregation and later left without giving reasons. The pastor reported no significant push-back from her members about whom she was quite praiseworthy. During the earlier years the average worship attendance was twenty but has since doubled.

Rev. Edwards described her church as traditional Methodist congregation. In terms of the worship experience, there was exuberance in the service. The worshipers could be meditative when needed. For the most part, they experienced their worship in the black Church tradition.

The Mount Sinai AME Church in April 2002 experienced a devastating tornado that destroyed their worship center. With the loss of the building and two subsequent temporary locations to conduct services were factors that caused the congregation to scatter. To exacerbate the situation, she experienced breast cancer. Nevertheless, Rev. Edwards testifies that God brought her and the congregation through the challenges that confronted them. Presently, the congregation is in a permanent location in Waldorf, Maryland.

In reference to the matter of financial compensation Rev. Edwards did not appear to be overly concerned about her salary. She acknowledged that male clergy seem to be compensated more than female pastors. Her consolation was, in her words, "I believe they did the best as possible . . . most were tithers." [28]

The pastor's leadership style is that of being compassionate and nurturing. She has a maternal bearing about herself that can be assertive and firm when needed. Rev. Edwards served the congregation for nineteen years. She was a widow who had the strong support of her family members. They not only gave moral support but financial support as well. Since her retirement from active ministry, the family continues serve in the congregation. For nineteen years, she drove fifty-four miles round-trip to serve the people. In 2012, Rev. Edwards retired from active pastoring. Her closing reflection was: "Planting a church was very stressful; however, the work was divine and fulfilling." [29] The Rev. Melynda Clarkesucceeded Rev. Edwards and now serves as senior pastor of Mount Sinai AME Church.

Closing Thoughts about African American Women Clergy Colleagues

I sought in this excursus to give my observations of African American Clergy women in pastoral ministry in the Baltimore-Washington Conference of the United Methodist Church. Significantly, the late Rev. Dr. Emma P. Burrell was the forerunner and model of clergy women of color who would serve churches once only pastored by male clergy. The clergy women of color would be academically well-qualified with advanced degrees, served in professional careers, and some in nontraditional professional careers that were dominated by males. Each sensed the call of God to leave their secular professional careers and serve in pastoral ministry.

The mosaic presented by the African American clergy women is reflective of their male counterparts. They are single, married, separated, and divorced. Some are clergy couples who serve individual congregations while others have served as co-pastors in congregations. They serve congregations in the urban, suburban, and rural communities. While serving the various churches, some of the clergy women have had very strong support from their spouses and families. Contrary to this, there were spouses who were not supportive of their wives being in pastoral ministry; as a result, there were some break-ups of marriages. Some clergy women have served long pastorates in their local churches in various community settings.

Clergy women of color experience normal conflict as their male counterparts. However, there are cases in which certain congregations have initiated an abnormal degree of resistance to female pastors' appointment to their churches. In such circumstances the women pastors have suffered undue emotional harm and, unfortunately, premature cessation of the appointment. Churches of this ilk have the reputation of being "clergy killers." Sadly, there are still members who feel women should not serve as pastors, but the said sentiment is diminishing.

The corps of African American clergy women is contributing at every level of the annual conference and serving in integral areas of ministries such as district superintendents, chair of the Board of Ordained Ministry, District Committees of Ordained Ministry, and staff members of the Discipleship Academy and other ministry areas of the conference. Moreover, their performances in the various areas of ministry have been quite exemplary and will continue on into the future. Anthony Pinn writes regarding the future of women in ministry:

> The continuing large number of women in black churches combined with the massive increase in the number of seminary-trained women across the various denominations creates a tremendous paradox and surplus of talent . . . the more liberal opinions of the Episcopal and United Methodist churches may

entice some women to leave historically black denominations in order to advance their ministerial interests. [30]

Lincoln aptly summarizes the case for African American clergy women:

> In spite of the great difficulties and obstacles they have encountered in their attempts to become professional ministers, black women have forged ahead to answer their own spiritual calling to serve and to provide their own contributions to the church as a liberating force in American society. [31]

Tips for Newly Appointed Women Clergy

I offer tips for the African American clergy woman as she prepares to assume her first congregation or cooperative parish:

- Attitudinally, many churches are changing and becoming more accepting of female pastors. Some suburban and rural congregations that have not had a woman pastor will possibly be resistive at first. Seek the help from seasoned clergy women and conference help to navigate through the waters of resistance. "It takes time to turn an aircraft carrier" is my favorite saying when beginning ministry in a new setting.

- Do not hesitate to request the judicatory to provide advance training to the leadership of the new appointment in preparation of receiving a female clergy person.
- Be flexible in your leadership style and adapt to your situation.
- Do not make immediate changes in the leadership unless absolutely necessary.
- Work with congregation where they are spiritually with the intent to help deepen their spiritual formation.
- Be able to receive criticism, and do not be defensive.

Chapter 7

Leaving the Regional Guide Ministry

The year 2011 brought a shift in my life. For some time, I entertained the idea of retiring, but when my friend and colleague, the Rev. Dr. Otto Kent, suddenly passed and I saw the profound grief and pain of his wife Gwendolyn, I felt the urge to retire and get some "R and R" (rest and relaxation). I still did not want to completely give up ministry. What was I going to do? The Rev. Dr. Rodney T. Smothers and the Saint Paul United Methodist Church, Oxon Hill, Maryland would probably let me do some ministry, I thought. However, the Rev. Vicky Starnes, guide, shared during our regional team staff meeting the problem she was having with Smith Chapel-Alexandria Chapel UMC Charge. In a communication addressed on November 8, 2010, to the leadership of the congregations their options based upon 2545 of the Book of Discipline were to merge or discontinue one of the churches. While the pastor was sick, lay speakers were filling in during the worship services. There was some difficulty in securing an interim elder who could care for the sacramental responsibilities of the churches. Finally, the Rev. Evelyn Manson, retired elder who was familiar with the area, agreed to serve on a temporary basis.

More problems developed at the Smith Chapel-Alexandria Chapel Charge. In an exasperated manner, Rev Starnes reported that during a joint meeting of the churches on the last Sunday January 30, 2011, the majority of the members attending voted to negate merging after months of preparation had gone into preparing for the merger. It was an apparent communication issue as some of the participants at the said meeting did not realize or had not been in ongoing attendance of what was about to take place. Rev. Starnes was upset. After the meeting, Vicky said, "They need a real, seasoned pastor like you, George!" At that moment I chuckled and went to my office. I began to meditate and pray about the matter. I had thoughts of being on staff at Saint Paul UMC with a light obligation for ministerial duties. Then, I recalled during a prayer meeting, a lay woman spoke about a man standing on the shores beckoning to come over to Macedonia and help them. At that point I went to Rev. Starnes' office and chatted about the two churches. I finally agreed to take the assignment, but I would need an assistant.

The Annapolis Southern Region (ASR) Leadership Day at Good Shepherd UMC, Waldorf, Maryland on March 5, 2011, provided an opportunity for me to enlist an assistant that would be a part of the pastoral ministry team to the two churches in Western Charles County. I was in discussion with Dr. Mills about the two congregations and the assistance I would need. I was willing to work a year or more with the churches. At that point Dr. Mills alluded to Kermit C. C. Moore, Certified Lay Minister, who had great potential and at some point might be considered in the future for a church. I knew him and some of his family. It was a fortuitous moment as no sooner than she spoke his name, he walked through the narthex of Good Shepherd UMC.

I said, "Let me have him as my assistant." Dr. Mills replied, "Good, talk with him, but let him know that he has to be quiet about this until we meet with the churches." I approached and shared with Kermit the prospects of him joining with me as a team member that would serve Smith Chapel and Alexandria Chapel UMCs. He willingly agreed with an appearance of restrained excitement and promised to keep quiet until the appropriate time. I gave Kermit my contact information with the intent to speak about my vision for the pastoral team ministry with the said charge. I felt very comfortable with the certified lay minister, a musician, with anticipation of doing a great work together with the rural congregations. We met at Bob Evans in Waldorf, Maryland, on March 28 for purposes of getting to know one another more fully and to discuss the vision I had for the two congregations that currently formed the charge. It was my contention at that time that we should work to strengthen both churches and possibly empower them to become station churches. I could hear and see the excitement Bro. Moore had for this new upcoming ministry opportunity. We both looked forward to the meeting time with the members of the Staff Parish Relations Committee of both churches.

My planned retirement, which my wife Lila planned to perfection, would be celebrated on April 16, 2011, but would be shorted lived. On April 26, 2011, at 7:30 p.m., Dr. Mills conducted the "take-in," that is the official introduction of the pastors to the congregational leadership. Each of us introduced ourselves to the leadership and our experiences in ministry along with the gifts and graces that we brought to share with the congregations. Further we introduced our spouses, Lila DeFord and Paulette Moore, both who gave comments; Mrs. DeFord was surprised that I was taking on a new pastorate while being in retirement, she was not feeling it! Needless to say, I had a lot of explaining to do because of my neglect to consult with my wife. Later through much prayer, my wife eventually gave complete support to this new ministry while I was in the retirement phase of life.

The take-in meeting concluded with prayer followed by completing final details in preparation for the joint worship service on Sunday, May 1. My impression, as I observed the interactions of members from Alexandria Chapel, was they finally had gotten their own pastor. As keys were given to me and Pastor Moore, no keys from Alexandria were issued to mealthough I was the lead pastor and had overall responsibility for both churches. When I inquired about the keys to Alexandria, it was an afterthought by the lay leader from the church: "Oh, we will have your keys by next week."

It was an awkward moment. The keys to Alexandria were given to me after the joint worship service at Smith Chapel on the first Sunday in May.

The gathering of the Baltimore-Washington Annual Conference began on May 26, 2011, in Baltimore City. On the last day of annual conference the celebration of the appointments took place. I was listed under the Washington East District "Retired Elder, District Superintendent Hire" and Pastor Moore as Part Time Local Pastor for Smith Chapel-Alexandria Chapel Cooperative Parish (WE). Meanwhile the churches were moving ahead in preparation to begin ministry as a cooperative parish.

The designing of a covenant agreement had already begun prior to the annual conference that would take place in Baltimore, Maryland. The members of the Covenant Agreement Drafting Team brought together a covenant agreement that would guide both churches for a two-year period subsequent to which an evaluation of the churches progress would be made, and a mutually determined path forward would be identified. The members of the drafting team were: Carolyn M. Simmons, Jacqueline L. Baker, Rhonda L. Taylor, Joyce Gray, Perry Taylor, Nancy M Burroughs, Roland C. Chase, and Audrey Chase. The signatories agreeing to the covenant agreement were Rev. Dr. Ianther M. Mills, District Superintendent; Rev. Dr. George F. DeFord, Senior Pastor; Pastor Kermit C.C. Moore, Associate Pastor; Vera M. Littlejohn, Chair, Smith Chapel Church Council; Christine S. Washington, Chair, Alexandria Chapel Church

Council. The Covenant Agreement was signed on June 30, 2011 and put into effect July 1, 2011. The Covenant Agreement was based upon five objectives:

- Make disciples of Jesus Christ and bear fruit as found in Acts 2;
- Grow in relationship and commitment with one another as we come together with unity of purpose to serve in ministry for the good of all within our congregation and our community;
- Increase the vitality and health of both congregations through the shared gifts and graces of each individual as well as through shared ministries and shared leadership resources;
- Educate each person within our congregations regarding the benefits to be derived from this multisite ministry and demonstrate those benefits over the two-year period of the covenant; and
- Preserve the identity of each individual congregation even as we pursue common goals and objectives and share ministries and leadership resources.

The congregations followed the objectives of the covenant agreement.

My last week at the Baltimore-Washington, Conference Mission Center in Fulton, Maryland, was a time of clearing up all loose ends and mixed emotions. I was enthusiastically looking forward to doing ministry in the rural setting, but at the same time I was having second thoughts about this new phase of ministry. To add to the mix, I was having separation pains from leaving the persons with whom I had developed friendships and enjoyed being with in extension ministry. I did a lot of reminiscing during the final days while chatting and chuckling with the co-workers who reminded me I was not to forget bringing them chocolate candies whenever I should visit the Mission Center because I owed them to refill their candy jars because of the many occasions when I visited their offices, looking for candy in the middle of the day. Finally on June 29, I turned in my keys, said my goodbyes, and left with a feeling of relief complicated with an uncertainty of what lay ahead. One thing was certain: I did not have to drive the beltway again! The only matter remaining now was to meet with Dr. Mills DS, Pastor Moore, chairpersons of the respective church councils, and members of the Covenant Draft Committee to sign the Covenant Agreement on June 30; the matter was completed in that evening.

Sunday is coming for the official start of the new conference year 2011–2012 with the Smith Chapel-Alexandria Chapel Cooperative Parish.

Chapter 8

Smith Chapel-Alexandria Chapel Cooperative Parish

The Context

We officially began the new conference year on July 1, 2011, as the Smith Chapel-Alexandria Chapel Cooperative Parish. I served as the senior pastor while Pastor Kermit C.C. Moore, served as the associate pastor. On July 3, 2011, a joint unity service was conducted with good representation from both churches. There was a sense of great hope as the new configuration of ministry as a cooperative parish was officially beginning to be lived out. It was during the unity service that Jocelyn Moore, Pastor Moore's sister, transferred her membership from Asbury UMC, Brandywine, Maryland, to Alexandria Chapel UMC, Indian Head, Maryland, and she would be the first new member to join this congregation. Ms. Moore's joining signaled a renewed vitality and "a new day" in Alexandria Chapel, which is the older of the two congregations.

Alexandria Chapel and Smith Chapel have interesting histories that are representative of small African American rural churches. C. Eric Lincoln points out from his review of the literature that the majority of black rural churches were organized in the late nineteenth and early twentieth centuries. The majority of those churches studied in the South were organized by blacks while a lesser number were established by whites. Still a lesser number of the churches were organized on plantations. He continues to comment that a significant number of the churches were "wooden frame buildings." [1] Both Alexandria Chapel and Smith Chapel fall into the profile Lincoln alludes to in his scholarly research. Both congregations are located in rural communities with postal zones associated with the larger area: Alexandria was assigned to Indian Head but was actually situated in Rison, and Smith Chapel was assigned to La Plata but was located in Pisgah.

I have referred to Alexandria Chapel and Smith Chapel as rural churches. Precisely what is a rural church and do the two congregations fall within the parameters of the definition? Several authors offer definitions that help us have greater clarity regarding the two congregations focused upon in this writing. Kent R. Hunter in his informative work on the rural church cites that the United States Census Bureau designates rural as a nonmetropolitan area where less than a given number of people reside. [2] Hunter argues, "A rural church is a congregation of Christian people who live an agriculturally oriented life-style. It is made up of a people group who belong to the agriculture community." [3] As amplification to his position on the definition of the rural church, Hunter offers, " . . . Rural is a mind-set . . . a way of life . . . not poor or rich . . . not necessarily educated or uneducated . . ." [4] A strong characteristic of the rural church is it is a close-nit family unit. It is not uncommon to hear, " . . . everyone here is related . . ." [5] There is a mutual care and support while each family has its tribal chief and its patriarchs and/or matriarchs. Rural is informative of the mindset of the people and not only their worldview but their perception of the church.

The average worship attendance (AWA) is an indicator of a church being classified as small, mid-size, or large. "Protestant churches averaging fewer than forty-five members a Sunday should be classified as small "says Lyle E. Schaller. [6] Still there is another description of the small church.

The consultant-trainer in the field of parish development, Alice Mann, views congregations with an AWA up to fifty as a family-sized church. She describes the said type church as a single-cell organism—a social system resembling an extended biological family. Each member knows the other. New additions to the family are by means of birth or marriage. Further, others are incorporated into the family by means of adoption—after careful scrutiny. Mann further points out that the clergy who serve these congregations typically are less than full-time and/or are short-term in their tenure. Moreover, the clergy function primarily as chaplains while leadership is actually carried out by the matriarchs and patriarchs.

The said leaders are the glue that holds the congregation together, and they are the opinion makers within the tribal community. [7]

Carl S. Dudley sums it up regarding the rural small church:

> It is an image of serenity in the American culture: in summer, the crossroads church under the spreading shade tree; and in winter, at the heart of the Christmas season, surrounded by driven snow . . . issuing a warm 'Season's Greeting!' Small churches are intentional fellowships that will resist moving, merging, yoking, or teaming . . . Small churches are the toughest: they won't grow and they won't go away .[8]

In light of the foregoing, Alexandria Chapel and Smith Chapel fit within the parameters that qualify them as rural small churches but with an exception. Although both churches are in areas that are designated as agriculture, the majority of the members of the community are employed at the nearby US Naval facilities, Indian Head, Maryland, and Andrews Joint Base, Camp Springs, Maryland. Other residents are employed by local, state and federal government agencies and the private sector in metropolitan Washington, DC, and nearby Northern Virginia areas. Whatever farming that is done is mainly for personal interest or in pursuit of maintaining the community's agriculture zoning. Anecdotal to the above, a number of the members of both congregations are property owners with a member who owns approximately 140 acres of farming land.

Therefore, it is without a doubt that both Alexandria Chapel and Smith Chapel UMCs are rural small churches in every sense of the word.

History of Alexandria Chapel

Alexandria Chapel was formally known as Jordan Chapel that was established by ex-slaves, William and Eliza Jordan. William and Eliza were slaves on the plantation of William B. Mathews. History discloses that after emancipation from slavery in 1865, William Tubman changed his last name to Jordan because he liked the name and thought of going to heaven to hear "Jordan Roll." [9] The ex-slave couple purchased thirty acres of land on August 28, 1868 from George and Virginia Wheeler (white) of Chicamuxen, Maryland for one hundred sixty dollars. They built a log house in which most of the ex-slaves would gather periodically to have prayer services. For a period of sixteen years (1868–1884), other Christians hosted the prayer services in their homes until, due to the large gathering of worshipers, a decision was made to buy more land for a church building. Frederick Dorsey, James Tyler, and Bailey Lemon were selected to meet and negotiate a purchase for one acre of land from George Wheeler at the price of ten dollars.

The Jordan's donated logs from their property to build the church in addition to contributing money to pay the salaries of the carpenters. Eliza prepared food daily to feed the workers. Once the church was built, it was decided to name the church Jordan Chapel in honor of William because of his Christian spirit, inspiration, generosity, dedication, and his work to the cause of kingdom building.[10] The church's deed was recorded in the courthouse in Port Tobacco, Maryland, on May 19, 1884. Port Tobacco was the county seat of Charles County at that time. The deed was recorded under the name of Colored Methodist Episcopal Church of Chicamuxen of the Washington Annual Conference. It was recorded as such due to there being an already established white Methodist Church in Chicamuxen. Local people called the church Jordan Chapel, but it was never recorded as such. [11] The Jordan's loved their land so much that they wanted to be buried on the same. It is reported that William Jordan at the age of eighty-nine died in September, 1890. His wife Eliza died in January, 1900. Both are buried on the family plot.

Jordan Chapel, similar to many other African American churches of the era, served as a public school. The church was utilized as a school room for black children from Monday to Friday. The obligation to sweep and clean the church was a weekly requirement in preparation for Sunday worship service. Soon, the peopled became tired of the shifting from school to church; as a result, because the old church frame building was difficult to heat and keep the mud out of the crevices of the log floor, a decision was to build a new frame church.

The first trustees of Jordan Chapel were Frederick Dorsey, James Tyler, and Bailey Lemon. Church records reflect that trustee Lemon died on October 7, 1928, and was buried in Jordan Chapel cemetery. He was the last of the original trustees. The Rev. Daniel Wheeler was the first pastor to serve the Chicamuxen Charge under the Colored Methodist Episcopal Church Conference. He was appointed to four churches: Pomonkey (Metropolitan), Emory Chapel, Smith Chapel, and Alexander Chapel. His successors were: Rev. C. Cecil, Rev. H. Reed, Rev. J. A. Warmes, Rev. S. M. Qualley, Rev. C. Price, and Rev. R. H. Alexander.

Two churches of the Chicamuxen Charge would separate from the Charge and become station churches, that is to say, each church would have its own pastor. Smith Chapel and Pomonkey (Metropolitan) were the congregations that left, leaving Alexander and Emory churches on the Charge.

The Rev. R. H. Alexander would usher in a new period. A new church building was built on the same ground where the old log church stood. Rev. Alexander was noted for his hard work in getting the new church built. Because of his great work, the congregation honored him by naming the new church Alexander Chapel. The church was constructed in 1891, the last year of his pastorate; he served for five years (1886–1891). In addition a school was built on the adjoining property for the black children of Chicamuxen.

A succession of itinerating pastors followed Rev. Alexander from 1891 to 1941 during which time made significant contributions and events took place in the life of the church. Rev. Smith and Rev. Davis served the congregation. Anecdotal to Rev. Davis is that his first wife passed away and was buried at Pomonkey Church. He later married Nettie Lemon, sister of Mrs. Mary Jane Butler of Chicamuxen. Subsequent pastors were Rev. Coin, Rev. Barnett, and Rev. Cole. Rev. Brown served the congregation from 1914–1916. Rev. Walter Dorsey was appointed to the charge in 1917, and following him were Rev. Stevenson and Rev. Rudolph Wheeler. During Rev. Wheeler's administration, a three-room bungalow was purchased for the parsonage. The record reflects that Rev. R. H. Riley who served the charge for a six year period (1928–1934), was the first pastor to occupy the new parsonage. The living quarters were located on two acres of land and contained one bedroom, kitchen, and dining room. It is to be noted that the parsonage was without electricity or running water.

Succeeding Rev. Riley, Rev. Robert E. Burnett served a two year period (1935–1937). This pastor had a large family, which created a problem because of the small parsonage. After much discussion, the church decided to remodel the parsonage by raising the roof and adding three bedrooms. Members volunteered to finish the renovation of the parsonage in addition to donating furniture and household items. Significantly, electric lights and a gas stove were added after 1936. (The record reflects: rural electric lights were not available in Charles County until 1936 and were only erected along the main highways.) Rev. Burnett was followed by Rev. William E.

Brooks (1937–1939) whose successor Rev. R. A. Fray, died a month after his appointment to the charge. This would lead to the appointment of Rev. Thomas H. Reed who would serve the charge for six years (1939–1945). Significant change would take place during the pastorate of Rev. Reed. The members launched into a program of moving Alexander Chapel onto the main highway.

The road leading from the highway to the church was almost impassable at times, especially during the winter months. Land was available but the church was financially unable to make the purchase. Rev. Reed and his wife, Agnes, purchased the land—eight and one-fourth acres. The land was obtained from Clinton Wheeler's widow. [12]

The trustees of the church carried out their fiduciary responsibilities. The property was deeded to the Trustees of Alexander Chapel: Rev. Richard Davis, Joseph Smallwood, Sylvester Gray, and Otten Swann on October 24, 1941, according to the land records of Charles County (Liber W.M.A. 71 Folio 401). [13] Anecdotal to Rev. Davis is that he was a lay minister and assistant to the pastor, who was described as a lay leader, church school superintendent and an assistant pastor. He was a "great Christian leader and helper to all the ministers that he served.

The groundbreaking ceremony was conducted for the new church with the oldest descendant of William Jordan, Sr., Mrs.

Delscina Jordan, lifting the first shovel of full dirt. The lumber from the old church was dismantled and taken to the new site. The congregation built a new hall that would serve as a worship center until such time the new edifice was completed.

There would be four ministers to succeed Rev. Reed in the persons of Rev. William H. Tyler (1946) and Rev. Richardson (1947). Unfortunately for the church, Rev. Richardson would be another pastor to die prior to completing his conference year. Rev. Charles Page (1948) and Rev. Alfred Munnerlyn (1949) each served one year. There were several pastors that would serve extended periods of time. Rev. Norman Goolsby served the charge for seven years (1950–1957). The church was completed and the mortgage paid off in three months. The corner stone was laid in 1951. The historical record exhibits: "It was during this period that the Chicamuxen Charge set a remarkable record for paying conference claims in full for seven years. Pulpit furniture was purchased as well as a piano. A youth program was organized and Rev. Goolsby planned weekly activities for them". [14]

Rev. J. O. Grayson (1957—1961) succeeded Rev. Goolsby. Significant for his ministry was that the debt on the hall was liquidated, interior of the church refinished, and the floors carpeted. Rev. Albert Luckett followed Rev. Gray and served for two years.

Rev. Thomas H. Reed returned for a second pastorate and served from 1964 to 1971. Bathrooms were installed in the church in addition to a new chancel railing. It is further noted that his wife,

Mrs. Agnes Reed, continued to be a great supporter of the church. The appointment of Rev. Harvey Custis would usher in a new era and a phenomenal period of ministry for twenty-four years during which time Alexandria Chapel, Emory Chapel, and Smith Chapel would reunite to form the Pisgah Charge. I turn to recapitulate Smith Chapel's history.

History of Smith Chapel

The following is an abstract as presented in *The Smith Chapel Church History.* Some of the critical documents are no longer extant; therefore a disclaimer is offered:

> "The actual date and year of the inception of the Church is unknown. Although we do not have documentation to support this, we believe the first Church on this site began in the late 1890's or early 1900's with a vision by Mr. Robinson and Mr. Swann. In the year 1902 under the Pastorship of the Reverend Smith that vision became a reality culminating in the building of the church, and the church being assigned to the Pisgah Circuit, under the Colored Methodist Episcopal Church Conference.
>
> "Although the dates are not known some early members of the Trustee were: Thomas Barbour, James Julias Hawkins, Thomas Bowman, George Greer and Samuel Marbury. Other officials of the Church during that reign were the Stewards:

James Queen, Thomas Barbour, Walter Hawkins, George Hackerson, Thomas, Mary Dyson, and Carrie S. Hackerson.

"We also had:

- President of Ladies Aid Mary Dyson
- President of E. L Gertrude Miller
- President of Foreign Mission Maidie Queen
- President of Home M. S Carrie S. Hackerson

It is the year 1922 we find:

- Carrie Hackerson President of Women's H.M.S.
- Consul Thompson President of Education
- Maidie Queen President of Foreign Mission
- James Queen District Steward
- Maidie Queen Communion Steward
- Annie Henson President of Epworth League

The Conference appointed the following pastors:

- 1902–1907 Rev. Smith & Rev. John
- 1907–1909 Rev. James S. Cole
- 1909–1911 Rev. George W. Cohen (Rev. Coin at Alexander?)
- 1911–1914 Rev. L. E. Nash

- 1914–1916 Rev. A. D. Brown
- 1916–1920 Rev. Walter Dorsey
- 1920–1921 Rev. David Pleasant
- 1921–1923 Rev. Fred Myers
- 1923–1925 Rev. C. D. Hughes
- 1925–1926 Rev. E. D. Venture
- 1926–1930 Rev. Fred Myers
- 1930–1937 Rev. George L. Nelson

"Previous Superintendents of Sunday school were Brother Thomas, Sister Alice Brown, Brother Robert Brown, and Sister Veronica Milstead. Sister Brenda Chase is currently serving as the Church Superintendent of Sunday School. Previous Sunday schools teachers were Mildred Williams, Jeryle Dorsey, and Brother Perry Taylor. Sunday school teachers currently serving are Sister Sandra Bowman, Kia Hicks and Bridgette Taylor. Smith Chapel was also a member of the Sunday School Union.

"In 1932 the parsonage was torn down, and in July 1932 a new parsonage was built under the leadership of the Reverend George Nelson at a cost of $800.00 The chairman of the building committee was Brother James Brown who have a donation of $75.00, other recorded donation were Brother Henry Barbour $5.00, J. E. Hackerson unknown amount and Ophita $10.00.

"Mrs. Carrie Hackerson organized the choir and was the choir president. The organist was Mr. Thomas Hackerson, succeeding presidents were Sisters Alice Henson, Eleanor Washington, and Ida Williams Woods. The current President is Sister Clara Washington. Previous organists/pianists were Goshen Butler, Ollie Lancaster, Hazel Lucks, Bertha Key, and Anita L. The current pianist is Sister Inez Schoolfield.

"Rev. Joseph Marbury, Sisters Edna Simmons and Amelia Brown donated the first communion set.

- 1937–1938 Rev. William Manor
- 1938–1942 Rev. Charles Coleman
- 1942–1948 Rev. B. F. Hall

"Under the leadership of Rev. Hall two new rooms were added to the Parsonage.

- 1948–1950 Rev. Joseph Cater

"Under the leadership of Rev. Joseph Cater the Parsonage was refurnished.

- 1950–1951 Rev. Charles Randall
- 1951–1953 Rev. William H. Tylers

"Due to illness of Rev. Tylers, Rev. Joseph Marbury completed his appointment. Under Rev. Marbury's leadership Brother Daniel Williams Sr. installed a new Choir Loft.

- 1954–1955 Rev. Henry J. Lewis

"Under the appointment of Rev. Lewis, Sister Doris Barbour Monk, organized a Youth Choir, and also was the Choir Director. The pianists were Goshen Butler and Ollie Lancaster. Succeeding Sister Doris as Choir Director were Elnora Milstead, Judy Estep, Deborah Chase-Wells and Kia Hicks. The current Choir Director is Lisa Marshall. Previous pianists were Brother Albert Ford, and Sister Judy Estep. Currently the pianist is Patricia Wallace.

"In April 1955 Rev. Lewis died during his appointment on the Charge.

- 1955–1956 Rev. Robert Simmons
- 1956–1961 Rev. Charles Page
- 1961–1964 Rev. Donald Ford
- 1964–1966 Rev. Albert Luckett

"Under the leadership of Rev. Albert Luckett in 1965, Sister Clara Washington organized the Usher Board. Sister Washington was voted president and remains president today. Before the Usher

Board was organized Sister Lucille Bowman was the only usher for many years until her illness.

- 1966–1971 Rev. William Simms

"In 1966 it was discovered that the property of the Church was never deeded. Rev. Simms along with Trustees Theresa Swann and Vincent Washington traveled to and from the deed office in La Plata, Maryland, for many months until all the paperwork was finalized and the property was deeded in the name of Smith Chapel United Methodist Church. A new parsonage was built and bathrooms were installed in the Church December of 1970.

- 1971–1995 Rev. Harvey Custis

"Under the leadership of Rev. Custis the following was accomplished:

- 1971–The Parsonage was finished and furnished.
- 1972–Mr. Thomas Bowman, Mr. Levi Bowman, and the Men of the Church built a Fellowship Hall. A duplicating machine was purchased.
- 1973–The H.A.R.M.O.N. Social Club was organized for the youth of the Church and the Community.

- 1974–New Pews were purchased and installed in the Church, some of the Pews were donated by family members and friends of the Church members.
- 1976–The Chancel Choir was organized by Rev. Custis.
- 1978–New Air Conditioner units were installed in the Windows of the Church and Fellowship hall.
- 1983–Wall cabinets were installed in the kitchen, and a P.A. system was installed in the Church with speakers connecting the hall.
- 1986–A school bus was donated to the Charge by Mr. Hart to be used for the Charge. The Men of the Church participated in helping with the repairs.
- 1989–Mr. Robert Linkins built a lectern and donated it to the Church.
- 1989–Brother Earl Barbour, a member of the Trustees, was instrumental in installing an artesian well, he and members of the Church worked diligently until it was completed." [15]

A subsequent undated Smith Chapel History document reveals the following:

"Although we do not have dates to support these accomplishments, under the direction of Rev. Harvey Custis; the church had a very active Sunday school, youth Bible classes and vacation Bible study. The church received a new communion set, new Bibles, new carpet was installed, and folding tables were donated by the Methodist Men.

"Previous members who served on the Trustee Ministry were Sisters Barbara Washington and Theresa Swann, Brothers Luther Stuckey, Lloyd, Earl and Willie Barbour, Sylvester Smith, Robert Parker, Richard Lewis, Jerome Williams, Lawrence Dyson, Roderick Milstead, Jr., Charles Bowman and Almalita Robertson. The current members of the trustee ministry are Chairperson Perry Taylor . . . Vice Chairperson Rachel Johnson, Secretary Leslie Taylor, Iretha Irwin, Nancy Burroughs, Roderick Milstead, Sr., Roland Chase, and Asia Robertson.

- 1995–2003 Rev. Dr. Shirlimarie McAroy-Gray

"In 1995 Rev. Dr. Shirlimarie McAroy-Gray a native of Cleveland, Ohio, was assigned by the conference to the Smith Chapel United Methodist Church. During her tenure, she has encouraged the officers of the church to attend the leadership training offered by the District. She also instituted in-house Leadership Training for the officers and members of the congregation. She instituted the Cemetery Policy.

"She instituted the Cemetery Policy.

"(She) revamped the Sunday School which resulted in increased attendance, the youth having opportunity to attend

Manidokan and West River, yearly field trips, and twenty-five children taking a trip to Orlando, Florida for a week. [16]

Changes were effected in both the worship service and physical changes in the building:

"Activated the transformation of the Worship service to amplify the spiritual participation for the Congregation.

"The Sanctuary was renovated, and the bathrooms were upgraded.

"There was a Cooling System added to the Central Air unit.

"Rev. McAroy-Gray was instrumental in Smith Chapel's Men taking an active role in affairs of the Church, and the Men being a role model for the youth.

"The year of 2002 the members of Smith Chapel United Methodist Church under the Pastorship of the Reverend McAroy-Gray have a shared vision, a vision deeply rooted in both the physical and spiritual growth within the Church, with God's blessing and guidance, that vision will become a reality.

"Under the leadership of the Building Committee Chairperson Brother Lawrence Dyson and the expertise and workmanship of Brother Zachary Bowman, the fellowship hall was renovated. Brother Zachary is the Grandson of Thomas Bowman, and the Nephew of Levi Bowman, the two men who were instrumental in the planning and building of the original fellowship hall.

"The Smith Chapel Men of 2002 were also instrumental in the renovation of the fellowship hall. They gave blood, sweat, and honor for the Church and at the end of the day the accomplishment was worth the effort. Also the Trustee Women have taken the lead role in donating, and the solicitation of donation for the equipment, fixtures, and the furniture for the newly renovated hall . . ." [17]

- 2003–2010 Rev. Lucius Ross, Jr.

Rev. Ross' pastorate was noted for the initiatives that he inaugurated that continue as part of the current ministry:

"Pastor Lucius Ross, Jr. was [appointed] by the Conference to Smith Chapel United Methodist Church. Pastor Ross' inaugural sermon at Smith Chapel Church captivated the members of the congregation with the preached word.

"He instituted the grogram Becoming Disciples through Bible Study about ways your life and the life of the congregation reflect the marks of discipleship.

"He encouraged the congregation to increase tithes and offering, as opposed to fundraising.

"Under Pastor Ross' leadership the following were accomplished:

- Upgrade of the security system at the church
- Installation of a security system at what is now the Smith Chapel Annex
- Started a visionary movement with the Vanguard work committee
- An amiable supporter of the Lifestyles Program
- Developed a vision statement each year he served
- Members developed a partnership with Lifestyles to feed the homeless during Safe Nights Project
- All Saints' Sunday—stared (sic) a memorial service to honor the Saints
- Mrs. Washington died on January 29, 2016, thirteen days short of her 99th birthday.
- Started the monthly birthday celebration
- Instituted the church Picnic Ministry
- The Chosen Few Choir (an acapella choir)
- Spirit in Motion Dance Ministry
- Used the Certified Lay Speakers and lay members to bring the Preached Word
- The feasibility of merging (blending) process between Smith Chapel and Alexandria Chapel Churches.

"The current members of the Trustee ministry are Chairperson Perry Taylor . . . other members are Vice-Chairperson Rachel Johnson, Secretary Leslie Taylor, Iretha Irwin, Nancy Burroughs, Roderick Milstead, Sr., Roland Chase and Asia Robertson."[18]

- January 2011–April 2011 Rev. Evelyn Manson

"Due to the illness of Pastor Ross, Pastor Evelyn Manson in 2011 served as interim until the end of April 2011. She introduced anointing with oil as part of the worship service. Fellowship hall windows were installed while serving as interim pastor." [19]

Profile of the Pastors

Harvey Raymond Custis, Sr.

(1929–1999)

The late Reverend Harvey Raymond Custis, Sr., was the much beloved pastor of the Pisgah Charge (Smith Chapel and Alexandria Chapel) where he was the only pastor in the history of either church to serve an impressive twenty-four years of pastoral ministry. He benefitted from academic experiences at Baltimore Junior College and Morgan State University in addition to pastoral training at Bennett College and Duke University. ([20] He was married to LeVurn (nee Corporal) Custis, and they are the parents of Harvey, Jr., Steve, and Yolanda. They resided in the parsonage. Rev. Custis responded to his call to pastoral ministry while a member of West Liberty United Methodist Church. He served the Liberty Town Charge and Poolesville Charge 1960 and 1964 respectively prior to his appointment to Pisgah Charge in 1971. The Pisgah Charge was comprised of Alexandria Chapel, Emory Chapel, and Smith Chapel United Methodist Churches. Eventually Emory Chapel UMC would be disestablished, and the members of the said congregation transferred into either Alexandria Chapel or Smith Chapel. Some of his accomplishments in ministry at the Pisgah Charge have been enumerated in the abstracts from the history of Smith Chapel Church.

Rev. Custis is fondly remembered by members and nonmembers as a man of God who was visibly present in the community.

> Rev. Custis would visit and pray for patients in the hospital . . . He would go from room to room and pray for them. Their denominations did not matter" was comment by the late James Chesley, Sr., a Roman Catholic. His statement is further corroborated by Lay Leader Littlejohn: " . . . visited the hospitals weekly and prayed with the patients whether they were members of Smith Chapel or not. ([21]

He had the reputation of being the unofficial greeter at a local community store where he would give a dollar to patrons with whom he would speak. Rev. Custis was the embodiment of the world being his parish. Being connectional and ecumenical are adjectival adverbs that best describe Rev. Custis in terms of ministry beyond the walls of the church. A connectional relationship with West Liberty UMC originated with Rev. Custis, and members from the charge would journey by bus to Carrol County, Maryland to celebrate Custis Family Day. He frequently spoke at revival services and participated in pulpit exchanges; he initiated a pulpit exchange with Pisgah United Methodist Church, a white congregation. (I was reminded by a member at Pisgah UMC when we had a joint service due to Smith Chapel UMC being unavailable because of rest room facilities being repaired that Rev. Custis many years ago had pulpit exchanges with them.) Both congregations are now routinely have joint services on Thanksgiving Eve and Christmas Eve Candlelight service. This is a legacy left to us by Rev. Harvey Custis.

Another description that is quite apropos to Pastor Custis is he was a people person. He readily visited the homes of members who were slack in their attendance at worship services and those on the periphery of membership but claimed Smith Chapel as their church because of family ties although not active in their commitment or support. It was not uncommon for him to visit and minister to the residents of nursing homes in the community and beyond. To say the least, Rev. Custis was a people person who enjoyed his role as a visiting community pastor.

Rev. Custis was active with community groups and the Ministers Alliance of Charles County and vicinity. He was a member of the NAACP, Hospice of Charles County, Housing Coalition, and AARP. He also served as a chaplain at Civista Hospital, La Plata, Maryland. He represented the United Methodist Church in the Ministers Alliance, predominated by clergy of the Baptist church. In fact, mention Rev. Harvey Custis and an immediate association is made with Smith Chapel and Alexandria Chapel UMCs.

An adult member described Rev. Custis as a compassionate pastor. She reminisced about her teenage years when Rev. Custis would pick up children and transport them in the back of his pickup truck to Smith Chapel. More significantly, when she became pregnant, he did not put her out of the church as was the practice in "those days" but extended grace unto her by allowing her to attend worship services. He affirmed her personhood as a child of God. She and the father of her child eventually married and continue to be married; in fact they are grandparents who are very active in the ministries of the church. She has only praise for the late pastor.

I met Rev. Custis during the early to mid-1980s when I served St. Marks UMC, Laurel, Maryland. At that time I was a member of the Black Methodist Clergy group of Metropolitan Washington, DC. Rev. Custis served as a coordinator for reminding clergy members of scheduled monthly meetings and the location. He faithfully called each member the day or evening before the meeting to remind us of our obligation to attend. His scripted message was: "Rev. De Ford, this is Rev. Custis calling to remind you of our Black Methodist Clergy meeting on tomorrow. The meeting will be held at (time and place). We look forward to seeing you there . . ." The said routine telephone advisory came monthly until my appointment to Mt. Zion UMC, Baltimore City in 1993. During the time of my association with the Black Clergy group, I was impressed by Rev. Custis faithfully transporting to each meeting the late Rev. Donald Adams, a blind colleague who served the Newburg Charge. In fact I cannot recall an occasion that Rev. Adams was not with Rev. Custis, even at annual conference. The last occasion I saw Harvey Custis was at the 215th Annual Conference at the Renaissance Hotel, Washington, DC. I was cognizant that he had been ill, but why did he push himself to be present at conference? It was quite apparent that his health was failing although he was still actively pastoring at Bethesda UMC, Valley Lee, Maryland. Sadly, I learned that Rev. Harvey R. Custis, Sr. transitioned on August14, 1999.

The legacy Rev. Harvey R. Custis, Sr. leaves for many clergy to emulate is compassion, commitment, faithfulness, generosity, gracefulness, kindness, and his genuine love for people and for Jesus Christ. He touched the lives of many people in the Southern Maryland region of the Baltimore-Washington Conference.

Shirlimarie Mahalia McAroy-Gray

(1948–2011)

The late Reverend Dr. Shirlimarie M. McAroy-Gray was a part of the "Surge" in the 1990s. She was the first woman pastor of the Pisgah Charge. A native of Cleveland, Ohio, she was well qualified academically with degrees from the University of the District of Columbia and George Washington University, with a Bachelor of Arts in Psychology and Juris Doctor Degree, respectively. She matriculated at Howard University School of Divinity and United Theological Seminary, receiving Master of Divinity and Doctor of Ministry, respectively.

In terms of her conference relations, Rev. Dr. McAroy-Gray was ordained deacon in 1994 and as elder in 2003. In 2009, she expressed an interest and joined with the staff of instructors while I served as Director of the Discipleship Academy where the initial cadre of Certified Lay Ministers (CLMs) would be trained. Rev. Dr. McAroy-Gray was noted for her no-nonsense, thorough approach to teaching the subject matter and giving additional assignments that were meaningful to the students and their ministries in the local church. Moreover, she emphasized that the role of CLMs were to assist the pastors, not attempt to be the pastor. She served a subsequent term in 2010, but her health began to militate against her continued teaching ministry with the Discipleship Academy. Pastor Kermit C. C. Moore was trained under her as a CLM, and he eventually became my associate with the Smith Chapel and Alexandria Chapel Cooperative Parish.

The Rev. Dr. McAroy-Gray was the first woman pastor in the history of the Pisgah Charge. With her appointment in 1995, there was push-back; some of the women members of the charge were at the forefront in opposition to her appointment to the charge. It is reported that some of the women from the charge went to the conference office to protest Rev. Dr. McAroy-Gray's appointment. Eventually the disturbance quelled as the new pastor began her ministry with the Charge. She would bring innovative ministry along with emphasis upon women's issues, especially domestic violence. Her accomplishments during her pastorate with the Pisgah Charge have already been listed in the historical abstract.

Rev. Dr. McAroy-Gray ushered in a unique dynamic in her role as the first woman pastor of the Pisgah Charge. She served as a less than full-time pastor and continued her professional career as a senior litigator in the District of Columbia Superior Court Public Defender's Office. ([18] In addition the pastor, who was single, adopted two young sisters; many in the congregation questioned the wisdom of this but nevertheless gave assistance to her by caring for the children and babysitting. During outside speaking engagements and/or during regular services, it was not uncommon to see certain members caring for the children in the audience. When the pastor moved from one residence to another, the members of the Board of Trustees assisted her by providing their trucks and manpower. Trustees also stood ready to provide home repairs and snow removal service at her home in Prince George's County, Maryland. Being the first female pastor, single mother of two young girls, and a professional bi-vocational woman became less of a concern as she gave effective pastoral and teaching ministry to both congregations.

I initially met Rev. Dr. McAroy-Gray in the winter of 1994 while I was a member of the Board of Ordained Ministry at the Deacons' examination retreat in New Windsor, Maryland. The chatter among members of "the Board" was one of the candidates was an attorney; my immediate impression of Shirlimarie was that she was cautious, observant, attentive to every word spoken before answering a question and not reluctant to engage in discussion; perhaps that was her legal training. Succinctly, she passed the Deacons' retreat and was received on probation and ordained deacon at the 1994 Annual Conference.

My next contact with her would not be until July, 2000, when I was appointed to Metropolitan UMC. One of our first connectional activities would be the Summer Breeze Bible Study, a joint Bible study on the first epistle of John. Together, we team taught the one-week Bible study; it was quite evident that she had a gift for teaching. From that venture we arranged for Watch Night services for the next three years in addition to revivals and Good Friday services. In June 2003, I attended her farewell celebration at Middleton Hall, Waldorf, Maryland, as she prepared to go to her next appointment, Wards Memorial UMC in Owings, Maryland.

In 2008, I became Rev. Dr. McAroy-Gray's regional guide until her untimely death in 2011. She had a greater distance to travel from her home in Fort Washington, Maryland to Wards' Memorial in Owings, Maryland. The stress of pastoring a church, rearing a family, and maintaining her career as a public defender, in my opinion, were contributory factors in the decline of her health. Moreover, push-back from the church eventually led to her appointment to another congregation much closer to her home. She would be the first African American female pastor of Lanham UMC, Lanham, Maryland. The said congregation was multicultural and had just come out of a conflictive situation with a previous pastor. She was a breath of fresh air to the congregation that warmly received her and her daughters. However, her health declined resulting in an extensive hospitalization. I arranged for lay speakers to fill the pulpit until such time Rev. Dr. Alfonso J. Harrod was hired as interim pastor. Rev. Dr. McAroy-Gray expressed deep appreciation for and confidence in Rev. Harrod's assuming the pastorate in her absence. My last recollection of her was at her home where she expressed concern for her adopted daughters and their well-being. I prayed with her and with our last good-bye her hand was pointing heavenward. Shirlimarie transitioned on August 18, 2011 at the Washington Hospital Center, Washington, DC.

A postscript is that the oldest daughter is currently enrolled in college and the youngest is in her senior year of high school. Both are left in the care of a guardian designated by their late mother.

Lucius Ross, Jr.

(1948—present)

Pastor Lucius Ross, Jr. is a retired local pastor who served two congregations during his ministerial career: Chesapeake Beach: Wards Memorial, 1996–2003 and Pisgah Charge: Smith Chapel and Alexandria Chapel UMCs, 2003–2011. He retired on November 13, 2011 and a part of the Class of 2012 Retirees. He maintains his charge conference affiliation with Simpson-Hamlin UMC, Washington, DC. His accomplishments are enumerated in the abstract of Smith Chapel's history.

I met Pastor Ross by way of the District Committee on Ordained Ministry during the fall of 2000. During that time, he was appointed to Wards' Memorial, Owings, Maryland. He is a tall gentleman who is candid and direct, a no-nonsense and stoic individual. (He gives the distinct impression of being a NFL player.) While some members of the DCOM were anxious about his presence, I soon learned that Pastor Ross was a very cordial and respectful minister. I was assigned to be his mentor and would periodically make telephone contact with him. A year later when he appeared before the DCOM, his candidness remained but expressed appreciation for having me as his mentor.

Pastor Ross was appointed to the Pisgah Charge and began his ministry with the said charge on July 1, 2003. Pastor Ross would bring to Smith Chapel and Alexandria Chapel congregations an emphasis on tithing as opposed to fundraising and social justice ministry. While the fundraising activities decreased, revenue increased due to tithing. Those in leadership positions were expected to be in Bible study in addition to carrying out their responsibilities as leaders while not being in positions for ceremonialism's sake. Pastor Ross held leaders accountable for their areas of ministry. He was very direct with his people. This did not set well with some, resulting in their vacating their membership with Smith Chapel. In a telephone conversation with him, he reflectively commented, "My being direct was a problem."

Social justice was one of Pastor Ross' priorities of ministry. He was a very strong supporter of Lifestyles, a social justice agency in Charles County, Maryland that provides service to the marginalized of the community. It is reported that he regularly gave monetary support and/or clothing to help the agency meet the needs of the homeless. In addition he gave leadership in supporting the Catherine Foundation Pregnancy Care Center, Waldorf, Maryland. The offerings received by the Pisgah Charge during the series of Route 210 Lenten Services were designated for either Lifestyles or the Catherine Foundation. He was instrumental in bringing clothing to the Thanksgiving community dinner for the persons who were refugees from the Katrina Hurricane disaster in 2005. To say the least, the pastor demonstrated an ongoing passion to fulfill the mandates of the Final Judgment pericope: "for I was hungry and you gave me food, I was thirsty and you gave me something to drink, I was a stranger and you welcomed me, I was naked and you gave me clothing" (Matthew 25:35, 36a NRSV).

Pastor Ross was connectional in his ministry. His congregations fully participated in the series of Lenten Services with the Route 210 Corridor of Churches; the sermons he delivered were excellent, very biblically based and challenging to the hearers. Each New Year's Eve while I served as pastor to Metropolitan UMC, Pastor Ross preached the sermon in preparation for the New Year and reminded the many assembled of what they used to do on New Year's Eve in the secular world before accepting Christ as their Lord and Savior.

In the late fall of 2011, Pastor Ross became ill and would remain out of the pulpit for an extended period of time. Lay speakers filled in during his incapacitation until such time Rev. Evelyn Manson, retired elder and former pastor of St. Matthews, La Plata, Maryland, became the interim pastor from January 1, 2011 to April 30, 2011. Pastor Ross did not return to the pulpit; I and Kermit C. C. Moore, CLM, became the interim pastors until July 1, 2011. Pastor Ross eventually retired on November 13, 2011.

Matter of Unresolved Issues

The Pisgah Charge, although established in 1971 during the pastorate of the late Pastor Harvey R. Custis, Sr., was in need of reorganizing into a more efficient means of ministry. Merger, a concept broached by Pastor Custis, was emphatically turned down during the early 1990s. The idea was resurrected again by Pastor

Ross, and efforts were set in motion to have the concept to become a reality.[22] However, to recapitulate, the effort was thwarted on January 30, 2011, when during a joint meeting of the two churches, members voted down the plan to merge as one church. The question raised: "Why was the merger rejected?",[23]

I contend there are multiplicities of reasons that contribute toward congregations not wanting to merge with another church even though the members may be related. In a two-church configuration all too often one congregation will feel that it is being neglected by the pastor. The pastor does not have time after worship service to chat, care for and mingle with the people and in many cases the said congregation is the smaller of the two. Lyle Schaller in his assessment gives the following analysis:

> Church members especially like to have the complete attention of their pastor on the Sabbath . . . the minister serving a two or three-church parish has limited availability in each church on the Sabbath . . . the small church wants its minister to be a "lover" . . . the second church in a two-church parish may be perceived as a rival for our lover's affections. ([25]

Meanwhile, the larger church may have feelings that it is not getting its total money worth from the pastor that is spending too much time at the other church. The pastor can find him- or herself in a catch twenty-two situation.

Some congregations resist merger because of the intrinsic values held regarding the church building. Fond memories of individuals who donated certain items of altar-ware, furniture and/or musical instruments all factor in the intrinsically valuable property as viewed by the members. It is very difficult to separate from such, and as a result they become a source of resistance to merger. A member of another church continued to resent the fact the old church was razed in order to provide for the new edifice even in light of the fact that the old church building was termite infested and unsafe to occupy. Her ongoing mantra was: "My father, the first black licensed carpenter in this county, put so much workmanship into the woodwork of the sanctuary . . ." [26] Separation from the sources of affections and memories will cause trauma to individuals, even a sense of death!

Judicatories at times find themselves in a predicament when making available full-time positions for pastors. When there is a shortage of full-time pastoral positions, denominational officials find themselves establishing mergers or yoking together churches to create a full-time appointment. At times this is very beneficial especially when the churches are receiving a seasoned minister; however, there is also a downside. "Pressure from on high for congregations to merge or yoke together is a recipe for disaster." is a comment by Steve Willis.[27] Bennett says, "Some yoked ministries are still able to support a full-time person, but they are increasingly rare and are often fraught with tension of a leadership style that is out of harmony with the congregational setting or that bears conflicting expectations."[28] What denominational officials overlook sometimes is the small church is not a bureaucratic system but a tribal system based upon relationships; each tribe does not want to be forced together as if it were a "shot-gun" wedding.

Small churches, like Alexandria Chapel and Smith Chapel, that are linked together by family ties have been in competition with one another over the years and have been in conflict tend to resist mergers. Families talk among themselves as to what is taking place in their particular church where something new is occurring or progress is being made in certain areas of ministry become a source for spurring the other on to out-do the other. Or there may have been a certain occasion of conflict among the members and through the years the cause of the problem was forgotten, but still there was lingering animosity that contributed to the preventing of the churches to come together even for the improvement of ministry. Such ongoing competition and deep-seated resentment between two churches can be illustrated by but not to the level of what Cardinal Roger Etchergary of the Vatican experienced on his visit to Rwanda in attempt to bring peace between warring tribes. He commented during a meeting with Rwandan religious leaders in 1994: "Are you saying that the blood of tribalism is deeper than the waters of baptism?" One leader responded, "Yes, it is." ([29] While friction was not to the magnitude as was with the Hutus and Tutsis, there is some tension, and quietly kept, for unknown reasons serves as a means of obstructionism between the two congregations that prevent them from completely working together in total harmony.

In light of the foregoing, it appears to me that the reasons for Alexandria UMC's backing out of the merger with Smith Chapel was predicated upon the church's members' unwillingness to relinquish the property because of intrinsic values they held and apparent unresolved interpersonal congregational issues dating far back in the histories of the congregations. Moreover, there may have been some competitive issues that lingered and engendered feelings of low self-esteem. Members of Alexandria Chapel only wanted to have their own pastor. The solution to the problem was the implementation of the cooperative parish ministry based upon the Book of Discipline, Section II, paragraph 206, 2, 3.c. With the introduction of the cooperative parish model for the two churches and the assignment of me as the lead pastor at Smith Chapel Campus and Associate Pastor Moore to the Alexandria Chapel Campus, the prayers of members of Alexandria Chapel were answered.

Alexandria Chapel Key Families and Players

The rural small church is typically made-up of several dominant family groups. Alexandria is no exception. There are five family groups represented within this congregation: the Milsteads, Savoys, Grays, Diggs and Washingtons. The Milsteads appear to be the most dominant in terms of serving in ministry areas of the church. The key players in the life of the church serve as inspirational models of faith and faithfulness in using their gifts and graces to the glory of God. The following players have integral roles in the life of Alexandria Chapel:

Ruth Milstead Simmons is the senior matriarch of the church. She is a lifelong member of the congregation where she served in a number of ministry areas and is noted for being the lead communion stewardess of Alexandria Chapel for years. She is the Mother of the Church and is well respected by all in the community. She is affectionately referred to as Aunt Ruth. In an interview with Aunt Ruth, she shared with me the various ministry areas that she served in, namely, Communion Stewards and secretary of the Administrative Council and Usher Board. She also was a Sunday school teacher and was noted for giving the morning announcements. There was noticeable exuberance in her voice as she reflected on the coming of Pastor Moore; the church in her view is growing with an increase in the number of choir groups, Bible studies, and the administrative structuring and organization of new ministries

She finds Pastor Moore to be a very personable minister who is not autocratic and visits the members of the church. The only occasion she was disappointed with the pastor was when he forgot to bring his robe to the Ash Wednesday Service in 2012; though the other pastors were robed, he wasn't. (I explained that there was a communication breakdown on that occasion.) I questioned Aunt Ruth about the attitude of the church with the introduction of its first woman pastor; she admitted there was resistance by some of the members but eventually accepted the fact of having a woman pastor. Aunt Ruth was uncertain as to the reasons for some of the tension between Alexandria and Smith. At the conclusion of my interview with her, it was very clear that Alexandria Chapel has a very positive self-esteem due to having their own pastor. "Our pastor is doing a wonderful job!" was her comment.

Royce Milstead is the senior patriarch of the Alexandria Chapel. He is a lifelong member of the church and the brother of Ruth Simmons. He is affectionately called Uncle Smack. He is the uncle of Roderick "Squeaky" Milstead, Sr., member of Smith Chapel.

Rhonda Taylor is the Lay Leader and Lay Member to the Annual Conference. She is representative of the lay person, besides the Mother of the Church that has been a longtime member with a vast amount of knowledge of the corporate history of this local church. Rhonda carries out many of the administrative functions; she is in effect the church administrator that is of invaluable assistance to the pastor. Rhonda affectionately known as "Easy Rider" because she has her own motorcycle and is a Certified Lay Servant Minister. As a trustee and because she lives nearby, she frequently is the person who opens and closes the church for scheduled meetings. She benefits from a baccalaureate degree in Biblical Studies from a local institute. Rhonda participates in speaking engagements to include biblical story-telling at other churches, at Smith Chapel, and at the Charles County Nursing Home, now Sagepoint. Rhonda coordinates with Vera Littlejohn of Smith Chapel on the monthly nursing home order of worship. She also serves as Coordinator of the Outreach Ministries. The Lay Leader is the niece of the mother of the Church and the sister of Roderick Milstead, Sr.

Rita Simmons is the daughter of Ruth Simmons and serves as the chair of the Church Council. Rita is a Lay Servant Minister who serves as a worship leader.

Maureen Diggs is the daughter of Ruth Simmons and serves as the Church Council Secretary and is noted for the variety of worship bulletins created weekly.

Jacqueline Baker serves as treasurer and is the niece of the Mother of the Church.

Wendy Noble Burns serves as Financial Secretary and the niece of Jacqueline Baker.

Shawn Lee is the Chair of the Board of Trustees; he is the grandson of the late Mother of the Church, Catherine Day Lee.

Rose Chase is the Financial Secretary and Certified Lay Servant Minister. She is the sister-in-law of Roland Chase, member of Smith Chapel. Rose serves in several other ministry areas: Staff/ Pastor Parish Relations Committee, Committee on Lay Leadership and Development. She delivered inspirational messages at the Sagepoint Nursing Home.

Christine Washington serves as Chair of the Staff/Pastor Parish Relations Committee and Coordinator of Children's Ministries.

Wayne Washington is the president of the United Methodist Men's unit and the husband of Christine Washington.

Paulette Moore is the Chair of the United Methodist Women's unit and wife of the pastor.

Jocelyn B. D. Moore is Coordinator of Youth and Family Ministries. She orchestrated several plays involving the members of Alexandria and Smith congregations and is a published author of several Christian plays. She is the owner of JM Entertainment. Ms. Moore is the sister of Pastor Moore.

Jennifer Dorsey, a fraternal twin, serves faithfully as an usher and established a reputation at the nursing home as the member from Alexandria Chapel that closes out the order of worship with the praying of the Lord's Prayer. Significantly, Jennifer was among the first volunteers from Alexandria Chapel and Smith Chapel to participate in the Local Establishment Ministry (LEM). The said ministry's focus was taking inspirational materials to local bars and taverns, church events calendars, newsletters, and invitations to visit the churches.

There are other members of Alexandria Chapel who played vital roles in the scope of ministries that enable this congregation to meet the needs within and beyond the wall of the church.

Church Administration

The Charge Conference reports of 2011 and 2012 exhibit a very upbeat tone pertinent to the ministry taking place at Alexandria

Chapel. There is a clear sense of revitalization of ministry as the pastor narrates the accomplishments within the church in each of the conference years. The theme for 2011 was: "It's a New Day." The parishioners enthusiastically proclaimed the theme as their pastor took every opportunity to remind them. He prefaced the new initiatives that were started by saying, "It's a new day!"

Lay Leader Rhonda Taylor previously shouldered the weight for administrative duties in the church. With Pastor Moore's assignment to the church, he immediately began organizing the "A-Team" that would be comprised of key leaders in the church. Although an office was available at the annex of Smith Chapel Campus, he preferred to establish his own office at the Alexandria Chapel Campus where the "A-Team" met. Meanwhile Aunt Ruth had a meeting with her daughters and informed them that she would be stepping down from serving as the secretary for the Administrative Council; moreover, she wanted Rita to become the chair of the Administrative Council while Maureen served as secretary and Carolyn work with the Trustees. While this may not have comported with conventional wisdom and polity that is what happened. (This was a demonstration of the power of the Mother of the Church.) Anthony Pinn comments:

> (T)he church Mother . . . is a title bestowed upon older wise and spiritually strong women who have distinguished themselves through service in numerous capacities. Once a woman receives this title, she receives new status, based on moral and spiritual authority . . .

'Church Mothers are also consulted with respect to the spiritual direction of the church . . . other members of the congregation may walk out when they disagree with the pastor, but their actions will be ignored. The Church Mother is never ignored . . ."[30]

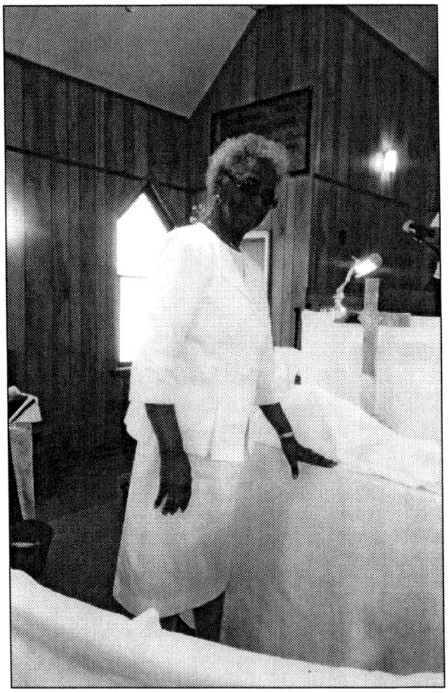

Ruth Milstead Simmons (Mother of Church)

Pastor Moore organized his A-Team to consist of the Lay Leader, Administrative Council Chair, Secretary, Treasurer, Trustee Chair and S/PPRC. He would conduct regular meetings with the team for purposes of keeping them informed of district and/or conference matters in addition to planning and executing new initiatives. The team was also the de facto church council that could approve any major actions. The implementation and ongoing use of the A-Team method worked very effectively for Alexandria Chapel.

In preparation for Charge Conference 2011, the leadership of Alexandria and Smith churches developed mission and vision statements in addition to short-term and long-term goals during the first joint planning retreat that was conducted at Metropolitan UMC and under the guidance of Rev. Victoria Starnes, Regional Guide on August 20, 2011. The Mission Statement was: *"Working together as one body in the Spirit of Christ."* The Vision Statement was: *"To be a cooperative parish, expanding in faithful service, fellowship, and growth to reach a needy world.*[31] The mission and vision statements would guide both congregations for the next two and half years.

The goals for Alexandria Chapel were ambitious, necessary, and achievable. The short terms goals were:

1. Increase average worship attendance by twenty through returning and/or new members by March 31, 2012.
2. Increase Christian educational opportunities by adding adult and teen classes by September 30, 2012.
3. Increase two small group experiences (Bible study and prayer meetings) by January 31, 2012.
4. Increase tithing members at least one-third by January 1, 2012.
5. Develop two new ministries (Dance and Big Brother/Big Sister) by April 30, 2012.

6. Organize a minimum of two fundraiser activities to support the ministries of the church by June 2012.
7. Construct to expand the church's physical plant with additions (multipurpose area, pastor's office, choir loft, windows, and carpet) by December 30, 2012.
8. Increase participation in the parish United Methodist Men by January 31, 2012.
9. Increase participation in the parish United Methodist Women by January 31, 2012.
10. Increase by two persons in the area of worship ministry (ushers, lay speakers, worship leaders, children's church teachers) by April 30, 2012.
11. Hire a full-time minister of music by December 30, 2012.
12. Survey church properties, especially cemetery to include identifying and marking graves by May 30, 2012.
13. Inquire of grants from federal government and other sources to be used in advancing church ministries by June 30, 2012.

The long term goals were:

1. Develop by December, 2014, the following: church park, church parking lot, and walkway from church to fellowship hall.
2. Renovate the fellowship hall to bring to county code to include running water and kitchen by December 2013.

3. Install bathroom with approved county code at fellowship hall by December 2013.

The foregoing goals would serve as sources of guidance for the ensuing year 2012.

Alexandria Chapel would have as it new theme for 2012: "Look Where He's Brought Us From." The goals established for 2012 were repetitive and/or an extension of 2011's goals. The short-term goals for 2012 were:

1. Increase average worship attendance to 60 by December 2013.
2. Increase Christian educational opportunities by adult and teen classes by December 2013 (i.e., children's church, bible study and prayer meetings, computer classes, confirmation classes, Sunday morning adult Bible study, VBS)
3. Increase tithing members at least one-third by December 2013.
4. Develop two new ministries (i.e., dance, Big Brother/Big Sister, Lifestyles) by December 2013.
5. Establish better communication plan (i.e., phone tree, newsletter, updating website, directory)
6. Organize a minimum of two fundraiser activities to support the ministries of the church by December 2013. (i.e., Trustee Day, ROCK, Community Day, fashion show, talent show)

7. Expand the church's physical plan by refurbishing and renovating (i.e., multipurpose area, pastor's office, choir loft, windows, carpet, doors, and furniture) by December 2013.
8. Increase participation in the parish United Methodist Men by December 2013.
9. Establish United Methodist Women individual charter at the Alexandria Campus by December 2013.
10. Increase participation in the area of worship ministry (i.e., ushers, lay speakers, liturgist, team Alexandria teachers, lay readers, prayers, communion stewards, and nursing home volunteers) by December 2013.
11. Continue to build on the music ministry by December 2013. (i.e., musician, additional choir members for all choirs)
12. Survey church properties, especially the cemetery to include identifying and marking graves by December 2013.
13. Inquire of grants from federal government and other sources to be used in advancing church ministries by December. (To be addressed)

The long-term goals established for 2012 were limited and have not been realized:

1. Develop by December 2014 the following: church park, church parking lot, and walkway from church to fellowship Hall. (Rev. Love has church deed for review.)

2. Purchase church vehicle by December 2014.

I mentioned early on that the goals were ambitious, necessary and achievable while in some cases were repetitive. Overall under Pastor Moore's leadership, the majority of the goals established were achieved. I will point of some of the accomplishments later on in this writing.

The Parish Council periodically met once a quarter. The meetings generally were conducted at the annex (old parsonage) at Smith Chapel. Usually members of Alexandria's A-Team were present as well as members of Smith's Chapel's Church Council. Reflectively, the meetings for the most part were perfunctory. Goals and objectives for the two churches were discussed and progress made relative to them. Scheduled joint activities were discussed. However, I sensed a growing desire on the part of Alexandria's membership to become independent of Smith Chapel to which I occasionally responded with the comment, "It costs to be free." Further, I mentioned to the leadership of Alexandria to strive to increase the pastor's financial support to a level of half-time status. Some replied, "We are doing the best we can now."

At the beginning of our venture as a cooperative parish, Pastor Moore and I met weekly at the Bob Evans Restaurant in Waldorf, Maryland, for purposes to debrief each week on our ministries at each campus. These were most fruitful times as we discussed the activities on each campus and how to support one another in ministry. Periodically, I offered advice and did some coaching with him pertinent to issues at the local church. Pastor Moore was open, shared what he did and observed what happened, and then he would extract from me, study my responses, and later try them out. Periodically, I still receive calls from him on certain matters of ministry.

Nurture

Worship services at Alexandria Chapel dramatically changed. There was increase in their average attendance. Before Pastor Moore was assigned to the congregation, it is reported that attendance was very low, but with his neophyte-like enthusiasm, inactive members began to return and new members joined. By 2013, the average worship attendance would be forty-four worshipers each Sunday morning. A change in the worship time from 9 a.m. to 10 a.m. contributed to the increase of attendance, and a new musician was hired. The former musician left before service was over in order to get to Smith Chapel where he would play for our morning service scheduled at 11 a.m. Three new choirs, Spirit of Alexandria, Male Chorus, and Youth Choir were added. The Children's Church met in the fellowship hall during the regular worship service. An added touch to the worship experience was the weekly bulletins that Maureen prepared with a picture theme associated with the sermon. Mrs. Paulette Moore, pastor's wife and an artist, made banners with seasonal themes for the sanctuary.

Performing wedding ceremonies is a sacred responsibility. For local pastors, it becomes problematic when it is outside the jurisdiction of the immediate local church. To this end, I assisted Pastor Moore with a wedding ceremony that took place in Annapolis, Maryland, in 2014. He did the marital coaching phase with the couple, but on the day of the wedding I served as the officiant of the ceremony and signed the license as required by law.

Administering the sacraments is very important to the members of Alexandria Chapel. Aunt Ruth retired as the lead communion steward. She was succeeded by Paulette Moore and by Romaine Savoy who prepares the pastor's communion kit for the sick and shut-ins.

Funeral services for members of Alexandria were typically handled by Adams Funeral Home out of Aquasco, Maryland. Other services were conducted at Thornton's Funeral Home in Indian Head, Maryland. Certified Lay Servant Minister Rhonda Taylor assisted the pastor, and occasionally I would help the pastor during such occasions. Pastor Moore frequently reciprocated with me when Smith Chapel's members died. Interments are at the old church grounds' cemetery—Jordan Chapel.

Funeral services in the African American experience are community events. Whenever services are conducted at the funeral home, the chapel is usually filled to capacity. The gatherings are made up of people from the community and come from different religious backgrounds. It is not unusual to have family members who are Baptists, Roman Catholic, and other Protestant communities of faith. Clergy from other churches usually offer "Words of Comfort" but all too often have to be reminded not to exceed two minutes and that there is only one eulogy to be given and that is by the pastor; however, at times the statement falls on deaf ears. Some of the clergy have to get their "whoop" in with a little sermonette. Personally, I get very irritated when this occurs. The person reading cards, family papers, and the obituary need to be reminded also about time limits, especially if the decedent is a veteran that is to be interred at a veterans' cemetery and an honor guard is scheduled to be present. Once the order of worship is over, the interment takes place, usually at the church cemetery contingent upon cemetery policy. (I will address this matter separately.) Then the repast takes place either in the fellowship hall or a rented facility. All bring together a sense of community and support for the bereaved family.

Another aspect of nurturing ministries is Christian Education. At the start of Pastor Moore's ministry at Alexandria Chapel there was only one child in the church. With the help of his sister Jocelyn and Christine Washington, the Sunday school began to grow to an enrollment of nineteen. Further, both ladies worked with the young people to develop several plays that included youngsters from Smith Chapel. The plays were sources of fundraising for the youth ministry. In addition the children were taking active parts in the worship service where they could demonstrate their development in Christian Education. To further advance them, several of the youngsters were able to attend the annual youth event in Ocean City, Maryland; ROCK was very transformative for the two attendees who gave testimonies of deepening their faith in Christ upon their return from the weekend event. The following year, 2014, youngsters from Smith Chapel would join with them.

Initially, Bible study was a joint venture with the members of both churches and alternating monthly between the two campuses. After one season with two or three members from Alexandria attending, it became clear that it would be beneficial for us to just meet at Smith Chapel campus. More Alexandria attendees began to come to Bible study on Sunday mornings at their own church. Bible study class for the adults now take place on Sunday mornings before worship service. The thrust of their study is in the Genesis to Revelation series. Rhonda Taylor, CLS, teaches the adult class that consists of five members. Meanwhile Jocelyn Moore and Christine Washington conducted Sunday school in the fellowship hall that is a two-minute walk along the pathway from the parking lot of the church. (The fellowship hall is a historic structure that was used while the main edifice was being built.) In addition other community and church school activities are conducted in the fellowship hall.

Vacation Bible School activities were joint ventures with Smith Chapel members. The joint VBS events took place for several years at the annex of Smith Chapel Campus where the attendance was in excess of thirty youngsters. Church school staff worked harmoniously together as they taught the children each year.

The nurturing ministries at Alexandria Chapel have affirmed the overall self-esteem as the needs of the parishioners are being met under the leadership of Pastor Moore.

Outreach

Pastor Moore successfully implemented a joint nursing home ministry with the Charles County Nursing Home, now Sagepoint. The first Saturday in the afternoon of each month with exception of August, members from both congregations join together in an order of worship for the residents. With his musical skills, Pastor Moore plays the keyboard while members take part in singing and giving testimonies and inspirational messages. The Nursing Home Ministry is a significant ministry that both congregations strongly support and harmoniously work together. Rhonda Taylor, CLSM, gets the various members assigned to the slots for the month while Vera Littlejohn, Lay Leader Smith Campus, prepares the program. During Advent, residents and staff members gather in the lounge where the order of worship is carried out; in December 2012 liturgical dancers in addition to youth participated in the service. The congregations have established a very positive reputation with the nursing home whose residents look forward to the special ministry these churches provide at the first of the month.

Alexandria once a month, usually on a Thursday evening, provides meals at the Robert Fuller Transition House in Waldorf, Maryland. Members provide home-cooked meals and/or purchased dinners from local restaurants for the men of the said establishment. The residents are very grateful for the meals provided by the members of Alexandria Chapel Campus. The time also allows for members to be in conversation with the residents. Charles County has a number of homeless persons that need shelter during the fall and winter months. Lifestyles of Maryland a social justice ministry, provides what is known as "Safe Nights." Under the leadership of Sandy Washington, Director, and Corae Briscoe Young, Assistant Director, the said ministry coordinates with local churches for them to house the homeless persons for a week during which time the congregations provide breakfast, lunch packs, and dinner. While Alexandria is unable to house the individuals, the church does work in concert with Smith Chapel that houses the guests by providing breakfast for them. This is another situation in which the two congregations harmoniously work together.

Indeed, the two churches work together to fulfill the mandates of the Final Judgment Pericope, Matthew 25:31–46, of meeting the needs of those marginalized in society.

Witness

The witnessing aspect of Alexandria's ministry was expressed its participation in the Route 210 Corridor of Churches Lenten Season. In January 2012 Rev. George Hackey, Jr. of Metropolitan UMC was coordinator of the annual gathering of churches. Plans were made, and Smith Chapel and Alexandria Chapel Cooperative Parish were assigned a date when we would take care of the order of worship on Good Friday during an evening service. We brought together a joint choir with Karleen Powell, Pastor Moore's sister, serving as the choir director and musician. Before a full sanctuary at Grace UMC, to use the vernacular, the combined choirs of the two churches "showed-off" during the service and demonstrated what could be done when they worked together. We left the service on a high note.

The United Methodist Men and United Methodist Women units were organized as charge units. Participation was not up to par. The UMM did not meet regularly, but once an effort was made to get them rechartered, there was a sluggish response to work together. As of this writing, the men of Alexandria have chartered and are meeting regularly. The UMW on the other hand, at least the women of Smith Chapel, met regularly each month, but there was no representation from Alexandria. As of this writing, the women of Alexandria Chapel are in the process of being chartered separately.

The Nursing Home ministry can also be representative of the Witness ministry. When members from both congregations get together, it is quite apparent what the Spirit of God does through the participants. Truly, there is evidence of what God can do through us when we are yielded and waiting for the Spirit to do a mighty thing in our collective lives.

Pastor Moore's Reflection

Pastor Moore reflected back on his ministry in an interview pertinent to Alexandria Chapel. His approach to serving the congregation was being a "hands-on" pastor that would be inclusive in his ministry. That is to say he would practice a participatory style of ministry that included laity working alongside with him. The response he received from the leadership was good. With his assignment to them, there was an expectation of change that was further amplified by his call for "It's a New Day."

There was an increase in the average worship attendance. He estimated that the once-eleven persons in attendance would no longer be the norm. Attendance soared to range from forty to fifty worshipers per Sunday. While the congregation was not emotive as he hoped them to be, the members were paying attention to his messages. Additional programs were initiated to attract more people and address the needs of the community along with spiritual nurturing.

On a personal note, Pastor Moore indicated that the church was very welcoming to them and especially to his wife who adjusted well because the congregants wanted a "First Lady." The Moore's live twenty-four miles away from the church, but that is not problematic for them. In fact C. Eric Lincoln comments, "The absentee nature of rural pastoral leadership means that church members are more independent and must develop their own networks of spiritual care and nurture . . . the pastor is often regarded as a necessary but an occasional visitor . . ."([32] He could see progress taking place within the bounds of Alexandria Chapel.[33]

Closing Thoughts on Alexandria Chapel Campus

My original impression of Alexandria Chapel was the congregation felt ignored, angry, and pushed aside by the pastor because of greater obligation to Smith Chapel that was the larger of the two and because Smith was paying the required conference benevolences. However, with Pastor Moore's assignment to them, a great turn-around was experienced. Not to sound secular, but just a little loving them went a long way. It also corroborates what Schaller contended regarding the fact that rural congregations would prefer having their own pastor as their leader and not sharing the person. Like other small rural congregations, Alexandria Chapel preferred having its own pastor whether, bi-vocational and/or an absentee, that would care for the sacramental obligations while the laity would carry on with the necessary leadership responsibilities. The fact that they had their own pastor bolstered their self-esteem.

The cooperative parish configuration gave Alexandria Chapel a tolerable method of ministry that allowed them to have "their own pastor." For the church, the cooperative parish model worked to their benefit as they received an energized and motivated young pastor, relatively speaking, who was committed to doing God's will. Their prayers had been answered.

I now turn my attention to Smith Chapel Campus.

Smith Chapel Key Families and Players

Similar to Alexandria Chapel, the Smith Chapel congregation is comprised of the following family groups: Bowman-Butler-Burroughs-Mason-Milstead-Robertson, Chase-Swann-Washington, Lewis-Taylor, Williams-Richardson, Smith-Littlejohn, Erwin, Johnson, Proctor, and White. Some of the families are linked with families at Alexandria Chapel, namely Chase, Milstead, and Washington.

The Senior Matriarchs

Clara Barbour Washington is the ninety-eight-year-old lifelong member of Smith Chapel and the Mother of the Church. She is currently home-bound and declining in her health. She is the grand matriarch of her five-generation family. "Ms. Washington" or "Ms.

Clara" as she is referred to by members of the church is affectionately called, "Granny" by her family members; some pastors greet Ms. Clara as "Mother Washington." I greet her as Ms. Washington and have done so since the time I met her in 2000 while I was serving as the pastor of Metropolitan UMC. When United Methodist Women's meetings convene on the second Sundays, the ladies will defer speaking until Ms. Washington speaks and/or gives advice on certain topics discussed in the meeting. The Mother of the Church has a very influential presence at the meetings. Rightly did Pinn aver, "The Church Mother is never ignored."[34]

In May 2011 Ms. Washington was attending Grace UMC, Fort Washington, Maryland, where her daughter, Judy and granddaughter Cynthia were members in addition to other local churches. I visited Ms. Washington during my first week of serving as the interim pastor of Smith Chapel; we had a very candid discussion about the ministry at the church and closed with prayer. "The hinges on my door always swing open, Reverend. You are always welcome." was her comment to me as I was leaving her home. The next Sunday Ms. Washington along with her granddaughter Brenda came and took seats in the next to last row of the sanctuary. After service, I went to greet and shake her hand. She held my hand tightly and said, "God bless you Dr. DeFord. I am glad you and Mrs. DeFord are here." A few Sunday's later Ms. Washington moved from the rear of the sanctuary toward the front. As the fall of the year approached, she seated herself next to my wife. This continued until her legs became weak, and she was brought into the sanctuary by wheelchair. On extremely cold days she did not come out.

My impression of what took place as Ms. Washington returned to Smith Chapel was a process of approving of the pastor and his wife as the servant leaders in the church. Moving from the rear of sanctuary toward the front served as an indicator that she was approving of the ministry; moreover, seating herself next to my wife was the final step in her complete approval of the pastoral family. I am certain that members of the congregation were paying close attention to this and took their cues from her actions.

Mrs. Clara Washington, Mother of Church

Each Sunday after service, members of the congregation would come to speak to Ms. Clara seated in the pew in front of church and near the small ramp built by the trustees so that her wheelchair could move from the sanctuary to the fellowship hall. A line formed as members went to speak with her. It was not uncommon for five generations of her family to be present. The routine that developed was adult members of the family came to greet Granny, followed by some members of the church, and finally the great grands and great-great grands. Two of the youngsters quarreled between themselves as to who would push Granny in her wheelchair to the car. In the event that the great-grandchildren were not in attendance, she only allowed Roland Chase to push her to the car. The ritual of greeting Ms. Clara could be akin to members of a tribe giving honor and respect to the elder Mother.

Ms. Washington had been very active in various ministry areas of the church. She was the Lay Leader and lay speaker. Both she and her late sister Rosie Theresa Swann, "Ms. Theresa or Aunt T" served as lay speakers in the congregation. Ms. Washington distinguished herself as being the president of the United Methodist Women for a number of years, a reason for the respect she received at meetings in recent years. She served in other leadership roles such as president of the Choir, the Usher Board and Council on Ministries. As recording secretary, she would, call the roll as persons in the sanctuary publicly stated what they would give for the offering. She and her late sister Theresa sang duets during morning services.

There were a plethora of other church activities she participated in over the years, and some of which are no longer conducted in some churches; for example, Camp Meetings in which she would sing with the praying bands. (Anecdotal to this is when Rev. Leon C. Kess, a retired pastor and friend of mine, preached a homecoming service in November 2012, and he began to sing some of the old praying band songs. Ms. Clara and he joined in together to sing some of the old familiar prayer band songs and had a delightful time in the Lord. She occasionally asks about him.)

Ms. Washington established a reputation as a leader in the church and in the community. She is still remembered by Rev. Robert Rodeffer who served as District Superintendent of the Washington East District from 1990 to 1998. In the social organization, the Eastern Stars she served in leadership capacity and invited me during my early pastorate at Metropolitan UMC to be the guest speaker at their special celebration. The Mother of the Church at Smith Chapel UMC is a remarkable lady who is a linkage to the past and an iconic expression of determination and faith of a people who have come through some challenging times, especially as it relates to the African American rural church. Mrs. Washington died on January 25, 2016, thirteen days short of her 99th birthday.

The late Ms. Rosie Theresa Barbour Swann was the sister of Clara Washington. Both were viewed as being inseparable. Ms. Theresa, also known as "Aunt T," served in a variety of ministries in Smith Chapel where she was a lifelong member. Known for her affable disposition and gentle patting of one's hand as she greeted persons, Ms. Theresa was the kind of Christian woman many enjoyed being around. She was the first woman of the church selected to serve on the Board of Trustees and eventually was elected to serve as the co-chair of the trustees. Like her Sister Clara, she was a member of the Senior Choir and served at its secretary; also she served as the president of the United Methodist Women. During the 1960s, organizing baby contests, Tiny Tot Weddings, and Mock Weddings were some of the fundraising activities that she gave leadership to raise monies for the church. When she and her husband relocated to St. Mary's County, Maryland, Theresa continued in faithful service to Smith Chapel.

I met Ms. Theresa while I served as pastor of Metropolitan UMC, Indian Head, Maryland. Routinely, she came to collect bread from our bread ministry with ultimate distribution to members in Pisgah, Maryland. I found her to have been a great conversationalist and never failed to pat my hand while talking. I was very delighted to see her on my first Sunday as interim pastor of Smith Chapel; there was no change in her disposition, always with a word of greeting and thanks to the Lord. The joy of the Lord was her strength as she met various individuals and continued giving out the periodical, *The Daily Bread*. Ms. Theresa transitioned in February 2014. In the days leading up to her death, Ms. Theresa continued to maintain her good-natured disposition that was indicative of the presence of the Spirit of Christ within her. We miss her presence.

The late Mrs. Mary Laurette Smith, mother of Lay Leader Vera Littlejohn, was a lifelong member of Smith Chapel and the lay member to the Annual Conference for a number of years. She was a very unique woman; I refer to her as, "the Indomitable Ms. Laurette." She was a federal service employee who was employed with the Department of the Navy; later she became a biological laboratory technician at the National Institutes of Health in Bethesda, Maryland and the Food and Drug Administration in Washington, DC, before retiring in 1977. In addition, she was an astute businesswoman and farmer. There are not enough words to describe Ms. Laurette, also known as, "Mary L, Ret, Loretta, and Mama." She was noted for not being afraid to drive anywhere! (In her late 90s, the family hid the truck keys from her.) Adventuresome, committed, determined, faithful, generous, helpful, hospitable, intelligent, loving, and self-reliant are just a few of the words that describe the character of Ms. Laurette. She was willing to drive anywhere and take whoever needed a ride.

Ms. Laurette was committed to the church and support of its ministries. Without question, she had faith in God and practiced the principles of Matthew 25 of doing acts of kindness to those marginalized in society. She provided housing for several men who worked her farm. During the fall of the year, Ms. Laurette, along with the men and her daughter, would prepare various meat products from the slaughtered hogs: bacon, sausage, scrapple, and souse, to name a few. I received a large aluminum pan of scrapple that I shared with other clergy colleagues; one of whom asked for more because he had never tasted such good scrapple. In addition, vegetables from the garden were given to us. She exceeded, "pounding the pastor" with meats and vegetables from her farm.

There were episodes of sudden hospitalizations during the early part of 2012. On one such occasion, Vera received an emergency call because Ms. Laurette was being transferred from the regular ward to the intensive care unit. By the time church service was over, my wife and I went to the hospital expecting the worse. While walking toward the intensive care unit, we met Iretha in the hallway, and she was noticeably distraught. Iretha tearfully said, "I don't think Mama is going to make it." At the unit, several of the family members were standing outside of Ms. Laurette's room. On the inside of the room, Vera was teary eyed as was Kevin, the grandson.

Lila and I approached the right side of the bed and began rubbing her right arm and called her name. "Ms. Laurette!" I said. She opened her eyes, smiled, and spoke in a normal tone of voice, "How are you Reverend and Mrs. DeFord?" Vera and Kevin appeared dumbfounded. Ms. Laurette proceeded to tell us that she did not want to be in the hospital and was trying to get up, but the nurse tried to restrain her then called for security. Ms. Laurette continued to tell us and demonstrated how she punched the fat security officer in the stomach and he doubled over. They restrained her. At our arrival, Ms. Laurette apparently was just pouting.

Vera comments, "1968 was an interesting year." She talked about her mother's commitment to help her and her sister get an education and home ownership. When she was entering college, her mother was helping Carolyn, Vera's older sister, who completed nursing school, purchase a house. Ms. Laurette helped other members of the family in a similar manner.

Laurette Smith, Former Lay Member to BWC

Ms. Laurette transitioned in August 2012. Normally, funeral services for Smith Chapel's deceased members take place at Metropolitan United Methodist Church, which has a larger sanctuary and seating capacity or at Thornton's Funeral Home Chapel. Ms. Laurette's wake and funeral took place in the sanctuary of Smith Chapel. Needless to say, the church could not accommodate all of the community members, former co-workers, and family. Moreover, the number of pastors could not be seated in the pulpit area. The service flowed as expected with the exception of a young Baptist preacher who did his sermonette and "whoop." As we departed from the sanctuary to church cemetery, the crowd parted like the Reed Sea in order to bear her remains to the final resting place. There was an extremely large crowd at graveside. What a unique woman—the Indomitable Laurette Smith.

Mrs. Norena Toyer

Norena Toyer, Choir Coach

Mrs. Norena Toyer is next senior matriarch in the congregation. She recently lost her husband Edward after sixty-eight years and seven months of marriage. Norena's daughter Barbara continues to bring her mom to weekly services. Mrs. Toyer is well known in the local church community for her alto voice. She has been a member of the Senior and Chancel Choirs for years and led many selections, her favorite Gospel songs were "On Time God" and "Get Away Jordan." At funerals one can expect that she will sing a selection before giving witness about the decedents. On an occasion, when we were having a joint service with Pisgah United Methodist Church, our neighboring white congregation, one gentleman specifically asked for her and whether she would be singing that evening.

"It is good to be here, children!" is her mantra on Sunday mornings during worship services. I have begun to call her the "choir coach" because although she must use a walker to help her along; her voice is still strong enough that she is able to sing along with the choirs during prayer and praise service. If the choir is a bit timid in their singing, Mrs. Toyer will encourage them by saying, "Come on, children, sing, sing!" One readily notices that Mrs. Toyer wears some rather flamboyant hats. Ms. Norena is a very determined lady who presses her way to come to worship services despite how inclement the weather might be on that Sunday. Once inside the sanctuary door, the familiar voice echoes, "It's good to be here, children!"

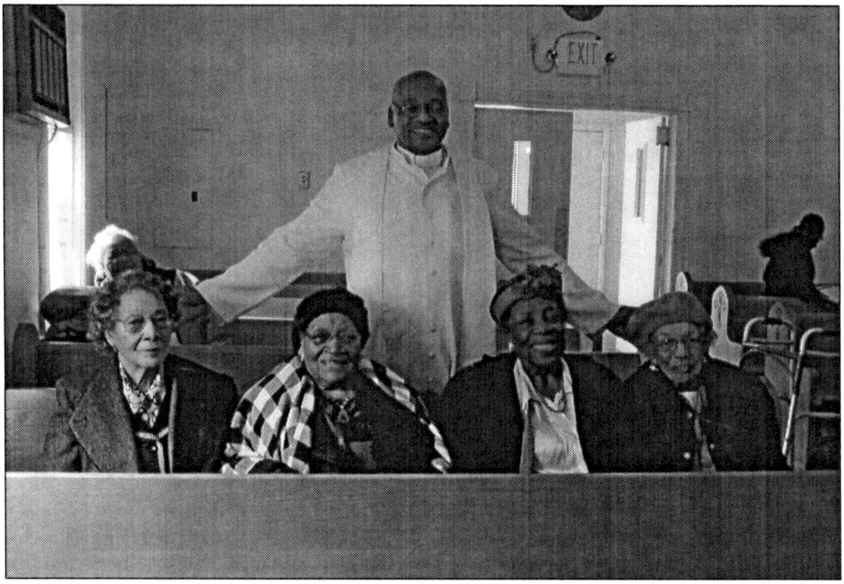

Grand Matriarchs of Smith Chapel UMC with Pastor

The next group of matriarchs and patriarch, seventy years and older, is composed of Elizabeth (nee: Bowman) Butler, Annette (nee: Baker) Bowman, Rosetta (nee: Dorsey) Bowman, Yvonne (nee: Washington) Chase, and Charles Bowman.

Elizabeth "Lizzie" Butler is a lifelong member with adult children who are members of other churches. She is noted for the stylish hats that she wears. She is the senior matriarch of the Bowman family.

Annette Bowman joined Smith Chapel during the pastorate of the late Rev. Harvey Custis, Sr. She has adult children who are active members: Gail Robertson, Deborah Swann, Joyce Thomas, and Wanda Price. Several of her sons, Leroy and Ivan, periodically attend worship services and special programs. Gail is the chair-person of the Staff Parish Relations Committee, and Deborah sings with two choirs and part of the Sagepoint Nursing Home ministry. Annette sings with the Chancel Choir, loves good gospel music, and readily responds when the music is good.

Rosetta Bowman is a lifelong member. The majority of Rosetta's adult children have joined other United Methodist Churches and other communities of faiths. Almalita remains very committed and faithful to Smith Chapel; she serves as the treasurer of the church and is one of the coordinators of children's ministries. I affectionately call her "the Sheriff" as she strives to keep the youngsters in line within the church and while on outings. Also Almalita's husband, Luther, and adult children and grandchildren are active participants in the church. Rosetta occasionally sings with the Chancel Choir when she is not having health issues. Rosetta gives and looks for hugs from the pastor and the first lady. Moreover, she periodically calls to check on the pastoral family.

Yvonne Chase, the daughter of Mrs. Clara Washington, is a lifelong member with the majority of her adult children, grandchildren, and great-grandchildren active in the church. Brenda, Carlotta, and Kim are active members with Brenda serving as president of the United Methodist Women and a teacher with our Sunday Morning Learning Session. Kim is a member of the Nominations and Lay Leader Development team. Kim's husband George Swann II and her son George Swann III both sang with the Male Chorus. Kim's son is currently matriculating at Morgan State University as a civil engineering student. Yvonne is the maternal figure for her nieces, Carolyn and Rose Washington and their children.

Charles "Tiny Baby" Bowman is the brother of Veronica Elnora Milstead and the father of Phyllis Bowman. Charles sings with several of our choirs and serves as an usher. He is a very open gentleman who shares his struggles and gives God the praise.

On any given Sunday morning I can look over the audience and see the matriarchs and patriarch seated in certain areas with their families that allows me to take a mental attendance of the members. At certain times, I can anticipate the arrival of certain members such as Rose with vision impairment whose son Larry escorts her in and seats her. These are the individuals that make up Smith Chapel United Methodist Church.

Key Players

Smith Chapel benefits from members that use their gifts and graces in the ministry of the church. The majority of the key players are members of the Church Council while others simply serve as volunteers to help the church maintain its vitality of ministry within and beyond the walls of the church.

Vera M. (nee Smith) Littlejohn, lifelong member, is the daughter of the late Ms. Laurette Smith. Vera serves as lay member to the Baltimore-Washington Conference of the United Methodist Church; like her mother she faithfully serves in this capacity and has done so for many years. In addition she is the Lay Leader of Smith Chapel, former chairperson of the Church Council and ex officio member to other ministry areas of the church. As church administrator, the Lay Leader cares for the final preparation of charge conference reports that are submitted electronically to the administrator of the Washington East District. Characteristically, Vera is a high-energy retired educator who usually goes the second mile in whatever tasks that are before her—the fruit does not fall far from the tree. She serves as secretary to the Church Council and Board of Trustees, taking copious notes that are available for the leadership. Vera is a member of two choirs, taught our middle school youth, and is very active with outreach ministry. She is the "Ever Ready Bunny" of Smith Chapel. Vera sees the church as insular but will rally for a cause and hopes for a larger facility in order to be more missional in the community and beyond.

Veronica Elnora (nee Bowman) Milstead is a lifelong member of Smith Chapel. Elnora served for a number of years as the chair of the Finance Committee until elected to serve as chair of the Church Council and Worship Committee. She enjoys singing on several choirs with her husband Roderick (Leon) for a number of years. Elnora wants things done decently and in order and will call into question if there is a lack of clarity in the process of discussions on church matters. She and her husband Leon are parents of two adult children: Roderick, Jr. and Lisa. (Roderick, Jr. is a former National Football League Super Bowl player with San Francisco 49ers.) Leon expresses a hope that the church will enter into a new building program in order to prepare for the needs of the future.

Perry Taylor joined Smith Chapel during the pastorate of the late Rev. Harvey Custis, Sr. Perry and his wife Leslie, lifelong member, are very active in the ministries of the church. Perry serves as the chair of the Board of Trustees, and Leslie works along with him. It is not usual to find them and two other trustees cleaning the church on Saturday morning in preparation for worship service on Sunday. In addition, Perry is the president of the United Methodist Men's unit, Lay Servant Minister, worship leader, and president of the Men's Choir. Leslie meanwhile serves as a communion steward and usher. Both serve as photographic historians of the church. I would not be surprised to see or hear of Perry's response to the call for ordained ministry in the not-too-distant future.

Audrey and Roland Chase are former Roman Catholics who joined during the pastorate of the late Rev. Dr. Shirlimarie McAroy-Gray. Audrey serves as membership secretary, having previously served as chair of the Worship Team and secretary to the Church Council. She initially guided me around the parish to be introduced to the members during the beginning stages of my ministry with Smith Chapel and Alexandria Chapel. She is a very personable lady, easy-going with an occasional laugh, and when she delivers a sermon, it is substantive and reflects the depth of her spirituality. Audrey is emotive and inspires the congregation that gives quite a bit of talk-back. Audrey is a member of our Kairos Prison Ministry team.

Roland, on the other hand, is quiet and reserved; one can describe him as Madeba, "quiet strength," based on Numbers 21:30. He serves as a member of the Board of Trustees, chair of the Finance Committee, treasurer of the United Methodist Men's unit, assistant teacher in the adult Sunday Morning Learning Session, and member of the Men's Choir. My wife calls Roland, "Professor," as he too will go the second mile in studying the Sunday adult class lessons and has rather profound questions and comments relative to the lesson. Roland is affectionately called "Uncle Roland" as he is the next most senior man in the congregation. He is the gatekeeper of the congregation. He checks the parking lot for new guests and invites them to worship with us.

Almalita (nee Bowman) and Luther (Pete) Robertson are the parents of three adult sons and grandparents of six. Almallita is the treasurer who is meticulous with the church's finances. On Sunday mornings, she occupies several roles: member of the choir, Sunday Morning Learning Session teacher with the smaller children, and treasurer disbursing salaries and/or reimbursements to the church staff. Almalita grew up in Smith Chapel while her husband, Pete, recently joined in 2014. Pete is a member of the Board of Trustees and a welder who built a cage for our air conditioning unit to prevent further thefts of the equipment. Peter is known for his barbeque skills.

Dorothy (Puddin, Mama) and David Mason are long term members of the church. Dorothy and the girls, Gail and Phyllis (Frosty) form the major part of the hospitality team. Dorothy and Gail sing on several choirs. On special Sunday mornings after service, they will immediately leave the choir loft and go to the kitchen to heat up foods brought to the church. Phyllis will care for the set up in the fellowship hall while Mama and Gail, the cut-up, will prepare the foods along with other members of the hospitality team. Mama and the girls typically travel together in addition to Gail's daughter. Gail, a tall young woman, was invited to play women's professional basketball but suffered an injury preventing her from playing. Gail can be quite comical at times and keeps the atmosphere light.

Jocelyn (nee Williams) Richardson joined during the administration of the late Rev. Harvey Custis, Sr. Jocelyn serves as a Lay Servant Minister, worship leader, and usher. Her niche is prison ministry. She is the lead team member for our prison ministry area and has been trained by Kairos Prison Ministry staffers. Jocelyn is a very passionate speaker as she delivers a sermon that reflects earnest preparation that was put in to it. She readily responses when asked to preach. She was a member of the Chosen Four, an acapella quartet that sang on the fourth Sundays but disbanded during my first year at Smith Chapel.

Iretha Erwin is a very faithful usher who serves as a back-up communion steward. She joined during the pastorate of the late Rev. Harvey Custis, Sr. Formerly, she served as a member of the Board of Trustees. I can depend on Iretha to have orange juice in the pulpit area so that I can counteract my blood sugar from dropping after my preaching. She gives attention to details in whatever she does. Iretha is connected to the Bowman Family.

Nancy Burroughs a recent retiree joined Smith Chapel during the pastorate of the late Rev. Harvey Custis, Sr. Nancy serves in a variety of ministry areas: vice-chair of the Board of Trustees, back-up communion steward, member of several choirs, and serves with hospitality team. Further, she collects the church's mail from the post office.

Rachel Stewart Johnson, a comparatively newcomer and registered nurse, joined during the pastorate of Pastor Lucius Ross, Jr. Rachel is the daughter of an African Methodist Episcopal retired pastor. She is married to the son of a former late member of mine at Metropolitan UMC. Rachel brings a wealth of gifts and graces particularly in the area of Christian education; she serves as the superintendent of the Sunday Morning Learning Session. Significantly, Rachel thinks outside the box and because of this has conducted several Christmas plays, organized trips for the youngsters, organized the Vacation Bible School, and developed learning stations in the fellowship hall for the youths. She has the gift of praying and serves as a lay servant minister and worship leader. Rachel has a calling upon her life to serve as clergy; she is in effect Smith Chapel's de facto youth minister.

Marva (nee Lewis) Smith is the older sister of Leslie Taylor and assistant in the Sunday Morning Learning Session. Marva recently completed her term as the president of the United Methodist Women. The church sponsored a trip to Ocean City, Maryland, this past winter for the gathering of young people for ROCK. Marva was one of the chaperones who kept the kids in check. She is a lifelong member of Smith Chapel.

Gail (nee Bowman) Robertson is a lifelong member of Smith Chapel and the sister-in-law of Almalita Robertson. She is the chair of the Staff/Pastor Parish Relations Committee, member of the Nominations and Lay Leadership Development Team, and president of the Chancel Choir. Gail serves as worship leader and brings with her a level of spirituality that stimulates praise.

Brenda Chase is the granddaughter of Clara Washington, Mother of the Church. Brenda's niche is working with young people. She conducts the middle school class in the Sunday Morning Learning Session. Taking pictures at church events is part of her ministry. Further, she is a dedicated sorority member of Alpha Kappa Alpha Sorority, Inc., Nu Zeta Omega Chapter, where she guided young ladies preparing to become debutants.

Bridget Taylor is the daughter of Perry and Leslie Taylor. Bridget is one of ten young adults in our congregation who serve with the Sunday Morning Learning Session. She works for a local community college while matriculating in a master's degree program at the University of Maryland University College.

All of the key persons that serve in the various ministries of the church, although related or incorporated into the families of Smith Chapel, use their gifts and graces to the glory of God in the rural setting of Pisgah, Maryland.

Smith Chapel UMC Family September 2012

Church Administration

The administrative machinery of Smith Chapel was led by Vera Littlejohn. Church Council meetings were scheduled to take place on the third Wednesday of the month. There were occasions, according to Vera, when not enough members of the council were present thus lacking a quorum. Vera typically prepared the agenda and sign-in roster for each meeting.

When I began my official pastorate for the conference year 2011—2012, I found myself attending Church Council meetings at Smith Chapel and Alexandria Chapel. The meetings were primarily information sharing times regarding the finances of the churches, need for more volunteers and recapitulations about maintenance issues. Every now and then the mantra was recited, "We need more fundraisers!" Here again fundraisers versus tithing and percentage giving was discussed.

I initiated at Smith Chapel the Smith Chapel Executive Team (SET) for the purposes of sharing information from the Ministers Alliance meetings on the second Saturday of the month. Usually there would be information pertinent to social justice issues and special events taking place in the community or at other local churches. During the Thanksgiving and Christmas seasons, donations, such as turkeys for marginalized families, were given to the churches specifically to be distributed to the needy families in their communities. The location of the distributions was given to the members of the SET to prepare accordingly. In the event special actions that required the Church Council to care for, the SET meeting transitioned into a call meeting of the Church Council. This worked very effectively for Smith Chapel in that the key members of the council were present, and there was not a lot of formal reporting on activities in ministry areas. In short, the SET was an informal meeting guided by the pastor.

At the Parish Council meetings that were scheduled for once a quarter at the Smith Chapel's annex, the participating members from either church came erratically. One of the reasons was some of the members worked in Washington, DC, and travel from the city was a chore especially for those who rode the commuter buses. Nevertheless, we were able to accomplish some items that contributed to the overall functioning of the Cooperative Parish: a parish directory, joint planning retreat, a parish newsletter, reorganizing the United Methodist Men's parish unit, having joint worship services, and a joint parish picnic at Stump Neck Regional Park, Indian Head, Maryland. In preparation for our charge conference scheduled for October 23, 2011, I urged the representatives of the Parish Council to have their members to work diligently on the preparation of their reports in a timely fashion. Pastor Moore was eager to prepare his first charge conference report along with the members of Alexandria Chapel, too. He was very upbeat in his Pastor's Report.

Similar to Pastor Moore, I was very enthusiastic regarding my 2011 Charge Conference report. I reported on the accomplishments of the church since July 1, 2011 and the strong signs of revitalization underway, such as increase in the average worship attendance and the upward swing in attendance in the Sunday Morning Learning Session (SMLS). Two other initiatives were pending: Saturday Evening Worship (SEW) and the Soup and Sandwich ministry that would take place on Wednesday afternoons from 12 p.m. to 2 p.m. Further I cited Smith Chapel's Goals for 2012:

1. To increase the average worship attendance to fifty worshipers by December 2012.
2. To increase giving to $32.05 per member per Sunday for repairs by June 2012.

3. To develop a plan for expansion of the physical structure of the church by June 2012.
4. To increase the participation of youth in the total worship experience by December 2012.
5. To continue the church's participation in social justice ministries, Lifestyles, Neighbors Eager to Serve (NETS), Catherine Foundation, Christmas Connection, and special offerings during 2012.
6. To restart the United Methodist Men's ministry as a cooperative parish unit immediately.

The majority of the above goals were accomplished. Goal No. 1 was exceeded with an AWA of 67.75 by June 2012 and sixty-two by December 2012. We did not achieve the increased giving rate of $32.05 by June 2012 as stated in Goal No. 2 and did not meet the development of an expansion plan by June 2012 as indicated in Goal No. 3. We met Goal No. 4 with the youth participating in the total worship experience; in fact, several of our young people routinely serve as worship leaders monthly and/or any other occasions. We met both Goals No. 5 and 6 and continue to be strong supporters of the social justice ministries identified in Goal No. 5. Conference year 2011–2012 was a time of revitalization and anticipation of greater achievements by both churches.

The Conference year 2012–2013 was a time of revisiting the goals that were not accomplished. Again I pushed for the physical expansion of the church and had great support. However, in February 2013, the restrooms were in dire need of repair. The Board of Trustees requested the Church Council to authorize a draw-down from the renovation fund to be used for the repair of the restrooms; as a result, the building fund was established for the purpose of constructing an addition to the church. Moreover, for two Sundays, we were in joint worship at Pisgah United Methodist Church.

Smith Chapel and Alexandria Chapel were making significant progress that could facilitate a change that would be beneficial for both. I, in conversation with Pastor Moore, concurred that while both churches were doing "parallel ministry" in the communities of Pisgah and Rison, Alexandria with a positive self-esteem, and the capability to sustain its own clergy, we submitted a joint letter requesting a change of status. We recommended to Rev. Dr. Ianther M. Mills, Annapolis-Southern Region Team Leader and Washington East District Superintendent, that the cooperative parish be dissolved and Smith Chapel and Alexandria Chapel United Methodist Churches become station churches. The request was granted to be effective July 1, 2013. Both churches as of this writing continue to serve in a connectional way with outreach and witness ministries.

Nurture

Worship

The gathering each Sunday at Smith Chapel can be compared to a weekly family reunion. Several members come from as far as Lanham and Temple Hills, Maryland. The drives for these members are forty-four miles with a fifty-minute journey and a forty-five minute drive respectively. A young adult family comes from King George, Virginia that requires them to come across the Governor Harry Nice Bridge, a toll bridge that spans the Potomac River, from Charles County, Maryland to Virginia. Their journey is approximately forty-five minutes to one hour. Other members come from neighboring communities where they could very easily attend churches closer to their homes, but their choice is to come to Smith Chapel, their family church. While a number of churches are passed by in route to Smith Chapel, in the Pisgah community where they grew up, the members look forward to return to the family church to experience a sort of family reunion each Sunday. After each worship service, the members linger around the church before returning to their homes or visiting with relatives in the community.

Bulletins are prepared weekly by Sis. Melissa, a member of Cornerstone African Methodist Episcopal Church, Indian Head, Maryland, and the sister of Perry Taylor. I directed Melissa to prepare a monthly announcement booklet in an effort to reduce the contents of the weekly bulletin. She did an outstanding job. A few months later, the members of the church although informed of the use of the monthly announcement booklet, complained about scheduled events not being in the weekly bulletin. With the increased cost of preparing the announcement booklet and complaints by some of the members, I returned to the old format of weekly announcements. Moreover, the worship leaders gave a summary of the announcements before the Praise and Prayer Service. Melissa continues to do an outstanding job in preparing our bulletins and special occasion bulletins.

In preparation for the coming Sunday, choir rehearsals take place on Wednesdays and Saturday mornings. At one point, we had the benefit of five choirs that each served a Sunday: Sanctuary first and second, Chancel, third, Youth, fourth and Men fifth but now Sanctuary first, Unity with Men, Second, Chancel, third, and Men, fourth and fifth. Larry Fletcher served as pianist on the first and third Sundays while Karleen Powell, a music educator with Prince George's County Public Schools, served the second and fourth Sundays. Larry served as pianist on the fifth Sunday with the men.

The Youth Choir consisted of eight boys and two girls under the guidance of Mrs. Powell. In the beginning the children were growing in terms of singing out and some doing solos. The youngsters bonded with Mrs. Powell, in fact one boy's behavior improved in public school because "Ms. Karleen" developed rapport with him. But conflicting issues crept into the situation. Organized sports with the youth football league in Charles County, Maryland hindered some of the boys from coming to rehearsals on Saturdays. To further exacerbate the problem, some of the youngsters went to stay with their other parents on the weekends. Rehearsals were changed to Friday evenings, but this did not work. Sometimes there were only two children at rehearsals. Meetings with the parents took place in which one parent said her child felt Mrs. Powell was to too hard (firm). In spite of the negativity that was present in one meeting, the parents agreed to have their children come to rehearsal. The choir dwindled down to four boys. This discouraged "Ms. Karleen," as the children called her. I convinced her to stay on for a couple of months, but in June 2014 we gave her time off to reflect on her future with us.

The Sanctuary choir was also experiencing problems. Mrs. Powell may have been viewed by some of the choir members as being too dogmatic in her teaching style. There was an up-tick in tension with the choir. As a result, some push-back came from some of the members. Mrs. Powell concluded that she could no longer work with the Sanctuary Choir; although I tried to persuade her to remain, she reneged. In retrospect I see Mrs. Powell's gifts are not only as pianist and organist but as a choir directress.

We have done some reshuffling of the choirs. The church was blessed to secure another gifted musician to fill the vacancy left by Mrs. Powell. Dr. Ray Petty, writer, composer, and musician, agreed to contract with us and serve for the first and third Sundays. He brings with him great people and teaching skills and a level of spirituality in his music that is infectious and readily brings worshipers to their feet. Both choirs enjoy him and after service, choir members linger around him in the choir loft.

Larry Fletcher serves the Sanctuary Choir on the second Sunday and the Intergenerational Male Choir on the fourth Sunday. Larry, from a charismatic tradition, certainly helps the preacher during the climax of the sermon by spontaneously playing on the keyboard and/or piano. Young males serve with the men on this choir. I contend that the men set an example for the youngsters as to what it is to be a Christian man. In one case, there was the father, son, and grandson singing together on the choir. We are still trying to perfect the male choir.

Robert Wayne Gass, drummer, is like a son to my wife and me. He has accompanied me over the years to several churches: Ebenezer and Metropolitan UMCs. With his tenor voice, he does a musical meditation for me prior to the sermon. He plays for the church on the third and fourth Sundays and occasionally during special services.

Each Sunday morning after having prayer with the choir and musician, I return to my office with the adjacent door to the choir loft open. The choir enthusiastically ushers in the praise time. I hear members that are given opportunity during the praise and prayer service to express their thanksgiving to God and share joys, concerns, and make petitions. This is a very significant moment in the life of the household of God. Members without hesitation will disclose circumstances that are occurring in their lives, sometimes given very tearfully with a request for prayer. This confessional, petitionary, and testimonial time is not only emotionally cathartic but spiritually renewing for the member. With tears shed and burdens lifted, a feeling of renewal comes over the individual. This is done in an atmosphere of openness with the church family that is empathetic and in some cases has experienced similar circumstances and conditions. At times, it is my impression that the assembled church family is serving in a corporate surrogate priestly function during the praise and prayer moment. As it may be, I am cognizant of the issues prevailing in the life of the household of God and can prepare myself to address their concerns appropriately during altar call.

The transition from the praise and prayer service is signaled by the leader of the service. The worship leader speaks words of thanks to the participants subsequent to which the acolyte/usher will come forth to light the candles on the altar table. The worship leader guides the congregation through the order of worship to the point in the service when Rachel Johnson, our lead Christian Educator, leads the youths into the fellowship hall for the Sunday Morning Learning Session; visiting youngsters are invited, too. (High school students can remain with adults in the sanctuary.) Periodically, lay persons read the Scriptures for the morning. The fourth Sunday is designated as Casual Dress and Youth Sunday. The young people are responsible for the worship service; they do a very fine job.

I am primarily a lectionary preacher, but on occasions will do a series of sermons such as the "Drama in Jerusalem, Acts 1, 2, and 3." The sermons focused on the events leading up to our Lord's crucifixion and resurrection. Each sermon closed as if all persons were witnessing a three-act play.

My delivery can be described as traditional African American with an expectation of talk-back, but also I want the listeners to learn something new each time as I proclaim the Gospel of our Lord Jesus Christ. Most of all, I hope that my message will help in the transformation of their lives for the better. I learned many years ago in seminary the acronym: P.R.E.A.C.H.(P-preach;Each-to each person under the hearing of your voice) We proclaim the message of God to reach each individual. That is my mission each time I preach the Gospel of Jesus Christ. After the sermon, I give the invitation or as some express, "The door of the church is open." Some who have not been active return and reaffirm their faith. With individuals who are not members, we invite them to come and be a part of the new members' class and upon completion of the new members' class are read in as full members.

Communion Sunday services tend to be longer. After the morning sermon, the worship leader assists me during the communion service, based upon Table II of the United Methodist Hymnal. My wife serves with the communion stewards, Leslie Taylor and alternates Iretha Erwin and Nancy Burroughs. (Anecdote: Lila prepares the communion paraments and chancel skirt on Friday afternoons before the first Sunday.) It is our practice to honor those with birthdays during the month to come to receive the elements first, followed by the rest of the worshipers. I, along with the communion stewards, go to those in the pews who are unable to come forth and the musician. Lastly, the communion stewards, worship leader, and the pastor receive the elements before concluding the service. The ladies strip the furniture in the pulpit area and take the communion elements to the kitchen where they prepare my visitation kit.

For the sacrament of Baptism, the lay leader, membership secretary, and communion steward join with me and the family as we go through the service of Holy Baptism as printed in the bulletin. This is always a very special occasion in the life of the household of God. It is my practice to coach the family of those who cannot answer for themselves, namely infants and young children. Once the baptism is finished, the information is entered in the membership book. Family and friends gather for the picture taking. It is always amazing to see the number of family members who turn out on these special occasions.

Confirmation classes start in January in anticipation of having confirmation on Easter Sunday or no later than the second Sunday of June. I use denominational resources. Each confirmand, upon completion of the training, is encouraged to be in conversation with their parents about becoming a full member or delaying until a more appropriate time for them. Confirmation Sunday typically is a well-attended worship service. Parents, whether married or divorced, have attended that service after which there is a gathering in the fellowship hall for refreshments. The youngsters are quite excited about their accomplishment and the mementos given to them.

The funeral service is a unique entity unto itself. It is a time of grief and celebration. Because of our relatively small sanctuary, most funeral services are conducted at Metropolitan United Methodist Church or at Thornton's Funeral Chapel, Indian Head, Maryland. Quite similar to the response given by members of Metropolitan UMC that I alluded to early on in this work, it is a community event in which there is sadness and laughter, especially recalling certain idiosyncrasies of the decedent and things that happened in his or her life. Participating members play certain roles from singing on the choir, ushering, reading resolutions and selected sympathy cards, to serving with the hospitality committee. All takes place in this mixed atmosphere of sorrow and celebration.

Some deaths trigger conflict with the church's polity. When persons who were previously members of the church years ago and have joined other churches, their family expects their deceased loved one to be interred in Smith Chapel's cemetery. In the family's mind, their loved one has the same rights and privileges of those who have remained in active fellowship. There are certain situations in which the pastor along with the lay leader and chair of the Board of Trustees can make exceptions. There was a recent situation in which we extended grace to a certain family.

An inactive member unbeknownst to me died in a tragic house fire in the community. The church responded by giving a generous special offering to the family in order for them to meet the required funeral expenses. The family wanted their loved one buried in the cemetery where the decedent's husband was interred. Upon reviewing the situation, we granted the family's wish. The following year, another member of the same family who moved from the community during the 1990s and had not returned to the church wanted the same privilege. We declined to give that courtesy, but I did offer to do her funeral. Needless to say, the family did not want my services.

There is an erroneous belief operating in the church and the community that if the family member leaves Smith Chapel and joins another church, the same rights and privileges apply to them. Some of their families will pay "church dues" on behalf of their absent family members. I dare say there is a theology of membership in absentia in the small rural church: the reason one maintains his or her membership is to be certain that when one dies, they have a burial place in the church's cemetery. Even those that have become dechurched and have not responded to invitations to reaffirm their membership vows, the families expect the church to extend compensatory justice [34] on behalf of the deceased, so they can be buried in the church cemetery regardless of the limited space. I argue that those that have remained in membership and did their fair share should also be treated justly; to me, it is a matter of justice. I have cynically said, "Being buried in the cemetery out there could be a trap-door to hell!" Tribal blood is greater than the waters of baptism; oh well enough of this.

I have conducted several weddings while serving Smith Chapel. After premarital coaching, I have conducted the wedding ceremonies off campus such as at a golf clubhouse and a mansion set aside for weddings and retreats. I initiate a followup with them six months after the wedding to see how they are coming along. Periodically, one couple comes to worship services while the other couple has had their first child and is getting adjusted to being new parents. I look forward to the other couple attending on a regular basis with their new child.

Special worship services such as Homecoming; Annual Trustee Day; and Friends, Relatives, and Neighbors Day (FRANS) are occasions for the church to have guests visit, celebrate, and worship with us. An invited preacher typically brings members of his or her congregation who support them. It is also an opportunity for the guest congregation to have their choir to minister to the host church. It is not uncommon for these worship services to be quite spirit-filled and reviving to all.

I invited members of my fraternity, Phi Beta Sigma Inc., Zeta Chi Sigma Chapter, to visit our church in November 2013. After the worship service, the members of the fraternity met with our young boys of middle- and high-school age, to encourage them in their studies and to pursue higher education or technical training but most of all keep out of trouble. It was a very positive experience for the youngsters to meet with college-educated men who were successful in their professional careers. George, one of our youngsters who was interested in engineering, was introduced to Bro. Solomon Isaac, an engineer. As of this writing, George is matriculating at Morgan State University and enrolled in the engineering program.

I have found during my ministry that special worship services are vital in the life of the church, especially in the worship ministry of Smith Chapel UMC.

Hospitality Ministry

Another aspect of the nurturing ministry is hospitality. Ms. Dorothy Mason and her two daughters, Gail and Phyllis, are faithful servants in the area of hospitality. "I love being in hospitality" was a comment Phyllis made to me one Sunday after church. All members of the hospitality team are very personable and eager to serve those assembled in the fellowship hall. I can always depend upon Iretha providing me with bananas and/or orange juice, especially since I am diabetic. Later, she has a cup of coffee for me. After special services, the hospitality team makes certain we have a little extra to take with us when we leave church. The same holds true for some of our shut-ins, such as Ms. Clara Washington. Her great-granddaughter Brenda will take her something home.

The hospitality team made a special impression upon the guests who stayed with Smith Chapel during Safe Nights last fall. Each night members brought in hot food along with various kinds of desserts. The guests expressed deep appreciation to the team and told us that we were the only church who provided hot meals each night and not cold sandwiches and soup.

Each time I see the members gathered in the fellowship hall and "breaking bread" together I am continually reminded of the family reunion motif with overtones of the Eucharistic meal. Senior members, such as Ms. Norena Toyer, are served while seated at the table while others go through the buffet line set near the kitchen entrance. Conversations with laughter and reminisces of bygone years pervade the air. Various members are called for one reason or another by their nicknames. While all are eating, members of the finance committee come into the fellowship hall to get their plates of food and sit with their families. Someone in the course of talking will say, "Remember what the Reverend said this morning!" It is a family reunion time.

Another aspect of the Hospitality Ministry, as I view it, is the cleanliness of our church but especially the restrooms. I recall during my days as a regional guide that some of the restrooms of the various churches that were visited were in very unsatisfactory conditions, if not unsanitary. I made a mental note that I would not want to revisit that particular church. With this in mind, I urged the church trustees to make certain that the restrooms were clean. In fact in February 2015, the restrooms of Smith Chapel were renovated to have a more commodious and hospitable appearance and sanitary setting.

Christian Education Ministry

When I began serving as pastor in May 2011, the Sunday school had only one child, Olivia. From the pulpit I expressed that I wanted to have some noise in here, meaning I wanted children in the church and participating in Sunday school. By September 2011 some children were coming out as their parents returned to worship service. I changed the name from Sunday school to Sunday Morning Learning Session for both adults and young people. We began to grow.

I took responsibility for teaching the adult class while Rachel, Vera, and Brenda cared for the elementary and middle-school youngsters. My prayer for having noise in the fellowship hall was answered; moreover, Vera who taught the middle school students took over my office, using it for a classroom. At one point, we had as many as twenty-five in attendance for the Sunday Morning Learning Session. When I began confirmation study in January 2012, I turned the adult class over to my wife. She did such a great job that the members of the class wanted her to continue, and she continues to be the adult teacher as of this writing.

Rachel Johnson, Christian education coordinator, uses United Methodist materials year-around, Vacation Bible School included. She uses her creativity to get the children involved in Christmas/ Easter plays. We set aside the Sunday before Christmas for the Christmas play; the children learn their parts and do not need to read scripts during the actual performances. Again the audience is filled with parents, relatives, and friends in support of the youngsters. Presently, the format changed this year, 2015. Youngsters transition from the main worship service to gather in the fellowship hall or around the table in the kitchen for instructions. The effect of this has impacted the adult class; some of the parents come only to the main worship because they know that the children will transition from the main service just before the reading of the Scripture lessons. (We will evaluate this at the planning retreat.) Overall, this area of Christian Education is working satisfactorily.

Bible study is very integral to one's growth and spiritual development. Initially, I conducted Bible study on Thursday evenings. In the beginning, ten to twelve persons would start in September, but by November or December, half of the number would be in attendance. One of the reasons was that Smith Chapel is located in the country, and it was a challenge for some to drive on Poorhouse Road at night. In fact while on his way home, Roland Chase hit a deer that severely damaged his car and killed the animal. Moreover, there were concerns about inclement weather. Bible study attendance was low during the winter.

The purchase of study materials became costly and on occasions the said materials were placed on back orders. Each became a contributory factor to cause a change to our Bible study routine. Each Monday evening, several of us participated in teleconference intercessory prayer service led by Perry Taylor. In the midst of speaking with Perry, I had a pop-up idea: conduct Bible study as we did the intercessory prayer service. Perry saw no problem with it. We began our teleconference Bible study and developed teleconference protocols for the participants to follow. Each member received an outline for the scheduled study and assignments. When on line, other participants put their telephones on mute to reduce the interference. Since using this system, we completed the three Gospels and Acts of the Apostles. In September 2015, we began studying the Gospel of John with the expectation of completing the study in January 2016.

The value of the teleconference method proved quite beneficial to us as a congregation earlier this year when we had two weekends of snow in February and March. On each occasion, the order of worship was modified, and I preached my sermons from my home office! Surprisingly, on each Sunday, there were thirty-eight persons on line and several from other congregations. The teleconference tool proved to be very valuable for our ministry situated in a rural setting.

Membership Care

I continue to hear the echo of the late Rev. Louis D. Conway who served with me at St. Mark's UMC, Laurel, Maryland. Rev. Conway said, "I rather be a good pastor than a great preacher." My sentiments are the same. Caring for the sheep is what a shepherd does. I recall an occasion at St. Mark's when one Sunday there was a noticeable absence of members. The following week I sent "We Miss You" cards to each of the persons who were not in worship service. To my surprise on the next Sunday, there was a significant increase, particularly from the previously missing members. Later my wife told me, attendees were laughing at one another and saying, "Did you get a card from the Reverend?" The members knew I was concerned about them and their whereabouts.

Members want to know that their pastor cares about them. A visit or telephone call helps to reassure that the pastor cares. I also learned to listen for the subtle hints from congregants, such as "How is (So and So) doing? I understand they went to the hospital." If the information was not given to me, I try to follow up as soon as I can.

I do visitations of sick and shut-in members on a regular basis. The shut-ins and sick are affirmed and encouraged that the church and the pastor still cares about their well-being and importance in the life of the church. I often hear the expressions of thanks from the homebound and hospitalized members, especially when bringing them the sacraments and updates on church activities by way of the bulletin. There are members of the congregation, on the other hand, who are very private and do not want their circumstance known. I respect their feelings about such. And there are those that want only the pastor to be aware of their circumstance, and I treat it in the manner they desire.

Membership care is reflected in supporting members during special times of their lives. Certain members retired from their jobs, and my wife and I went to support them during those significant milestones in their lives. When the time of appreciation was made, the person publicly thanked the pastor and his wife for coming to their event. Attending school programs is another avenue of membership care. What a joy it is to see Olivia perform in a play as one of the main characters or see Rachel play in the school band and orchestra. Each youngster demonstrated her gifts and talents in the presence of proud parents, relatives, friends, and other supporters, such as the pastor. I rejoiced with the families during the events. This also is an example of membership care.

There is much wisdom in the words of the late Rev. Louis D. Conway which guides me in my ministry to the sick and shut-in members: "I'd rather be a good pastor than a great preacher."

Outreach

Smith Chapel conducts several outreach ministries that engage the members of the congregation. The nursing home ministry, initiated by Rev. Kermit C. C. Moore, continues to be a joint ministry of Alexandria Chapel and Smith Chapel. The first Saturday of each month, volunteers from both congregations assemble at Sagepoint Nursing facility where a worship service is conducted from 1:30 p.m. to 2:30 p.m. I alluded to this ministry under Alexandria Chapel's ministry. I was the inspirational speaker for the nursing home ministry during the early part of 2015; it was very rewarding to serve in that capacity.

Vera Littlejohn serves as coordinator for the ministry to the residents of the Robert Fuller Transition House in Waldorf, Maryland, the second Tuesday of each month. She often speaks about the words of appreciation that come from the residents with whom she has conversation. Our church can be depended upon to be on time and have nutritional and delicious meals for the residents.

Another of Smith Chapel's outreach ministries is participation in the Safe Nights program sponsored by Lifestyle of Maryland. We are into our third year as a host church that welcomes homeless persons (guests). The same caterer will donate breakfast and lunch for our guests who will be staying at the church in October 2015. Ms. Dorothy and members of the hospitality team will serve our guests as was done in the past two years. Last year, we were told Smith Chapel was the only church that provided hot meals nightly. I make certain to be present and have meals with our guests each night. As a congregation, we are thankful for the opportunity to participate in such a meaningful ministry and fulfill the mandates expressed in Matthew 25:31–46, The Final Judgment of the Nations pericope.

I initiated the Local Establishment Ministry (LEM) for the purpose of visiting local bars, taverns, and carry-outs to advertise our ministries and invite persons to come our Saturday Evening Worship (SEW) service and/or Sunday morning worship services. The first of each month, Pastor Moore, Jennifer Dorsey, Gail Robertson, and I decide which businesses to take our invitational materials and give any further information to prospective visitors. We became quite familiar to the proprietors of the businesses in the community. After nearly a year, it was clear that our approach of using the attractional model to come to our churches did not work. Slowly, the effort petered out and we discontinued what was called, "The Bar" ministry. I will try the ministry again with the exception of only putting out materials such as the *Upper Room* and/or *The Daily Bread*; hopefully someone will get what they need for the moment of their need or interest.

A byproduct of the LEM ministry was some of the inactive members began to attend the SEW service. Slowly, the inactive members who visited on Saturday evenings began showing up on Sunday mornings. Eventually, we were able to reaffirm the membership vows of the inactive members as they began worshiping on Sunday mornings, seven persons in all.

The new and developing ministry with Smith Chapel is the Kairos Ministry, prison ministry. Sis Jocelyn Richardson is an excited member who volunteers for Kairos Ministry. She took training with Kairos Ministry and is deeply involved in this prison ministry; Audrey Chase was newly enrolled in this said ministry and looks for to become meaningfully involved with the said prison ministry along with Jocelyn Richardson in April 2015. Both members participated in a weekend event with the women who are incarcerated and came back highly motivated to enlist others in the ministry to women prisoners. Both Jocelyn and Audrey are seeking more volunteers to participate in the Kairos prison ministry. As adjunct to the prison ministry, the United Methodist Women participate in the Christmas Connection that attempts to meet the needs of youngsters whose parents are incarcerated during the Christmas season. I praise them for this effort.

The Macedonia Baptist Church of Bryans Road, Maryland, coordinated the Community Feast the weekend before Thanksgiving. In an ecumenical collaborative effort, fifteen or more members of Smith Chapel joined in with other communities of faith to participate in the two-shift serving of seniors and marginalized individuals in Bryans Road, Maryland. Members of our hospitality team served in various capacities with the ecumenical group.

In light of the scope of outreach ministry by the members of Smith Chapel, I am convinced that we are very vital in terms of ministry and missions beyond the wall of this local church and our particular context, a rural community.

Witness Ministry

I reiterate our connection with the Route 210 Corridor of Churches. Smith Chapel along with Alexandria Chapel as a cooperative parish participated in the series of Lenten services in the years 2012 and 2013. In subsequent years, the churches participated in the Lenten services as individual churches with the obligations to provide for the order of worship service on the scheduled Wednesday night. On the occasions that our church served as the host church, the offering received was donated to Lifestyles and the Robert Fuller Transition. Other congregations periodically refer to us as a cooperative parish; however, without hesitation members from Smith Chapel and/or Alexandria Chapel will quickly correct members of other churches that we are station churches. (The blood of tribalism is deeper that the waters of baptism.)

We as United Methodist congregations are connected. I noticed over the years that where there was an African American United Methodist Church, within a radius of one and one half miles there was a white United Methodist Church. Within the Washington East District in St. Leonard, Maryland, Brooks and Waters Memorial United Methodist Churches are within sight of each other, perhaps the length of a football field. In Washington, DC, Ebenezer and Capitol Hill United Methodist churches are just around the corner from one another, one on the southwest corner and the other on the northeast corner of the block. The appearance is that the churches are contented as they are.

In February 2014, we were unable to use the church building because of the renovation of the men and women's restrooms. Pisgah United Methodist Church, a little over a mile away from us and predominantly Caucasian, invited us to join with them in joint services while renovation was in process at Smith Chapel. The first Sunday I preached the morning message, and the following Sunday Pastor Parr gave the message. I found the experience very good for both congregations. I am reminded: "How very good and pleasant it is when kindred live together in unity!" (Psalm 133:1 NRSV) I took the opportunity after our joint worship services to get an impression of Pisgah's members about Smith Chapel UMC. One senior member of Pisgah UMC commented: "This little country church, known as Smith Chapel has been located in the bend of the road for all of my seventy-plus years . . . continues to be an inspiration to surrounding neighborhood . . ."[36]. Another member of Pisgah UMC said: " . . . A very hospitable and welcoming group of parishioners . . . passionate about their faith and love for the Lord . . ." The member continued, " . . . conduct joint Vacation Bible School . . . host Easter Sunrise service . . ."[37]. In an undated interview form, the interviewee wrote: "They are more traditional more lively songs to enhance worship . . . I'd like to do more with Smith Chapel . . ."[38]. The pastor echoes the sentiments of her members; she says, " . . . small African American traditional church . . . deep in the Word of

God . . . involved in homeless and incarcerated . . . fired up for the Lord."[39]. The pastor welcomes more connectional ministry activities between the two congregations.

Pisgah and Smith Chapel UMCs have Thanksgiving Eve and Christmas Eve Candlelight services that alternate between the two churches. Each year since November 2013, we have had joint services, and the attendance appears to be increasing, especially on Christmas Eve. These services witness to and emphasize our connectional relationship. The overall experience with Pisgah was very encouraging with potential for more connectional activities.

I do visitations of sick and shut-in members on a regular basis. The shut-ins and sick are affirmed and encouraged that the church and the pastor still cares about their well-being and importance in the life of the church. I often hear the expressions of thanks from the homebound and hospitalized members, especially when bringing them the sacraments and update on church activities by way of the bulletin.

Pertinent to men and women's ministries, the United Methodist Men (UMM) of Smith Chapel have their own charter. Meetings for the UMM take place on the last Saturday of each month after Men's Choir rehearsal. The men have joined in with the UMM of Pisgah during Advent when they visit the local nursing homes and sing together for the residents. The United Methodist Women (UMW) is a Gold Star unit that has an ongoing series of ministries during the year. The UMW meets the second Sunday after service and follows the agenda as prescribed. Significantly, the fifteen women participate in the nursing home ministry in conjunction with members from Alexandria Chapel. Thanksgiving baskets are assembled by the ladies and distributed to needy families. At Christmas time, the unit makes contributions to the Christmas Connection and prison ministries.

The youth of the church participate in the annual ROCK gathering in Ocean City, Maryland during a weekend either the last week of January or first or second weekend in February. Usually there are thousands of youths from the Baltimore-Washington Annual Conference that attend the event at the Ocean City Convention Center. It is a time of growing closer to Jesus Christ, introspection, small groups, and fun time for kids. It is the hope of the event to have attendees strengthened in their faith and share the love of Christ Jesus, our Lord. Our youth return energized and anxious to give their presentations to the church. The youngsters of Smith Chapel conduct fundraisers throughout the year to defray the cost for the trip to Ocean City, Maryland.

There are some memorable moments at ROCK. I enjoy the energy the kids bring to the event. It appears to be an endless sea of youngsters from all over the Baltimore-Washington Conference and some non-Methodist groups. There was an incident that Almalita and Gail periodically remind me of and get the greatest chuckle out of it. We just finished our Friday evening session and were preparing to go back to the hotel while our youngsters were really energized. One youngster, Kai Vaughn, was sliding down the center stairs handrail from the first landing to the main floor. Almalita told him to stop. Once again, to take a final slide, he went to the first landing and started again sliding down the handrail. As he was completing his slide, I turned to stop him as he came off the rail.

He had a lot of momentum; I intended to chastise him, but he unintentionally stepped on my right toe that was already suffering from gout. The pain I already had plus with his stepping on my toe was too much. I grimaced in my face, grabbed his right shoulder and through my teeth I snarled, "Kai—you almost made the preacher cuss!" What pain! The kid was startled. I went limping away toward the van. He was quite for the rest of the evening. The next morning when I saw him at breakfast, I told Kai, "Give me a fist bump." (This signaled we were okay with one another.) He did. Needless to say, when he is in my vicinity, Kai is very watchful as to where he walks.

Another aspect of the Witness Ministry is Smith Chapel's participation with the Ministers' Alliance of Charles County and vicinity, "the Alliance." The said ministerial organization was established forty or more years ago and is primarily Baptist, but now is quite representative of the various communities of faith in the African American community. "In small cities, towns, and rural areas there usually is one black ministerial alliance that includes all black clergy, regardless of denomination." comments C. Eric Lincoln.[40] The mission of the organization was to provide an opportunity for collegiality while addressing social justice issues in the community while not proselytizing for a certain community of faith. There was an attempt to make it a diverse group of clergy, but in my opinion that has not been successful.

I, as the pastor of Smith Chapel UMC, participated with the Alliance in various community events. The National Day of prayer in May of each year is a local news item. On the second Saturday of September, the Alliance sponsors the Annual Ministers Prayer Breakfast that is conducted at Metropolitan UMC. In September 2014, several of us of the Alliance organized a fall encounter that focused upon the role of the African American minister in collaboration with other community groups and social justice organizations to address the matter of the police shootings of men of color, such as in Ferguson, Missouri. It was a noble attempt but nothing significant materialized after the three-night encounter. We all agreed that something must be done and returned to our churches, status quo. Receiving and distributing turkeys to marginalized families during Thanksgiving is another ministry of the Alliance. We look forward to ongoing progress as the Alliance moves ahead to address the spiritual and social needs for the improvement of our community.

It is interesting to observe that some of the newer African Americans pastors in Charles County, Maryland, do not necessarily feel a sense of obligation to affiliate with the Alliance. Some visit with our organization, give impressive comments, and are not seen again. Perhaps there is a feeling of the lack of relevance of the ministers' alliance. Nevertheless, Rev. Reginald Kearney, president of the Alliance, continues faithfully to carry out his duties and responsibilities of the organization as did the former presidents: Rev. Frederick Lancaster, Elder Willie Hunt, and Bishop James Briscoe. Rev. Kearney is to be commended for his faithful leadership and service to the organization.

The Matter of Expansion

Smith Chapel, built in 1902, consists of timber framing on the exterior and drywall interior. Several additions have been constructed; a brick façade was installed and handicapped entrance ramps were added[41] Soon after my arrival as interim pastor in May 2011, I was made aware of the physical condition of the building that suffered some termite infestation, and that had been addressed. In addition, the most significant renovation occurred during the pastorate of the late Rev. Dr. Shirlimarie McAroy-Gray. The majority of other repairs were made as the need arose.

The increased activity with Christian education ministry caused the Board of Trustees and I to investigate the possibility of purchasing modular units that could serve as a multipurpose facility for use by the church and community. One company gave us a presentation on several scenarios and the cost of the units. For our needs and the available space, two units that totaled forty by eighty feet would work perfectly for our needs. But first we would need to meet disciplinary requirements and county and health codes before such could be undertaken. Moreover, we needed the funds to pay for the project.

An expansion committee was formed in the spring of 2012 with co-chairpersons Helen White and Carolyn Washington to serve in leadership for the expansion of the facility. A presentation was given by the co-chairs to the church; emphasis was placed upon the need for the multipurpose center modular units. Members were encouraged to give more to the renovation fund. The congregation enthusiastically gave to the renovation fund. By December 2012, we accrued $51,000 in the renovation fund. However, in February of 2013, we were confronted with an emergency situation: the need to replace the termite infested floors of the restrooms adjacent to the narthex. The emergency situation was addressed at the Church Council meeting with the decision made to divide the funds in half and establish a building fund, solely for the purpose of building an annex or a new church building. Subsequently in February for two Sundays, we were in joint worship with Pisgah UMC. The experience of joint worship was very good, but we were glad to return to Smith Chapel.

The church secured in July 2015 the services of Arro Consulting, Inc., Hagerstown, Maryland, a structural engineering firm. A structural engineer from Arro Consulting, Inc. conducted an evaluation of our building; a report was submitted to the Board of Trustees and the pastor. The detailed report confirmed what we suspected, and in addition several recommendations were offered, along with estimates of repairs and a recommendation to build a new building. The cost for minimal repairs would be in excess of $200,000.

The foundation beams, rotting due to moisture, along with the reoccurrence of termite infestation, created a very serious safety issue. The cost of repairing far outweighed the cost for building a new worship facility. On Sunday, September 20, I delivered the sermon: "What is Our Decision?" based upon selected passages of scripture from Nehemiah: 2:17–20; 4:1–6; 6:15–19; and Matthew 7:24–29. At the conclusion of my sermon, the Board of Trustees gave a video presentation of the structural engineer's report along with pictures taken by Trustee Luther Robertson that showed the serious damage to the foundation of the 113-year-old worship facility. Some of the members were stunned at the condition of the church. I made it very clear that no official action was being taken at this time, but very soon we would have to make some decision on what to do with the building. On the way home from church that afternoon, I recapitulated two or three times the situation, as if my wife and mother-in-law were not present during the service.

God works in mysterious ways and has a sense of humor, I believe. Later on Sunday afternoon, I attended the Omega Service funeral services of a long-time fraternity brother that the members of Zeta Chi Sigma Chapter performed. Our deceased brother's pastor, Reverend Darin Poullard of Fort Washington Baptist Church, Fort Washington, Maryland, preached the eulogy entitled: "Make up Your Own Mind" based upon the scripture text Revelation

3:14–22. I felt the Holy Spirit speaking directly to me to take the leadership role in guiding this congregation through the process of building a new edifice. The expansion team will need to reactivate. Questions would be raised as to how to fund the new endeavor. The Book of Discipline of the United Methodist Church, Paragraph 2544 stipulates what must be done when a congregation elects to enter into a building program. We would follow the guidelines as presented in the Book of Discipline, 2012.

In preparation for our annual charge conference in late October 2015, the leadership of the church represented the sentiments of the congregation in terms of entering into a building program.

Closing Thoughts on Smith Chapel

My initial impression of Smith Chapel was the church was part of a two-point charge in a rural setting, situated in a relatively remote location in Pisgah. Some of the members I knew previously through contacts with the former pastor, the late Reverend Dr. Shirlimarie McAroy-Gray and the series of Lenten services. I was aware when asked to serve as a DS hire that the church was in a conflictive situation with its sister congregation, Alexandria Chapel UMC. In light of my previous experience with a cooperative parish, I prayed about the method or praxis of ministry that would be most suitable for the two congregations. With Pastor Moore as my associate minister, we would be able to initiate a transition from a charge to a cooperative parish and subsequently to station churches. The general feeling, as of this writing, that is both congregations enjoy the status of being station churches, but Alexandria Chapel also feels the financial pinch of supporting a less than full-time pastor. It costs to be free.

Smith Chapel is very optimistic about providing a worship center for its future generation and community alike. The members are adjusting to the fact there will be many more families moving into Pisgah, and we as the church need to be ready for them. The insularity still persists; in time that will mellow to some degree but will not totally eradicate. I have bonded with the members of Smith Chapel. Rev. Dr. Alfonso J. Harrod says, "You have to love the people . . . pastor . . . and they will respond." This is what I have done in each of the churches that I have served, and indeed they have responded back in the affirmative.

Chapter 9

In Retrospect

I write this book in the spirit of Qohelet (Ecclesiastes) and not as an academic treatise. I reflect on experiences I had in local churches in various contexts for example: urban, town, suburban, and rural. The work is not written as a chronology but rather as selective experiences that happened over my twenty-nine years as an active ordained clergy. I hope that my lessons learned and/or recommendations to new clergy will be of benefit.

My journey did not begin at St. Mark's UMC, Laurel, Maryland, but on a cool crisp Friday evening in October, 1975. Having survived what could have been a fatal car accident a week before and my mother's tearful plea that I get right with the Lord, I went searching for a prayer meeting. By God's grace, the late John G. McNair, trustee of Macedonia Baptist Church, Baltimore City, came out to stand at the entrance of the lower auditorium where the choir was rehearsing. I asked him whether there was a prayer meeting being conducted. He said, "Yes, come on in and go to the left in the Ladies

Lounge." This man had never seen me before, but he extended what we call "radical hospitality" despite the fact that I could have been up to something devious and criminal. He welcomed me into the church.

The prayer meeting was attended by members I shall never forget: Deacons Walter Dickens, James Ford, and Clarence White; Rosie Holly, Arlene White, Deaconess Earlene Ford, Nellie Watts, Denise Tyler, Phyllis Rheubottom, and John G. McNair. On occasions, Deacon Jesse Sample and his wife Deaconess Deloris Sample were in attendance. Later during the prayer service, the late Dr. Willard Clayton joined the gathering. At a pause during the praying and singing, Deacon White asked my name; I told him, "George De Ford," and with excitement and a sense of relief, he said, "I know your father. We work together at Western Electric! What a small world!" (I guess they all were relieved in that they felt that I did not come to do them harm.) From that point on every Friday evening, I would be in attendance at the prayer meeting.

I am a strong believer in the power of prayer. Wherever I was appointed, I organized or continued to encourage prayer gatherings whether on Wednesday evenings, Friday afternoons, Sunday mornings, or teleconference prayer meetings at 7 p.m. The need for prayer is what brought me to our Lord and Savior Jesus Christ. Looking back, it was God's prevenient grace operating during a very difficult time of my life, but my circumstances changed for the best during the latter part of the 1970s.

On April 26, 1976 at 7 a.m., I was certain of the presence of the Lord in my life; I experienced God's justifying grace in my life. In September 1976, I enrolled in seminary at Howard University School of Divinity. Although my first marriage ended in divorce in the spring 1977, I resolved to remain in my son's life and be a responsible father to the best of my ability. In June 1977, I was licensed to preach, became a member of the pulpit staff, and served as assistant to the pastor. In June 1978, I met the love of my life, Lila A. Harris, on a humid, hazy Friday evening in Washington, DC. I was smitten at first sight; she wore a light baby-blue summer dress and matching shoes, with a modest amount of make-up, small earrings, and sunglasses on her forehead. We married on January 13, 1979. God is the God of the second chance.

After prayerful reflection, I felt led to the United Methodist Church and in June 1980 would join Ebenezer UMC, Washington, DC. In February 1982, I successfully completed the Deacon's Examination Retreat, New Windsor, Maryland, and was ordained Deacon on June 15, 1982 by Bishop David Frederick Wertz at the National Cathedral, Washington, DC, and appointed to St. Mark's UMC, Laurel, Maryland. I learned some important lessons while serving St. Mark's UMC:

- Learn as quickly as possible who are the key people and supporters.

- Listen with your second ear because you can pick up what is happening in the community and interpersonal relationships within the congregation.
- Do not voice your criticism or become judgmental of anyone because you could possibly be referring to a family member. Keep in mind the principles of Matthew 7:1–5 and James 3:1–12.
- Make certain that you give honor to matriarchs and patriarchs of the congregation.
- Learn the nicknames of persons and use them with only their permission.
- Be open to advice from seasoned, retired pastor(s) within the congregation and allow them to participate and/or play a role in the ministry of the church, but be certain to maintain parameters.
- Expect the parking lot committee (PLC) to meet after Church Council meetings.
- Take your Sabbath time with family and/or friends while engaging in recreational activities.
- Make certain the church does not become the "mistress" or paramour in your family life.
- Keep a keen eye open for those that are missing from worship service and follow-up with them.
- Maintain your professional integrity by observing rules concerning boundaries in your ministry.

- Be aware of community or school special events, and show enthusiastic support for youngsters in your congregation.
- Be aware of community needs and do not hesitate to initiate social action. (Do not encroach upon the responsibilities of law enforcement agencies.)
- Maintain personal Bible study, prayer time, and journal.

Ministry in the urban setting is slightly different than in the suburban or town context. There is less of the relational element. For the most part, members do not come from the immediate community and can have less of a vested interest in the various issues affecting that said community.

I learned some important lessons while serving the urban churches in two cities:

- Maintaining the physical plant is a priority, especially old buildings with slate roofs
- Protecting the physical plant from vandalism and thefts, particularly copper drainage and guttering systems and air conditioning equipment
- Being in compliance with the guidelines of the Americans with Disabilities Act
- Allowing funeral directors to care for the physical aspects of the funeral service

- Caring for some of the needs for homeless and marginalized persons
- Making available space for community groups and/or self-help groups
- Employing nonmembers as administrative staff persons and not limiting employment opportunities to members only
- Adjusting to new demographics in the community
- Practicing radical hospitality
- Provide meaningful Christian education experiences
- Keeping the traditions of the United Methodist Church, (Some of our pastors tend to dis-associate themselves from the UMC and influence some of their congregants to do the same and eventually leaving the denomination. I am a United Methodist because I choose to be and not a hireling that comes into the denomination to lead the sheep astray for personal aggrandizement.)
- Maintain personal Bible study, prayer time, and journal.

Pastoring in the bedroom community and/or suburban setting is unique, and I learned some valuable lessons:

- Knowing the history of the church, local cultural, and community
- Welcoming newcomers in the community to the church

- Establishing professional relationships with local businesses, civic groups, local schools, ministerial associations, social justice ministries, and political leaders.
- Connecting with other United Methodist Churches and other communities of faith.
- Maintain personal Bible study, prayer time, and journal.

I observed some of my clergy women colleagues who were successful and in some cases not so successful. I offer some recommendations that are applicable to both male and female clergy:

- Seek advice from seasoned clergy women colleagues and conference staff in order to navigate through the waters of resistance.
- Request the judicatory to provide advance training to the leadership of the new appointment in preparation for receiving a female clergy person.
- Be flexible in your leadership style and adapt to your situation.
- Avoid situations that have what I call the mutuality of toxicity, where both parties having toxic issues that are harmful to one another.
- Work with congregations where they are in order to take them to a new level.

- Avoid making immediate changes in the leadership of a congregation unless absolutely necessary.
- Be open to meaningful critique from colleagues, mentor, spiritual director, or certain of the laity.
- Maintain personal Bible study, prayer time, and journal

Ministry in the rural context is unique and some of the previous teaching points apply, however, there are some germane only to the rural small-membership church:

- The official or unofficial church administrator will likely be a woman with longevity as a member who has served in a variety of ministry areas and is the corporate memory of the congregation, besides the matriarch and/or patriarch. She is likely the person who will orient the new pastor to the culture of the church and/or community.
- The pastor's office will more than likely be a multipurpose room: administrative office, finance office, and sacristy. The office was organized on the basis of an absentee pastor or a pastor serving a charge. The pastor is fortunate when there is an office space designated specifically for him or her.
- In multiple-church charges, expect there to be feelings of resentment due to one or several of the congregations feeling neglected with the larger church getting more

attention from the pastor. Each rivals for the attention and love of the pastor.

- In some multiple-church charges, there will be interconnections of families in each church. Be mindful of what you say about any of them.
- Do not be surprised at the competitiveness between or among the churches on a multiple charge.
- Membership is very important, and conflicts occur when an inactive member is about to be removed from the active membership rolls. It can be seismic. The culture understanding is being listed as a member presumably guarantees burial rights with the rest of the family members in the church cemetery. Review the church's cemetery policy, and if one does not exist, develop a policy and stick with it.
- Keep your ears open for updates on what is happening within the community or families. Important information is given during the testimonial moments before the main worship service. (In my opinion the testimonial is a means of a confessional that is made in the context of the extended family, and the extended family serves as surrogate priest listening to the confessor. During the pastoral prayer or altar call, the pastor can make the specific intercessory prayer.)
- Visitations are very important, especially to the senior members who call other senior members and discuss the pastoral visit.

- Have written detailed contracts with paid staff members, especially musicians.
- Have annual evaluations of paid staff members.
- Fundraisers come in many different forms: selling dinners, going to plays, and so forth. The monetary goal is significant, but not as important as the fellowship involved in the process of achieving the financial goal.
- Church dinners have a Eucharistic character/quality that is very important to the members who bring and share their home-prepared meals with one another.
- The small-membership church consists of several dominant families that enjoy the comfort and security of being with one another. Newcomers will be adopted into at least one or at most two of the families. These churches are insular, and it is a chore to cultivate an attitude of openness to newcomers.
- Gifts to the church tend to be labeled with the name(s) of the donor(s).
- Articles and items donated over the years will clutter the pantry and other areas of the church. There is a hesitancy to throw away the articles and items for fear of repercussions from the donors. Get rid of the items during a general spring cleaning.
- Most small-membership churches prefer the traditional pastoral family: male pastor with wife, (the first lady), and

children. However, this model is rapidly changing as more women clergy persons, their spouses, and families are prevalent.

- The small-membership church will complain about insufficient funds to pay their pastor.
- Establish an office schedule, regardless of how often you will be present at the church.
- Return telephone calls and/or emails.
- When hospitality has been extended to the pastor to join the family in the kitchen, the clergy person is no longer ceremonially the minister of the church, but authentically their pastor.
- Clean restrooms are matters of hospitality.
- Signage on the marquis should be up to date and reflect care of the church.
- Maintain personal Bible study, prayer time, and journal.

The foregoing are experiences that I learned while serving as a pastor in the African American small-membership church in the rural setting. Other pastors may certainly have had different experiences and may not necessarily agree with what I said, but these are my experiences. I offer them as examples for new pastors, especially those appointed to rural congregations.

I have to pay tribute to my wife, Lila, although I was called to serve in itinerate ministry, she by default was called also. She has been faithfully at my side through the good times and not-so-good times. She has been like both active and passive social sonar, listening and picking up on things that I would miss around the congregation. My "girlfriend and wife who is one and the same" has been my helper in this ministry and been my encourager all these many years. My wife has had her stressors as a pastor's wife, but because of her praying nature has been able to overcome and not give up. Thank you, Lord!

I have heard over the years the expression, "Some were called and sent and others went." Ministry is not for everyone. It is not a job or part-time job; it is a calling upon one's life for God's purposes. It is not for the faint-hearted or one moved by the thrill of a spiritual moment. I have used the expression that ministry is a fatal attraction. Not only do we die to self, but some of the "stuff" that comes our way can harm us but will not deter us from doing God's will. I am reminded of some of John Wesley's experiences of being run out of town, told not to come back to certain churches, and even chased by a bull in the field where he had been preaching. He kept on preaching and serving God. Now in more recent times, as I reflect on the fatal shootings of nine persons including the senior pastor and associate minister in Emanuel African Methodist Episcopal Church, Charleston, South Carolina, the event dramatizes more the gravity of ministry being a fatal attraction.

On the flip side, there is a joy in serving the Lord. It is a joy to see persons accept Christ as their Lord and Savior. It is a joy to see transformation take place in the lives of parishioners. When the pastor sees an estranged couple reunite as a result of prayer, coaching, counseling, and more prayer, it is an absolute joy. When there is a physical and/or spiritual healing, it is joy. It is joy when unforeseen blessings come into the lives of congregants. To see youngsters grow and mature in their faith is a joy. When youngsters you have seen grow-up and go off to college, it is a joy. To see members of the congregation go out into the community and minister to the marginalized is a joy. It is a joy to see a once premature baby now in her two's romping around the church. It is a joy to have a couple that you provided premarital counseling and performed their wedding visit you twenty years later and remind you of the counseling session and are still married with a grown son, it is a joy. I can only echo the words and refrain of the traditional spiritual: "Well I would-n't take noth-in,' Mount Zion, for mah jour-ney now."[1] Rev. Dr. Alfonso J. Harrod says it this way: "Brother don't you know? I would not take nothing for my journey." Amen!

Prayer

Now, O God, I have written what You have put

on my heart to share with Your people.

May this writing serve as a guide as we serve You.

Amen.

Chapter 10

The Pastor's Wife: In Her Own Words

We have been blessed over the years to serve very loving, nurturing, and supportive congregations. However, on occasions when changes are implemented in the church that some members may dislike, they will be sure to express their displeasure to me with the intended purpose to convey their dissatisfaction to the pastor. In such circumstances, I have never found a diplomatic or Christian way of addressing this issue that would discourage members for using me as a "complaint messenger." I just quietly listen and try to make sympathetic sounds. I think members only view me as the pastor's wife and do not consider that he is my pastor, too!

This unique position makes me intensely loyal. I'm very sensitive to how persons interact with him. It seems there are always a few individuals in every church that are self-appointed thorns in the side. I know pastors' wives who refuse to attend the church their husbands are pastoring because they are so upset with the negative and disrespectful way the pastor is treated. I have tried to encourage those wives to continue being supportive. I am appreciative of those persons who join in and are supportive and committed to the ministries of the church. Conversely, I am not unaware of those persons who are more interested in the pastor than the ministries of the church. Unfortunately, such instances have brought us dangerously close to terminating our marriage. But, thanks to God, for His grace in leading us to Dr. Joyce Woods, Christian family counselor, who worked with us and helped us revitalize our marriage.

I view myself as an introvert and am very happy to stay in the background. However, over the years at the pastor's nudging, I am more involved in the ministries of the church.

I believe my husband has been called by God into the ministry. He puts his whole heart into serving the Lord. He's always seeking ways to reach as many people as he can to share the Good News of Jesus Christ. Also, my husband possesses a unique ability to discern spiritual gifts in persons. He is great encourager to develop those gifts to the glory of God.

My recommendations to pastors' wives:

- Invite and allow the Holy Spirit to guide and direct you in all you do.
- Pray fervently for your pastor and husband, your family, and church family.
- Finds ways to spend quality time together.

- Make sure you get sufficient rest (families in crisis will call at any hour).
- Be supportive (work hand-in-hand together to the glory of God).
- Communication is essential.

Pastors please listen to your wives! It is not unscriptural to do so. God told Abraham to listen to his wife (Genesis 21:12). There are many other instances in Holy Scripture where God has spoken through women: Mary, Deborah, and Priscilla to name a few. I do believe God gives us insight into situations and we can be a blessing.

Being a pastor's wife has proven to be very interesting. I have discovered there is no greater joy than serving Christ!

Pastors, my prayer is God will empower you with His strength, sustain you in the storms of life, and fill you with wisdom. Remain faithful, and you shall reap a great harvest for Christ. Amen.

End Notes

Chapter 1

1. Nolan B. Harmon, *Understanding the United Methodist Church (*Nashville: Abingdon Press, 1977), pp. 16–17.
2. Former Washington Conference Reunion: Celebrating the Past, Envisioning the Future: Celebrating 100 Years of Exciting Ministry and 40 Years with the Central Jurisdiction, pp. 9–12.
3. Ibid, p.10.
4. "Black Methodists for Church Renewal, Inc." Brochure.
5. Ibid.
6. Bill Kemp, *Holy Places, Small Spaces: A Hopeful Future for the Small Membership Church* (Nashville: Discipleship Resources, 2005), p.19.
7. C. Eric Lincoln, Lawrence H. Mamiya, *The Black Church in the African-American Experience* (Durham, N.C.: Duke University Press, 1990) pp. 98–99.

Chapter 2

1. Kevin E. Martin, *The Myth of the 200 Barrier: How to Lead Through Transitional Growths,* (Nashville: Abingdon Press, 2005), p.65.
2. Bill Kemp, *Holy Places, Small Spaces: A Hopeful Future for the Small Membership Church,* (Nashville: Discipleship Resources, 2005), pp. 58, 59.
3. St. Mark's United Methodist Church 97th Anniversary 1890–1987, p.11.
4. *The Centennial Anniversary Journal St. Mark's United Methodist Church 1890–1990: A Century of Performing God's Wondrous Works*, p. 14.
5. Ibid. p.15.
6. Lyle E. Schaller, *The Small Church Is Different!* (Nashville: Abingdon Press, 1982, pp 34–35).
7. Evans E. Crawford, *The Hum: Call and Response in African American Preaching* (Nashville: Abingdon Press, 1995, pp.43,44.____).
8. Charles Wesley, "Father, I Stretch My Hands to Thee" *Songs of Zion, Supplemental Worship Resources 12,* (Nashville: Abingdon Press, 1981, p.11).
9. Comment by the late Rev. Louis Conway, retired local pastor at St. Mark's UMC.

10. Julia Kuhn Wallace, *"Guidelines small-membership church: Serving with Significance in Your Context"* (Nashville: Abingdon Press, 2008, p.28).
11. Ibid., p.28.
12. Ibid., p. 28.
13. St. Mark's United Methodist Church 97th Anniversary, pp. 21, 27.
14. *The New Interpreter's Dictionary of the Bible Me-R Volume 4,* (Nashville: Abingdon Press, 2009), p. 218.
15. James L. Killen, Jr., *Pastoral Care in the Small Membership Church* (Nashville: Abingdon Press, 2005), p. 53.
16. C. Eric Lincoln p.113.
17. David Canada, Spiritual Leadership in the Small Membership Church, Abingdon Press, Nashville, 2005, pp. 57—66.
18. G. Lloyd Rediger, *Clergy Killers: Guidance for Pastors and Congregations Under Attack*, (Westminster John Knox Press, Louisville, KY, 1997), pp. 63–68.
19. *The United Methodist Hymnal, Book of Worship*, (The United Methodist Publishing House, Nashville, TN, 1989), p.12.
20. Carl S. Dudley, *Effective Small Churches: in the Twenty-First Century* (Nashville, Abingdon Press, 2003), pp. 51–52.
21. Randall C. Bailey and Jacqueline Grant, editors, *The Recovery of Black Presence: An Interdisciplinary Exploration: "Copher: What's in a Name?*, (Nashville, Abingdon Press), p.18 and Joe Stowell, *Our Daily Bread* July, August, September 2014,

"The Power of a Name," (Grand Rapids, Michigan, RBC Ministries), July 12.

22. Comment from the Rev. Dr. Calvin Morris, retired Elder, Baltimore-Washington Conference.
23. Julia Kuhn Wallace, p.28.

Chapter 3

1. The Historic Ebenezer UMC
2. Ibid. p.3
3. Harrod, Alfonso, "Worship and Its Effectiveness in Ebenezer UMC
4. *The United Methodist Hymnal*, p. 400
5. *Explanation of ROCK: It is designed as a retreat with a focus on presenting the Gospel message in an exciting, culturally appropriate way for young people . . .to be exposed to and have an opportunity to respond to an invitation to a life-changing relationship with Jesus Christ, The ROCK. (Taken from the Baltimore-Washington Conference Website.*

Chapter 4

1. Charles County Government document.
2. Kent R. Hunter, *The Lord's Harvest and the Rural Church* (Kansas City: Beacon Hill Press, 1993), p. 52.

3. *The New Scofield Reference Bible, Holy Bible Authorized King James Version,* (New York, Oxford University Press, 1969), p. 47. "Often used incorrectly as a benediction, in their original context these words were, rather, a malediction. Laban and Jacob distrusted one another. At their parting, Jacob had a heap of stones erected as a witness of his covenant with Laban, and Laban said that the stones would serve as a reminder that God was watching the way in which Jacob would treat Leah and Rachel in the future."
4. James L. Killen, Jr. *Pastoral Care in the Small Membership Church* (Nashville: Abingdon Press, 2005), pp. 53, 54.
5. *Book of Resolutions 2012,* p.180
6. Ibid, p.189
7. 4305. Sabbath Leave: The Baltimore-Washington Conference approves in principle the concept of Sabbath Leave for clergy to help restore perspective on God-given tasks, to bring a sense of appreciation for themselves and their church, and to assist in the restoration of effectiveness and balance in ministry. Such Sabbath Leave would:

   1. Be with the encouragement and approval of the District Superintendent and the coopration of the local church.

   2. Be for a period of three months, available every seventh year to those under full-time appointment.

3. Include a reflective report on its value and effects to the District Superintendent and Board of Ordained Ministry's Mid-Career Committee.
4. Encourage pastoral duties during the period of the leave to be fulfilled by supply ministers, Lay Speaker and neighboring clergy, with arrangements made by the local church and the District Superintendent.

4510.6 Sabbatical Leave: a. Deacons in Full Connection, Elders in Full Connection, and Associate Members who have served under full time appointment in the Conference with required MEP participation for at least six consecutive years since reception into full membership or six consecutive years from the time of their reception into associate membership, will be responsible for 10% of the active participant's premium cost and 50% of the dependent premium cost. The salary-paying unit will be responsible for 90% of the active participant's premium cost and 50% of the dependent premium cost for up to one year of Sabbatical Leave approved by the Board of Ordained Ministry and granted by vote of the Executive Session of the Annual Conference.

Policy and Procedures Manual of the Baltimore-Washington Conference of the United Methodist Church.

Chapter 5

1. Melvin Amerson, *Stewardship in African-American Churches: A New Paradigm* (Nashville: Discipleship Resources, 2006), p. 93
2. St. Mary's County document on St. Luke United Methodist Church, Ridge, Maryland
3. Anthony G. Pappas (Editor), John H Bennett, *"Rural Remnant: A Metaphor of Mission for the Rural Church": Inside the Small Church,* (Herndon, VA: Alban Institute, 2002), pp. 182–184
4. Lyle E, Schaller, *The Small Church Is Different,* (Nashville: Abingdon Press, 1982), p. 99
5. Ibid., p.99
6. C. Eric Lincoln, *Lawrence H. Mamiya, The Black Church in the African-American Experience* (Durham, N.C.: Duke University Press, 1990), pp. 98–99.
7. Ibid. p 106.
8. Comment by Lay leader Greene

Chapter 6

1. Cain Hope Felder, *Troubling Biblical Waters: Race, Class, and Family* (Maryknoll, N.Y.: Orbis Books, 1989), p.149.
2. 1989 Official Journal Baltimore Annual Conference Two Hundred Fifth Annual Session, p.39.
3. A rush is an occasion when sororities invite prospective new members to join their sorority.
4. Rev. Dr. Smith-Horn survey form dated April 3, 2014, p. 1.
5. Ibid, p. 2.
6. Ibid, p. 2.
7. Rev. Dr. Ianther Mills survey form date March 11, 2014, p.1.
8. Addendum to Interview/Survey of African-American Women Pastors in Small Membership Churches in Rural or Suburban Communities undated, p.1
9. Rev. Dr. Ianther Mills survey form, p.2.
10. Pastor Joan Jones survey form dated March 4, 2014, p. 2.
11. Ibid, p. 2.
12. Ibid, p.313.Steve Willis, *Imagining the Small Church Celebrating a Simpler Path,* (The Alban Institute, Herndon, Va., 2012), p. 61.
13. Pastor Eloise Newman survey form dated February 21, 2014, p.1.3
14. Rev. Dr. Sonia King survey form date June 4, 2015, p. 1.
15. Ibid.p. 2

16. Ibid. p.3
17. Tom Berlin and Lovett H. Weems, Jr. *High Yield: Seven Disciplines of the Fruitful Leader,* (Abingdon Press, Nashville, 2014), pp. 88, 89.
18. Rev. Dr. Priscilla Boswell survey form dated June 15, 2015, p. 1.
19. Member wishes to remain anonymous.
20. G. Lloyd Rediger, *Clergy Killers: Guidance for Pastors and Congregations under Attack.* (Westminster John Knox Press, Louisville, Kentucky, 1997), pp. 28, 29.
21. Rev. Dr. Boswell, p. 3.
22. Pastor Sandra survey form dated March 2014, p'1
23. Pastor Patricia Berry survey form dated April 2014, p. 2.
24. Rediger, p.58.
25. Pastor Berry, pp. 3, 4.
26. Ibid., p.6.
27. Rev. Patricia Allen survey form dated April 10, 2015, p. 4.
28. Rev. Johnsie Cogman survey form date May 2014, p.1.
29. Ibid, p. 3.
30. Rev. Beatrice Edwards survey form dated September 14, 2014, p. 3.
31. Ibid, p. 3.
32. Anthony B. Pinn, *The Black Church in the Post-Civil Rights Era,* (Orbis Books, Maryknoll, New York, 2002), pp. 130, 133.
33. C. Eric Lincoln, pp. 299–300.

Chapter 8

1. Kent R. Hunter, *The Lord's Harvest and the Rural Church,* (Kansas City, Missouri, Beacon Hill Press of Kansas City, 1993), p. 14.
2. Ibid. p. 16.
3. Ibid. p.16
4. Ibid. pp. 21–22.
5. Ibid. p.23
6. Lyle E. Schaller, *"Looking at the Small Church: A Frame of Reference," Christian Ministry 8, no. 4* (July 1977):5
7. Alice Mann, *The In Between Church; Navigating Size Transitions in Congregations* (Herndon, VA, The Alban Institute, 1998), p. 4.
8. Carl S. Dudley, *Effective Small Churches in the Twenty-first Century,* (Nashville; Abingdon Press, 2003), p. 25.
9. Alexandria Chapel Church History document undated, p. 1.
10. Ibid. p. 1.
11. Ibid. p. 2.
12. Ibid. p.3.
13. Ibid. p. 4
14. Ibid., p.5.
15. Ibid. p. 5.
16. Ibid. p. 5.
17. Ibid. p. 4.

18. The Smith Chapel Church History document undated, pp.1–5.
19. The Smith Chapel Church History document 2, undated, p. 4.
20. Ibid. p. 4.
21. Ibid. p. 5.
22. Ibid. p. 5.
23. *2000 Official Journal Baltimore-Washington Conference the United Methodist Church 216th Annual Session,* (Communications Department of the Baltimore-Washington Conference, Baltimore,) p. 592.
24. *2012 Official Journal 228th Session of the Baltimore-Washington Conference of the United Methodist Church, p. 606.*
25. Lyle E. Schaller, *The Small Church Is Different* (Nashville: Abingdon Press, 1992), pp. 90–91.
26. Comment made to me by a well-known trustee during his ministry at Metropolitan UMC, Indian Head, Maryland.
27. Steve Willis, *Imaging the Small Church: Celebrating a Simpler Path.* (Herndon, VA: Alban Institute, 2012), p. 83.
28. Anthony G. Pappas, ed, John H. Bennett *Developing Standards for Small-Church Mission Evaluation: Inside The Small Church"* (Herndon, VA.: Alban Institute, 2002), p. 184.
29. Shane Claiborne, Jonathan Wilson-Hartgrove, Enuma Okoro, *Common Prayer* (Grand Rapids, Michigan, Zondervan, 2010), p. 230.

30. Anthony B. Pinn, *The Black Church in the Post-Civil Rights Era,* (Maryknoll, New York: Orbis Books, 2002, p. 9. Cited in text Cheryl Townscend Gilkes, *Black Women's Experience and Womanist Culture in Church and Community*, (Maryknoll, NY: Orbis Books, 2000).
31. Smith Chapel-Alexandria Chapel Cooperative Parish, Alexandria Campus, p. 1
32. C. Eric Lincoln, p. 106.
33. Kermit C.C. Moore, Interview form dated March 12, 2014, p.2.
34. Pinn, p. 9.
35. Cain Hope Felder, *Troubling Biblical Waters: Race, Class, and Family,* (Maryknoll, New York: Orbis Books, 1989), p.73. "Compensatory justice is the moral process of correcting past or present injury, dispossession, exploitation, and the violation of rights. It makes restitution, offers reparation, seeks to restore persons to wholeness, and grants them rightful status in the community. It is an act of mercy and forgiveness."
36. Interview form dated 3/7/14 by M. P.
37. Interview form date 3/8/14 by J.G.
38. Undated interview form without signature.
39. Jeanne Parr, Interview form dated 3/15/14, p.1.
40. C. Eric Lincoln, p. 94.

41. Physical Evaluation by Arro Consulting, Inc., Hagerstown, Maryland, 2015, p. 1.

Chapter 9

1. *Songs of Zion: Supplemental Worship Resources 12.* (Abingdon, Nashville, 1981), p. 157

Bibliography

Amerson, Melvin. *Stewardship in African American Churches: A New Paradigm.* Discipleship Resources. Nashville, TN. 2006.

Bailey, Randall and Jacqueline Grant, editors, *"The Recovery of black Presence: An Interdisciplinary Exploration: "Copher: What's in a Name?,"* (Nashville, Abingdon Press).

Book of Resolution, United Methodist Church, 2012, Nashville, TN. The United Methodist Publishing House, 2012.

Claiborne, Shane, Jonathan Wilson-Hartgrove, Enuma Okoro. *Common Prayer.* Grand Rapids, Michigan, Zondervan, 2010.

Crawford, Evans E. *The Hum: Call and Response in African American Preaching.* Nashville, TN. Abingdon Press, 2001.

Daman, Glenn C. *Shepherding the Small Church: A Leadership Guide for the Majority of Today's Churches* (Second Edition), Grand Rapids, MI. Kregel Publications, 2008.

Dudley, Carl S. *Effective Small Churches in the Twenty-First Century.* Nashville, TN. Abingdon Press, 2003.

Felder, Cain Hope. *Troubling Biblical Waters: Race, Class, and Family.* Maryknoll, New York. Orbis Books, 1989.

Harmon, Nolan. *Understanding the United Methodist Church.* Nashville, TN. Abingdon Press, 1977.

Hunter, Kent R. *The Lord's Harvest and the Rural Church.* Kansas City, Beacon Hill Press, 1993.

Kemp, Bill. *Holy Places, Small Spaces: A Hopeful Future for the Small Membership Church.* Nashville, TN. Discipleship Resources, 2005.

Killen, James L. Jr. *Pastoral Care in Small Membership Church.* Nashville, TN. Abingdon Press, 2005.

Lincoln, C. Eric, Lawrence H. Mamiya. *The Black Church in the African-American Experience.* Durham, NC. Duke University Press, 1990.

Mann, Alice. *The In-Between Church: Navigating Size Transitions in Congre*gations. Herndon, VA. Alban Institute, 1998.

Martin, Kevin E. *The Myth of the 200 Barrier: How to Lead Through Transitional Growths.* Nashville, TN. Abingdon Press, 2005.

Official Journal 1989, Baltimore-Washington Conference, The United Methodist Church.

Pappas, Anthony G., editor. *Inside the Small Churc*h. Herndon, VA. Alban Institute, 2002.

Pappas, Anthony G. *Entering the World of the Small Church: A Guide for Leaders.* Herndon, VA. Alban Institute, 1988.

Pinn, Anthony. *The Black Church in Post-Civil Rights Era.* Maryknoll, New York. Orbis Books, 2002.

Rediger, G. Lloyd. *Clergy Killers: Guidance for Pastors and Congregations under Attack.* Louisville, KY. Westminster John Knox Press, 1997.

Schaller, Lyle E. *The Small Church is Different.* Nashville, TN. Abingdon Press, 1982.

Stowell, Joe. *Our Daily Bread:* July, August, September 2014: "The Power of a Name." Grand Rapids, Michigan, RBC Ministries, July 2014.

The New Interpreter's Dictionary of the Bible Me-R Volume 4. Nashville. Abingdon Press, 2009.

Wallace, Julia Kuhn. *Guidelines Small Membership Church: Serving with Significance in Your Context.* Nashville, TN. Abingdon Press, 2008.

Weems, Lovett H., Jr., Tom Berlin. *Over Flow: Increase Worship Attendance and Bear More Fruit.* Nashville, TN. Abingdon Press, 2013.

Wesley, Charles. "Father, I Stretch My Hands to Thee," *Songs of Zion, Supplemental Worship Resources 12.* Nashville, TN. Abingdon Press, 1981.

Willis, Steve. *Imagining the Small Church: Celebrating a Simpler Path.* Herndon, VA. Alban Institute, 2012.

Wimberly, Anne Streaty ed. *Honoring African American Elders: A Ministry in the Soul Community.* San Francisco, CA. Jossey-Bass Publishers, 1997.

Recommended Readings:

Byassee, Jason. *The Gifts of the Small Church.* Nashville, TN. Abingdon Press, 2010.

Crandall, Ron. *Turnaround and Beyond: A Hope Future for Small Membership Churches.* Nashville, TN. Abingdon Press, 2008.

DeKruyter, Arthur H., Quentin J. Schultze. *The Suburban Church: Practical Advice for Authentic Ministry.* Louisville, KY. Westminster John Knox Press, 2008.

Kujawa-Holbrook, Sheryl A. and Fredrica Harris Thompsett. *Born of Water, Born of Spirit: Supporting the Ministry of the Baptized in Small Congregations.* Herndon, VA. The Alban Institute, 2010.

Brochures, Historical Journals:

Alexandria Chapel Church History document undated

Black Methodists for Church Renewal, Inc.

Charles County Government (Maryland) Brochure

Former Washington Conference Reunion: Celebrating the past, Envisioning the future: Celebrating 100 Years of Exciting Ministry and 40 Years with the Central Jurisdiction.

Metropolitan United Methodist Church History document

St. Mark's United Methodist Church 97th Anniversary 1890–1987.

St. Mary's County (Maryland) document on Bethesda United Methodist Church, Valley Lee, Maryland

St. Mary's County (Maryland) document on Mt. Zion United Methodist Church, St. Inigoes, Maryland

St. Mary's County (Maryland) document on St. Luke United Methodist Church, Ridge, Maryland

The Centennial Anniversary Journal St. Mark's United Methodist Church 1890–1990: A Century of Performing God's Wondrous Works.

The Historic Ebenezer UMC

Harrod, Alfonso. "Worship and Its Effectiveness in Ebenezer United Methodist Church." Dissertation in fulfillment of Doctor of Ministry Degree, 1981.

Smith Chapel United Methodist Church History documents 1 and 2, undated.

Smith Chapel-Alexandria Chapel Cooperative Parish Covenant document July 2011.

Face-to-face, Telephonic and Written Interviews:

Clergy:

Rev. Kay Albury May 2015

Rev. Patricia Allen interview dated April 10, 2015

Rev. Patricia Berry interview dated April 2014

Pastor Irvin Beverly 2014

Pastor Leroy Boldley 2014

Rev. Dr. Priscilla Boswell interview dated June 15, 2015

Rev. Joan Carter-Rimbach interview summer 20015

Rev. Johnsie Cogman interview dated May 2014

Rev. Beatrice Edwards dated September 14, 2014

Pastor Joan Jones interview March 4, 2014

Rev. Dr. Sonia King interview June 4, 2015

Rev. Dr. Ianther M. Mills interview March 11, 2014

Pastor Kermit C.C. Moore interview March 12, 2014

Pastor Eloise Newman interview dated February 21, 2014

Rev. Dr. Dianna Parker interview date November 2014

Rev. Dr. LaReesa Smith-Horn interview April 3, 2014

Pastor Sandra Smith March 2014

Pastor Derrick Walton June 2015

Rev. Dr. Alfreda Wiggins Summer 2014

Rev. Mamie Alethea Williams Summer 2014

Laity

Rosetta Bowman Summer 2014

Brenda Chase March 2014

Roland Chase interview Summer 2014

Mrs. LeVurn Custis various 2014 and 2015

Maureen Diggs interview March 2014

Deloris Greene interview June 2015

Vera Littlejohn Summer 2014

V. Elnora Milstead Summer 2015

Karleen Powell interview March 2014/Summer 2015

Ruth Simmons interview March 2014

Rhonda Taylor interview March 2014

Clara Washington interview March 15, 2014

About the Author

Rev. Dr. George F. De Ford retired after twenty-nine years of ordained ministry in the Baltimore-Washington Conference, The United Methodist Church. He served on the Conference Commission of Archives and History, and District Committees on Ordained Ministry. As a member of the Conference Board of Ordained Ministry, he served in such capacities as Registrar for Probationary Members and briefly as chair of the Board of Ordained Ministry. Rev. DeFord was a Regional Guide for the Annapolis-Southern Region prior to his retirement in July 2011. Presently, he serves as a District Superintendent's Hire for Smith Chapel United Methodist Church, La Plata (Pisgah), MD.

CPSIA information can be obtained at www.ICGtesting.com
Printed in the USA
BVOW05s1413260216

438187BV00004B/6/P

9 781498 459693